Reforming Brazil

WESTERN HEMISPHERE STUDIES

Series Editor: Mauricio A. Font
The Graduate Center and Queens College
City University of New York

This series represents a joint publication initiative of the Bildner Center for Western Hemisphere Studies at the City University of New York Graduate Center and Lexington Books. The books published in this series endeavor to support the Center's mission of generating greater comprehension of contemporary issues in the Americas, creating an international dialogue on policy issues, and producing research on a range of topics that are both country and theme specific.

TITLES IN SERIES
Reforming Brazil, edited by Mauricio A. Font with the assistance of Anthony Peter Spanakos and Cristina Bordin

Forthcoming:
Cuban Counterpoints: The Legacy of Fernando Ortiz, edited by Mauricio A. Font and Alfonso Quiroz

Reforming Brazil

Edited by Mauricio A. Font
and Anthony Peter Spanakos

with the assistance of
Cristina Bordin

LEXINGTON BOOKS
Lanham • Boulder • New York • Toronto • Oxford

LEXINGTON BOOKS

Published in the United States of America
by Lexington Books
An imprint of The Rowman & Littlefield Publishing Group, Inc.
4501 Forbes Boulevard, Suite 200, Lanham, Maryland 20706

PO Box 317
Oxford
OX2 9RU, UK

A different version of chapter 5 appears in *Latin American Politics and Society*, 45 (2) (summer 2003): 41–46. Reprinted with the permission of the University of Miami.

British Library Cataloguing in Publication Information Available

Library of Congress Cataloging-in-Publication Data

Reforming Brazil / edited by Mauricio A. Font and Anthony Peter Spanakos, with the assistance of Cristina Bordin.
    p. cm. — (Western hemisphere studies)
  Includes bibliographical references and index.
  ISBN 0-7391-0586-8 (cloth : alk. paper) — ISBN 0-7391-0587-6 (pbk. : alk. paper)
  1. Brazil—Economic policy. I. Font, Mauricio A. (Mauricio Augusto) II. Spanakos, Anthony Peter. III. Bordin, Cristina. IV. Series.
HC187.R4116 2004
330.981—dc22   2003025453

Printed in the United States of America

♾™ The paper used in this publication meets the minimum requirements of American National Standard for Information Sciences—Permanence of Paper for Printed Library Materials, ANSI/NISO Z39.48–1992.

Contents

Figures

Tables

Acknowledgments

The Bildner Center for Western Hemisphere Studies is grateful to the many individuals and organizations who were involved in this book as well as in the international symposium on which it is based—"Reforming Brazil," held at The Graduate Center, City University of New York, on May 17–19, 2001. We thank all contributors and participants for their papers and comments, as well as for their patience in the effort to turn conference papers into a book. The staff at the Bildner Center played an enormous role in the entire process. Cristina Bordin provided effective overall coordination of the international seminar in which these papers were first presented, and of the arduous editing and lay-out work leading to the publication of this volume. We greatly appreciate Gary Aguayo's effective work in the organization of the conference. Sandra Black and Andrés Salas thoughtfully edited many of the texts. Danielle Xuereb helped edit and arrange texts and graphics, while Natalia Caruso and Sandra Black prepared the index. Rosa Maria Conceição provided valuable assistance in the early stages of this project. As a visiting fellow at the Bildner Center, Tony Spanakos assisted in organizing the symposium and in preparing the papers included in the book. We are grateful to the William and Flora Hewlett Foundation for financial support of this conference. Dr. Brian Schwartz and The Graduate Center at the City University of New York need to be thanked for their support of the Bildner Center.

This volume inaugurates the Bildner Western Hemisphere Studies series. We salute Jason Hallman and Lexington Books for their initiative in this effort. The series advances the Center's mission of generating greater comprehension, dialogue, and debate about contemporary issues in the Americas. In that spirit, authors are responsible for their own views; their positions do not necessarily represent those of the Bildner Center. Our hope is that by comparing different views, by confronting theory with evidence, the Bildner Western Hemisphere Studies series will shed light on key issues of our times. We look forward to adding several new and exciting titles in the near future.

Mauricio A. Font
Director
Bildner Center for Western Hemisphere Studies
The Graduate Center, City University of New York

Part I
Introduction

Dawn of a New Era

Mauricio A. Font

Throughout the twentieth century, many political movements adhered to the idea that the state should be the key historical agent to alleviate human misery and advance social and economic development. But by the end of the century, processes of reform radically changed or ended not only state socialism in Eastern Europe, the Soviet Union, China, and Vietnam, but also various types of developmental states throughout East Asia and Latin America. Chile and Mexico were pioneers in processes of state reform in Latin America. The reforms, embraced with varying degrees of success by a large number of countries, sought to open and liberalize the state-centered development model. Privatization, administrative change, and the push for fiscal adjustment initiated a major process of state reform and the search for new economic strategies. The perspective of time, reliable long-term information, and careful study will be necessary to draw mature assessments of these shifts and innovations. This volume seeks to contribute to that undertaking by documenting and probing the reform process in Brazil, a key country that came late to the reform process.

Significance of the Reform Process

Brazil is also a key case to study because of its sheer size: the largest country in Latin America in terms of geography, population, and economy. It embraced a distinctive form of state interventionism in the 1940s and 1950s, and only in the 1990s would it change its statist economic model.

Dirigisme grew deep roots in Brazilian society within a distinctive political context. The Revolution of 1930 initiated a long era of centralized rule, one etched into a national regime by the authoritarian Estado Novo of 1937–1945 and later refurbished by the military regime of 1964–1985. The twenty years of populist democracy between 1945 and 1964 witnessed some efforts

3

at decentralization and liberalization, but most governments after the early 1940s relied on elaborate development programs to justify their own versions of centralized rule. In general, the post–World War II developmental state relied on an industrial policy based on protectionism and subsidies, planning, state ownership, and extensive regulation. Shaped by clientelistic, corporatist, and populist practices, this regime prevailed into the early phase of the post-1985 democratizing era.

Brazilian statism became increasingly incompatible with the new era of democratization and experienced broad challenges in the 1990s.[1] The Fernando Collor government (1990–1992) placed a massive reform drive into the national agenda, but the bold proposals it advanced aborted with his impeachment. By 1993, a disastrous bout of hyperinflation and profound economic difficulties, building on the debt crisis of the 1980s, finally began to convince Brazilians of the need to embark on a sustained period of reform. The main impetus for sustained change came with the two-term administration of Fernando Henrique Cardoso (1994–2002). After putting in place the successful stabilization program known as *Plano Real* (*Real Plan*), the Cardoso government aimed at a broad and deep package of liberalizing reforms, articulating them in the framework of a fundamental transformation of the Brazilian state and economic regime. That the Luiz Inácio Lula da Silva presidency (2003–) subsequently maintained the course with regard to the core of the reform process tends to confirm Brazil's commitment to reforms as well as the view that the country is experiencing a complex process of realignment characterized by a new policy paradigm, institutional innovation, the consolidation of emergent political elites, and a new development strategy (Font, 2003).

A sustained focus on the lineaments and evolution of the Brazilian reform era opening in the nineties is hence of critical importance in understanding the country's present and probing what the future may hold.

Fernando Henrique Cardoso was elected president largely because of the success of the 1993 stabilization plan he implemented as finance minister. His presidency sought to deepen and broaden the process of stabilization and equilibrated fiscal model, reform the state and political system, liberalize the economy, and change Brazil's international role. The essays in this volume provide perspectives and information essential to the assessment of key reforms proposed and implemented by the Cardoso governments. They help determine the extent to which the latter succeeded in setting a new course for the country.

---

1.   My own account of the Brazilian reform process, with particular focus on the Cardoso years, is found in Font (2003).

The significance of an in-depth study of the policies of the Cardoso government also derives from the role of Cardoso as one of Latin America's best-known intellectuals and development analysts. Trained as a sociologist at the University of São Paulo, Cardoso embraced development as the central problematic of his intellectual career. His promising career as a professor of sociology at his alma mater was abruptly interrupted in 1964, when the military coup of March 31 of that year forced him into exile in Chile. Cardoso spent several years in Santiago, working at CEPAL (UN Economic Commission for Latin America) and also teaching and participating in various activities in Chilean universities and research centers. His work built on pioneering empirical studies of the role of entrepreneurs in Brazilian and Latin American development. His Santiago stay resulted in important contributions to the elaboration of the dependency approach to development and underdevelopment, particularly the influential volume *Dependency and Development in Latin America*. To many, he had become the leading intellectual in Latin America's search for its own distinctive approach to development.[2]

Upon his return to Brazil in late 1968, Cardoso and colleagues founded CEBRAP (Brazilian Center for Analysis and Planning), an independent research center focusing on critical assessments of Brazil's development model and military regime, the prospects for democracy, and the search for alternative economic strategies. As president of CEBRAP and as a public intellectual, Cardoso engaged himself with the struggle for democracy, as Brazil experienced gradual political liberalization in the 1970s. By the early 1980s he had emerged as a major political figure and was elected senator. His big political opportunity came in 1993, when he was asked to become finance minister with the charge to stop the vicious process of hyperinflation. Designed by a team of Brazilian economists under his supervision, the new stabilization plan led to monetary and macroeconomic stability. The success of the *Real Plan* made Cardoso an unbeatable candidate in the presidential elections of 1994 and 1998.

Several prominent academic or intellectual figures joined the Cardoso cabinet or occupied other high offices. The long list includes Pedro Malan (Finance), José Serra (Health, after a short stint as Planning Minister), Paulo Renato de Souza (Education), Francisco Weffort (Culture), Luiz Carlos Bresser-Pereira (Administrative Reform), and Celso Lafer (Foreign Relations). The first lady, anthropologist Ruth Cardoso, played a major role in social policy, while sociologist Vilmar Faria became a close adviser. Not a small number of cabinet positions were given to politicians from the parties allied to Cardoso's PSDB (Brazilian Social Democracy Party).

---

2.   For Cardoso's trajectory, see F. H. Cardoso [& Font] (2001).

Forming winning coalitions large enough for the congressional adoption of constitutional amendments (repeated two-third majority votes at the lower house and the Senate) would be a formidable challenge in any political system, but it is particularly so in Brazil due to its splintered party system. Cardoso's strategy was to form large alliances with parties of different ideological and regional bases. This permitted the passage of a round of critical reforms. But a series of financial and political mini-crises after 1998, deepening right after the elections, impeded a major breakthrough in such badly needed reforms as those of the social security and tax systems. Toward the end of the Cardoso years the broad alliance had been unable to make much progress in the reform agenda. The Cardoso years had put Brazil on a new course, but could not take all the steps needed to ensure the durability of the shift. In spite of its shortcomings, that government did succeed in more than a core of specific reforms. An important part of its legacy is the sea change with regard to political and economic thinking, as well as the inauguration of a more civil way of conducting politics.

Many feared that the 2002 victory by Lula da Silva and his Workers' Party (PT) would mean abandoning the course set by the previous government. But the Lula presidency moved rapidly to embrace stabilization, fiscal adjustment, and economic liberalization as priorities. Strikingly, it embraced the critical but politically difficult ideas of reforming the social security and taxation systems. The considerable continuity in policy tends to confirm the view that the 1990s indeed represented a major chapter in a new era of reform in Brazil (Font, 2003). While Brazilian policy making is still subject to great debate and challenges that should be expected to impact on the survival or adoption of specific policies, the country appears to have made difficult but lasting choices about its political and economic organization.

Democracy and Reform

One of the characteristics of the Brazilian case is that the liberalizing reforms have been designed and implemented by leaders with profound roots in the process of democratization. The military, who formally ruled until 1985, had been historically associated with the idea of a centralizing and interventionist regime—as were the elites allied with them, many of whom survived into the post-1985 democratic era. This contrasts with Chile, but also Mexico and Argentina, where the path to reform was defined and opened by technocratic elites working within authoritarian or quasi-authoritarian frameworks. The Brazilian case hence denies the alleged superiority of authoritarianism in matters of structural reform.

Brazil's path to reform thus far suggests that the democratic, consultative road can be effective and sustainable, but also that this approach is likely to be bumpy and slow. Brazil's process of democratization has shaped and will continue to shape the design and implementation of reforms. The political weaknesses of democratic presidents through 1994 partly explains the inability to arrive at new development strategies in the face of clear evidence that the old model no longer worked. The governing style inaugurated by the Cardoso administration emphasized dialogue, consensus-building, and the abandonment of a preexisting style inclined to shocks. The very design and adoption of the *Real Plan* came about in this manner—unlike the "economic packages" adopted in the period 1985–1992.[3] President Lula da Silva appears to adhere to a similar style. If so, this continuity of political style, together with the expressed commitment to liberalizing reforms, augur well for the reform process and its economic impact.

In fact, the government of the Workers' Party has certain advantages in advancing the reform agenda. The principal may be that, as the locus of the original reform drive, the PSDB and the PFL (Liberal Front Party), the core of the opposition, fully support the reform agenda.[4] So long as it stays the course, the Lula government should be able to make considerable progress in reforming Brazil.

In a nutshell, there is considerable consensus among the political elite about the need to reform Brazil. The general direction includes macroeconomic and fiscal stabilization, liberalization, promoting competitiveness and exports, forging trade alliances, creating conditions for rural development, emphasizing a social policy based on human capital (education and health), and eliminating flaws in the political system.

Toward a New Approach to Development

Reforms are justified by reference to a greater social value—in Brazil's case, creating conditions for sustained development. High rates of poverty still plague the country, and it maintains one of the most unequal distributions of wealth and income on earth. Creating propitious conditions for development is thus an urgent matter.

The core of the reforms has an external logic that centers on the country's ability to attract foreign capital and technology and expand exports. When the debt crisis of the 1980s led to the retraction of capital and investment from the outside, it brought out the inability of domestic actors to steer the economy toward healthy development. The government faced a fiscal crisis that made clear the need for major state reform—made all the more clearer by worsening inflation and economic woes. Meanwhile, the domestic private

---

3. See F. H. Cardoso "Além da economia: Interaçao de política e desenvolvimento econômico," paper delivered at CEPAL (Chile), August 8, 2003. In this essay, Cardoso also cites the success of the responses to the financial crisis after 1998 and to the energy crisis of 2001 as a result of extensive consultation.
4. The PSDB is on record as pleading support for the reform agenda even as the new government co-optatively embraced it.

sector, though it had continued to expand, lacked the capital and technology to generate the high levels of saving and investment needed for faster growth. The reforms adopted in the 1990s were not sufficient. If a balanced fiscal model is as essential as monetary stabilization to attract foreign investment, specific reforms such as that of the social security system are also unavoidable.

The inability to adopt a real reform of the social security system left the country's financial system vulnerable. After 1998, Brazil suffered four successive financial crises. Together with the energy crisis of 2001, and political turmoil within the ruling coalition, they generated a climate that impeded more substantial progress in the reform process.

In fact, the deterioration of economic conditions erased a significant portion of the progress made in the mid-1990s. As a result, the net rate of economic growth into the early years of the new century was nil. The liberalizing reform process had come short of ushering in and sustaining an era of high economic growth.

The climate of frustrated expectations following the sacrifices made in the 1990s helps explain the defeat of the ruling PSDB's candidate in late 2002. During the campaign, candidate Lula seemed to argue that the reform agenda as conceived would be abandoned in favor of a new model. However, the Lula presidency itself came to agree with original advocates of the reforms that they had to be completed in order to reduce the vulnerabilities of the financial system and in order to create conditions for sustained economic growth and the ability to attract foreign capital.

The Workers' Party government made a public commitment to pass the reforms of the social security and tax systems during its first year in office. If its actions and statements during the first few months in office confirm the existence of a Brazilian near consensus on key economic reforms, the PT government also declared social and overall development a national priority and continued the strategy toward international trade and integration sketched out by earlier administrations. While maintaining a number of the social programs begun in the 1990s, the federal government adopted the elimination of hunger as a key goal. The government reconfirmed Brazil's commitment toward South American trade integration (Mercosur) and began to develop a framework for the challenging negotiations surrounding the Free Trade Area of the Americas (FTAA) and the multilateral negotiations at the World Trade Organization (WTO).

Conclusion

This volume discusses in detail the Brazilian reform agenda sketched at the turn of the century, one that will occupy the country's political imagination for years to come. The essays provide perspectives and information *essential* to the assessment of key reforms proposed and partly implemented at the dawn of the new era of reform. Many analysts will no doubt deepen and extend the analysis of Brazil's overall reform process, its new approaches to social and sustainable development, and the evolution of the reform drive. Illuminating a critical phase in the reform process is in itself an important contribution. In addition, this volume provides what we hope is a solid base-line to probe the course of policy-mediated change in twenty-first-century Brazil.

CHAPTER 1

The Reform Agenda

Anthony Peter Spanakos

This book assesses the reform agenda that was proposed, contested, and legislated during the 1990s and the first part of the twenty-first century. The essays examine the economic, political, and social factors that have been the impetus and/or results of the reform agenda that emerged in Brazil during the last dozen years, particularly during the Cardoso presidency. That the Workers' Party government coming into office in 2003 maintained the general trajectory of the F. H. Cardoso's two-term administration (1995–2002) is indeed a considerable signal of how the reforms of the 1990s have been accepted, even by some of their fiercest critics. Written just prior to the election of Luiz Inácio "Lula" da Silva as president, the essays give insight into why the reforms have proven to be durable.

Background

In much of Latin America the importance of the state as a political actor expanded in the 1930s and peaked in the late 1960s. State activity and intervention in the economic realm followed a similar path. With the collapse of consumption in developed markets during the Great Depression, Latin American states shifted from a liberal trade regime and an export-bias to a more inward-oriented model of development (Diaz Alejandro, 1984; Cardoso and Helwege, 1995). The shift toward the development of internal markets and demand was justified by structuralist theories emerging from such scholars as Raul Prebisch and organizations like ECLAC (Economic Commission Latin America and the Caribbean) (Prebisch, 1954; Hirschman, 1981; Sunkel, 1993).

The structuralist argument implied that Latin America's lack of industrialization would cause it to suffer a permanent deterioration of terms of trade

(Prebisch, 1949). Industrialization was hence necessary. Investment in infant industries, not having the advantages of economies of scale, required that risks associated with entrepreneurial investment be absorbed by the government, since the private sector was insufficiently developed to support such risks. The structuralist prescription for development centered on the role of the state as a fundamental institution whose intervention was necessary to remove distortions and bottlenecks, to invest in public goods or in areas the private sector deemed too risky, and to maintain exchange rate and trade regimes that would facilitate the development of domestic markets.

Import Substitution Industrialization (ISI) was the program that emerged from these policy prescriptions. Through overvalued exchange rates, significant tariffs, and state investment and/or ownership in industry, ISI favored importers and domestic industries and consumers at the expense of exporters (Cardoso and Helwege, 1995). This shift in economic policy away from the landed oligarchs, whose political and economic influence was waning by the 1920s and 1930s, toward urban political actors, including industrialists and organized labor, led to the greater political salience of the latter. The center of power shifted decisively from the rural estates to the cities, and the construction of an active state and large bureaucratic organizations and state-owned enterprises served to both absorb and depoliticize new political actors while also contributing to a model of full employment. The political and economic goals of the interventionist state were hard to separate, but they were especially popular since ISI led to years of "miraculous" growth.[1]

In that context, foreign policy was constrained by an anti-export bias and by the imposition of Cold War rivalries onto the developing world. The former led to limited trade between developed and developing countries, and even less trade among developing countries. The Cold War imposed constraints on the diplomatic and security negotiations of Latin American states. In the shadow of the hemispheric superpower, Latin American states pursued foreign policies based on independence and sovereignty, as long as the threat to U.S. national security was limited.[2]

State budgets continued to grow through the early 1980s, but revenues were inconsistent and often considerably less than expenses. Chronic and growing fiscal deficits were indeed part and parcel of the state economic overexpansion. Fiscal imbalances led to increased borrowing from international capital markets and monetization. The former led to increasing indebtedness, the latter to higher levels of inflation. Following the oil shocks of the 1970s, most Latin American economies continued to follow ISI-based growth policies despite the fact that the oil shocks raised international interest

1.   Annual average growth in the region was 5.5 percent between 1950 and 1980 (Franko, 1999: 64).
2.   The major exception, of course, being Cuba under the Castro regime.

rates, and therefore the cost of borrowing. This was possible because the petro-dollars earned by oil exporters were recycled to areas of rapid growth, such as Latin America.

But Latin American governments suffered a profound shock when the U.S. federal reserve raised interest rates, forcing the United States into a recession while simultaneously increasing the cost of Latin America's existing loans. The fiscal deficits of Latin American states were made unsustainable by high levels of debt, high interest rates, and the closure of capital markets to Latin American borrowers following the announcement by the Mexican government in 1982 that it could not pay the interest on its debt.

In the early 1980s, international financial institutions emerged as powerful actors in Latin America because private banks were no longer willing to lend to Latin American governments and because negotiation of a loan with the international financial institutions added credibility and offered reassurance to international investors. Loans from the IMF (International Monetary Fund), however, were conditional upon significant restructuring of the economies of the borrowing countries. Liberal economics became hegemonic through international financial institutions, particularly liberal critiques of ISI and state development. Liberals claimed that state intervention created tremendous distortions, crowded out the private sector, and engendered rent-seeking behavior (Krueger, 1992). It also led to low levels of productivity, disincentives to invest, corruption, and capital flight (Cardoso and Helwege, 1995). Liberals proposed that inflation and government budgets be reined in; state-owned enterprises be privatized; exchange rates be made competitive; financial flows be liberalized; markets be deregulated; and governments promote exports as a means of bringing in hard currency (Williamson, 1990).

The first generation of reforms focused on stabilization, particularly giving attention to macroeconomic distortions, export promotion and stabilizing inflation. Most countries in Latin America have implemented, at least partially, these first-generation results. The more successful cases and the later reformers have begun a second generation of reforms which are designed to attend to social costs, by improving distribution through investment in education and health services, and toward building institutions, by improving the rule of law and governability. The importance of second-generation reforms is receiving considerable attention as comparative analysis of reforms in developing countries becomes increasingly available (Krueger, 2000). In fact, a recent article suggests that second-generation reforms may be not only more critical than first, but that second-generation reforms should come first (Scott, 2001: 171).

Liberalization of Latin American economies was juxtaposed to a liberalization of politics. Following shifts in domestic (failure of military regimes, loss of support, increased opposition in civil society, and economic crisis) and global conditions (the thawing of the Cold War, a redefinition of U.S. national security, democratization in Southern Europe and increasing global support for democracy), Latin America experienced a wave of democratization of unprecedented degree (Huntington, 1991; Diamond, Plattner, Chu, and Tien, 1997). One by one, authoritarian regimes collapsed and were replaced by democratically elected governments. These new democracies survived the economic crisis of the 1980s largely because of a change in political elites' commitment to elections and the nature of the return of the military to the barracks. Few of the new democracies are truly consolidated to the extent that political institutions are seen as defining the "rules of the political game" (Linz and Stepan, 1996), yet the democracies remain (Mainwaring, 1999).

Similarly, there has been a considerable liberalization in Latin American foreign relations as structural adjustment programs correct anti-export biases and as new security dynamics have emerged in the region, and the world. The increase in foreign trade in Latin America has been impressive: from a regional average of 4.7 percent of GDP (Gross Domestic Product) for the period 1970 to 1980, to 8.2 percent from 1990 to 1997 (Franko, 1999: 218). The shift toward exporting has led not only to increased exports to the United States and the EU (European Union), but also to increased intraregional trade. Initiation and participation in regional trading blocks and the rise in bilateral trade agreements is illustrative of far more open states. Additionally, multilateral organizations, such as the OAS (Organization of American States), have become more legitimate actors and there has been an improved spirit of partnership between the United States and Latin American states. This is largely due to the end of the Cold War, new discourses of security that focus on transborder issues (such as drug trafficking, trade, and immigration), and a new generation of political leaders (Spanakos and Wiarda, 2003).

The jury is still out on the reforms implemented during the 1980s and 1990s. While it is true that growth resumed by the early 1990s in Latin America after a very disastrous decade, liberalization of markets led to recessions and to increased vulnerability to international markets. It is difficult, however, to analyze the reforms as a whole since despite the consensus over the need for liberalization, the region's political and economic reforms were heterogeneous (Lora, 1997, 2000; Stallings and Peres, 2000). Analysis of the success of the reforms must consider a panoply of variables, such as speed of reforms, complementarity and the paring of reforms, governing coalitions, the role of federalism and decentralization, and the degree of indebtedness, among others. In addition to the methodological questions, there are theoretical concerns. Scholarly debate is quite intense about the question of the relationship between the liberalization of economies and politics, and whether the past two decades have been better than the era of ISI. Those with clear stakes in the neoliberal-neostructural debate will have clear answers to both questions (Oxhorn and Starr, 1999; Sunkel, 1993; Gwynne and Kay, 1999). Ideology aside, however, the answers are much more difficult and technical.

Assessing such issues necessitates evaluating specific reforms, how they were conducted, who participated in the discussions, who was excluded, what means of compensation were designed, and what distortions were corrected and created by them. Addressing the relationship between the reforms and their efficacy requires a careful examination of the reform agenda itself, and how it was implemented in a specific context. The authors in this book contribute, through their evaluation of political, social, and economic reforms in Brazil during the last decade, to the assessment of the reform agenda.

Reforming Brazil

With approximately 170 million people and a GNP (Gross National Product) of US$742 billion, Brazil is Latin America's largest democracy and most important market. Despite the size of Brazil's economy, Brazil is a developing country. A GNP per capita of US$4,420, life expectancy rates of 67 years, illiteracy of 15 percent and infant mortality rates of 33 per 1,000 clearly place Brazil in the developing world (World Bank, 2000). More pressing is that these statistics are the result of averaging the life expectancy, illiteracy, and infant mortality in a country where development and poverty are very regionalized, and even within regions, the distribution of wealth is among the most stark in the entire world (see Scheper-Hughes, 1992).

Although development has been a part of the strategy of authoritarian, democratic, and military governments in Brazil since the 1930s, few governments have had long-term success in improving the conditions for its poorest citizens. Until the 1990 Collor government, developmentalism (*desenvolvimento*) in Brazil was seen as a state-led process, consistent with import substitution industrialization strategies pursued elsewhere in the region. State-led growth was very successful in Brazil, leading to "miraculous" growth rates, particularly between 1968 and 1973 when GDP growth averaged 11 percent. Unlike many other countries in Latin America, Brazilian governments recognized the importance of exports and so exchange rates were not so grossly overvalued in Brazil as elsewhere. Favorable exchange rates coupled with high growth rates, tariffs, and quotas spurred the growth of a middle class and encouraged high levels of domestic consumption. Real wages increased even as productivity levels remained low due to union pressure and because most salaries are based on some multiple of the minimum wage.

As the world economy began overheating in the late 1970s, the military regime refused to sanction an economic program that would allow for a slowdown. Much of the military's political legitimacy—despite being a dictatorship—was the result of the spectacular growth rates of the late 1960s that continued throughout the 1970s. The pressure to continue to grow, even when it was no longer prudent, led to high levels of debt, a considerable fiscal deficit, and runaway inflation (Winn, 1999: 175). Economic crisis weakened the military's claim to political expertise and facilitated the victory of the opposition in 1985, ending the two-decade experiment in bureaucratic authoritarianism. Civilian politicians, however, were no more capable than their predecessors of controlling inflation. Efforts to generate growth led to higher levels of inflation and the introduction of a string of new currencies (Kingstone, 1999; Cardoso in this volume).

Like the military regime before it, the civilian government of José Sarney recognized the need to improve the economy. Political support for reform, however, was nascent and underdeveloped. The relative success of the Brazilian ISI model made Brazil less willing to follow the example of other Latin American countries and shed the state-led model of growth.[1] Additionally, indexation shielded certain politically salient sectors, particularly organized labor, from the damage of inflation, and financial institutions benefited considerably from currency volatility. These two key constituencies saw little need to support reform, especially in the case of labor, since it was believed that the costs of reform would fall squarely on the poor. The population had been wary of stabilization programs, particularly those sanctioned by the IMF. Between 1985 and 1994, Brazilian citizens witnessed nine failed stabilization programs. However, the hyperinflation of the late 1980s and early 1990s weakened the indexation mechanism's ability to correct wages, forcing unions to shift priorities in favor of stabilization (see Sandoval in this volume).

Popular support was not the only reason for the failure of efforts at reform during the 1980s and in the early 1990s. These reforms failed largely because of a lack of support among political elites, who saw clear costs without immediate returns. Critics have attributed much of the lack of support from the political elite on the fragmentation of the political elite (Faucher, 1999), on the institutional rules that discourage party discipline (Kingstone, 1999), and on the constraints placed by the constitution of 1988 (Power, 2000; Bresser-Pereira, 2001). All of this tends to encourage the creation of coalitions, and leads to rent-seeking behavior and political instability, conditions

---

1.   Paunovic (2000) notes that countries with the most successful experience with state-led growth, such as Brazil and Venezuela, were much more reluctant to reform than countries like Argentina and Chile, where state-led growth had not been so successful.

that have been identified as especially deleterious to reform efforts (Haggard and Webb, 1994).

Crises were not limited to economics, as both president Sarney and Collor's governments were also marked by considerable political instability. With the impeachment of Collor, Itamar Franco became the second vice president in the post-1985 republic to ascend to the presidency. Although Franco had more political support in Congress than Collor or even Sarney, Franco's government was no more successful than previous ones at stabilizing the economy. Monthly inflation stood at 50 percent in 1993, when Franco's fourth finance minister, Fernando Henrique Cardoso, proposed another new currency, the *real*. Popular support was not the only reason for the failure of efforts at reform during the 1980s and in the early 1990s. These reforms failed in part because of a lack of support among political elites, who saw clear costs without immediate returns. Critics have attributed much of the lack of public support on the fragmentation of the political elite (Faucher, 1999), on the institutional rules that discourage party discipline (Kingstone, 1999), and on the constraints placed by the Constitution of 1988 (Power, 2000; Bresser-Pereira, 2001). These factors tend to encourage the creation of volatile coalitions and lead to rent-seeking behavior and political instability, conditions that have been identified as deleterious to reform efforts (Haggard and Webb, 1994).

The *Real Plan* was a currency-based stabilization program. The one *real* to one dollar exchange rate was solidly backed by US$40 billion in reserves held at the Central Bank. As opposed to previous efforts, it was gradual, rather than imposed shock therapy, and it gave business and labor considerable time to calculate prices. Cardoso also made an effort to explain the program and to gain support for it from political parties and other politically salient sectors. As the program began to slow inflation, his political capital increased and he was able to shift revenues from states and municipalities, back toward the federal government (Kingstone, 1999: 140; see also Montero's chapter). The success of the *real* insured Cardoso's election. The economic success of the *Real Plan* was only the beginning. The Cardoso presidency (1994–1998, 1998–2002) has presented a broad consistent agenda for reform and development—including in areas of public administration, politics, economics and development, and foreign policy.

This Volume

The reform agenda of the F. H. Cardoso government was indeed ambitious and broad. This book examines political, economic, social, and foreign policy reforms. Each of these was a critical aspect of the reform strategy of the Cardoso government, and analysis of the specific policies that have been designed to address these areas will contribute to the more broad literature on reform in Latin America and the developing world.

Among the most immediate priorities of the Cardoso government was reforming the state. Considerable consensus existed among academics and politicians that the state ceased to be efficient and that economic recovery, democratic consolidation, and social development required a new state architecture. Although there had been attempts at reform during the 1980s, reforms were difficult to implement and sustain because of macroeconomic instability and hyperinflation.

One of the authors behind the constitution of 1988, Cardoso was very familiar with its shortcomings. It produced a constitutional bias against foreign investors, made privatization difficult, engendered an unweildy form of decentralized political rule, discouraged party loyalty, gave lavish protection for civil servants, and created an expensive social security system. Although Cardoso entered office in 1994 with considerable political capital, he recognized that he would be incapable of making immediate reforms in all these areas. Additionally, Cardoso preferred gradual reform to shock therapy, the loyalty of his coalition partners was not without its limits, and volatility in international markets kept the fear of a return of inflation lurking in the background.

With macroeconomic stabilization as its chief priority, Cardoso concentrated his efforts on easing sections in the constitution that limited foreign participation and investment in Brazilian markets, to lower tariffs and to make the Brazilian economic system less rigid. Not only did this lead to macroeconomic stabilization, but it encouraged a flood of foreign direct investment which was necessary to offset fiscal deficits and the cost of social security (sectors which would be much more difficult to reform).

Of all the reforms undertaken by Cardoso, the most significant, without doubt, has been the macroeconomic stabilization that was the result of the *Real Plan*. The costs of hyperinflation were widely distributed across society and the benefits of eliminating the scourge of inflation were equally broadly distributed. As a result, the *Real Plan* was immensely popular and it provided Cardoso with two presidential victories and more breathing room than any Brazilian president in recent history. Further reforms have been difficult since improvements in minority shareholder rights, social security reforms, labor and administrative policy, among others, involve concentrated costs and benefits that are more diffuse (Alesina, 1994). But the government has nonetheless progressed with an agenda to liberalize its markets, the macroeconomy, and to engage in regional trade associations (Mercosul and FTAA/ALCA).

Brazil experienced three important macroeconomic structural changes in the 1990s: the opening of trade at the beginning of the decade, the end of hyperinflation in 1994 to 95, and the floating of the exchange rate in 1999. Eliana Cardoso's "Monetary and Fiscal Reforms" examines these three periods and the policies that put an end to inflation and led to the adoption of a floating exchange rate. It also describes the institutional changes that underlie the new monetary regime of inflation targeting, as well as changes in fiscal balance and intergovernmental finance. The chapter then examines pension and tax reforms that remain incomplete, before concluding with an examination of recent macroeconomic developments. These points that Eliana Cardoso describes as critical are currently being discussed by the da Silva government, a telltale sign of the extent to which the reform agenda has been internalized as the paradigm of the Brazilian government, regardless of what parties are elected.

While many have argued that there are too many "veto players" in Brazilian politics and that deadlock is an inevitable result (Ames, 2001), Maria Hermínia Tavares de Almeida's analysis of the privatization process in Brazil suggests otherwise. In "Privatization: Reform Through Negotiation," she challenges the predominant theories which consider that the autonomy of the executive branch is a condition for successful economic reforms. The chapter contends that privatization in Brazil has been possible in the absence of an autonomous executive, through a negotiated process where results depended on the relevant actors' ideas about the role of the public sector, their strategies, and their capacity to use or circumvent institutionally embedded veto points. Though there have been significant changes and privatization has been relatively successful, she notes that liberalism is not hegemonic, and identifies the role that the state will play in post-stabilization Brazil as a major source of discussion and debate.

Despite criticisms to the contrary, the Cardoso government envisioned social policies and development as being central to reform efforts. It is true his initial concerns were with stabilization, and international financial institutions and investors have pushed for reforms that would liberalize capital flows and trade regimes, and flexibilize labor markets. But it would be inaccurate to describe Brazilian reforms as being dominated by fiscal adjustment at the expense of social policy.

A frequent criticism of structural adjustment programs is that in the name of orthodoxy and fiscal discipline cuts are made to state budgets.[1] These cuts fall disproportionately on the poor since the social sectors that receive government welfare are among the least organized. The economic crisis of the

---

1. Stallings and Peres (2000) show convincingly that reforms in 1990s led to net increases in social spending in all of the Latin American cases surveyed, including Brazil.

1980s and 1990s forced policymakers to recognize the importance of fiscal discipline, but not to the exclusion of social considerations.

No social science text on Brazil misses the opportunity to mention that the distribution of wealth in Brazil is among the worst in the world. That said, an investigation into the effects, positive or otherwise, that reforms have had on social development is critical. Reformers argue that stabilization is necessary for growth and that growth leads to development for society as a whole. Their opponents argue that liberalization worsens distribution of wealth. Studies argue that reforms have not changed the distribution of wealth in Brazil (Stallings and Peres, 2000; Dyer, 5 April 2001).

Sônia Draibe's "Social Policy Reform" argues that despite the claims of many critics of the Cardoso government and pundits who have posed the death of the welfare state, Brazilian social policy has survived economic crisis. She argues that although reforms to the social policy agenda began in the 1980s, it was not until the 1990s, particularly with the Cardoso administration, that reforms began in earnest. Brazil remains a country with terrible social indicators, even when compared against other middle-income countries, but there have been significant reforms, particularly in terms of elementary education and public health. The reforms have been progressive in orientation, have benefited from decentralization, and have encouraged the participation of nongovernmental organizations and the private sector. Other reforms in the area of social policy have been less successful and the results more contested.

In his contribution, Anthony Pereira addresses the controversial issue of "Agrarian Reform." He writes that the Cardoso government stood in sharp contrast to the first three post-authoritarian Brazilian governments in terms of land reform. While the first three could be characterized as mostly empty rhetoric with minimal accomplishments, the Cardoso government engaged in more land redistribution than any of its predecessors. But this claim is highly contested and misleading. Despite considerable movement in the area of land reform, Pereira argues that the Cardoso government continued the patrimonial politics of previous governments. This patrimonialism has been worsened by low levels of public authority and accountability, although rural violence has decreased.

The state has been and remains the chief institution that intermediates between key sectors in society and the two most salient sectors: labor and business. The state's intermediation in these sectors has been characterized by corporatism, which was perhaps the organizing principle of Brazilian politics and society throughout most of this century. But, as with other elements of the architecture of the Brazilian state, corporatism has been challenged by trends in global economics and by domestic reform efforts.

David Fleischer's "Political Reforms: The 'Missing Link'" argues that while the Cardoso government was successful at passing and implementing macroeconomic reforms, it has been much less successful with political reform, and it has relied on the traditional form of "pork-barrel" politics in order to govern. Fleischer's chapter emphasizes unresolved elements of the political reform agenda which would lead to more disciplined political parties and to better representation. He also gives special attention to the need to make changes within the judiciary system, particularly because of the increasingly high profile and cost of corruption.

Just as critics cite the constitution as an obstacle to investment, privatization, development, and reforms in general, political analysts have been critical of the decentralization of the political system that was part of the constitution of 1988. Although many scholars believe decentralization is fundamental to democratization, decentralization presents a very clear challenge to developing countries in that it shifts political and administrative accountability to a local level which can be a significant obstacle to the rationalization of national fiscal accounts and negotiation of standby loans. Yet, as Alfred Montero argues, scholars cannot account for the success of the Cardoso administration in recentralizing significant policy authorities and fiscal resources. In "Competitive Federalism and Distributive Conflict," Montero analyzes decentralization in Brazil as an intergovernmental distributive game in which the powers of the president and the weakness of horizontal coordination among the states has shifted bargaining leverage back to national regulators. Conditioning factors, such as changes in macroeconomic policy, the assertion of international constraints, and the reform and regeneration of central regulatory bodies, have reinforced central authority. The Brazilian case, he concludes, raises questions about the explanatory power of approaches that rely primarily on the structure of the party system, political careers, and legislative politics.

Corporatism aimed at the intermediation of business and labor interests. This was particularly important in Brazil where state intervention in the economy was considerable and had enduring effects. Corporatism and state intervention shielded Brazilian industrialists from foreign competition and also provided them with considerable rent. This should have engendered a block of business leaders that would oppose liberalization and that would cling to corporatist managerial ideas. But, as Peter Kingstone argues, in "Industrialists and Liberalization," the conventional wisdom is inaccurate in its depiction of the attitudes and complaints of industrialists in Brazil. He argues that: the industrial community was much more supportive of the economic reform process and goals than is generally assumed; many of the industrial community's complaints were justified and accurate diagnoses of the contradictions in the reform program rather than the criticism of threatened rent-seekers; and industrialists have reinvented themselves in important and meaningful ways in response to commercial liberalization. This reinvention has lasting consequences for business in Brazil, whose importance has increased significantly as the size of Brazil's private sector grows.

As Kingstone has argued elsewhere (Kingstone, 1999), business is a crucial group whose support for any reforms of the developmental model are essential. A case study of one particularly important business organization is provided by Eduardo Rodrigues Gomes and Fabrícia Guimarães's "Entreprenuers: The PNBE." Focusing on the oldest autonomous business association in Brazil's new democratic rule, the Pensamento Nacional das Bases Empresariais (PNBE), this chapter is aimed at assessing the reasons for PNBE's longevity, given that a number of other new collective actions business associations have been short-lived. It is suggested that PNBE's longevity and significance derives not only from the specific niche of small- and medium-sized entrepreneurs to whom it has appealed, but also from the dual role of political organization and a social movement. The chapter discusses implications of the case of PNBE for the politics of business in Brazil's democracy.

Salvador Sandoval's contribution to the volume, "Working-Class Contention," analyzes the impact of economic and state reforms that have contributed to the undermining of the Brazilian labor movement's capacity to mobilize workers in defense of their interests. He outlines how the economic changes in the 1990s affected elements of the progressive labor movement and how workers excluded from the growth stimulated by neoliberal economic policies have turned to other forms of collective actions in seeking redress of their grievances. In the ensuing conflicts, between these workers and authorities, the contradictions that have made organized labor less agile in formulating proposals at this point in history suggest a new set of conditions that have thrust organized labor into having to redefine key assumptions about its role as an effective representative of working-class interests.

The chapters by Kingstone, Gomes and Guimarães, and Sandoval highlight the importance of understanding the role that interest groups and actors play. Their influence is highlighted by the return of democracy, and the participation and support of business, labor, and other popular sectors, is necessary in the context of establishing a robust and fair democracy. This is especially important since the liberal reform agenda has been criticized for being imposed by international agents and domestic technocrats in a process that has excluded the bulk of the population (Oxhorn and Ducantzeiler, 1998; Oxhorn and Starr, 1999). This is a serious issue for any democracy but especially one that has such a historic problem with inequality and poverty.

João Paulo Peixoto's "Brazil and Hemispheric Integration" emphasizes the asymmetrical interests and ideological positions of the main actors, and the gains and losses that the FTAA presents to them. Regardless of position or interests, in the end, he argues, the FTAA is inevitable. As such, Brazil should seek to positively and actively pursue economic integration with the rest of the hemisphere, as suggested by the literature on the new political economy of international relations. But he also highlights the difficulties involved in negotiations, particularly by recounting the Embraer-Bombardier affair that led to Canada imposing sanctions against Brazil and with Brazil receiving permission in June of 2002 to retaliate.

Discussion

The reform agenda of the Cardoso government, as argued in various chapters in this book, was not exclusively "neoliberal" as often claimed. The aim of the reforms was to improve efficiency, not simply to minimize state size or responsibilities (Bresser-Pereira, 1996). It is precisely this notion of a pragmatic liberal reform, one which actually allows for a net improvement of welfare, that the da Silva government has adopted.

Studies of democratization consider democracy to be consolidated when all major political actors accept democratic rules of the game as the only possible means to attaining power. The accession to government of opposition forces and the acceptance of this by previous governors and the military is usually the mark of a mature democracy. Similarly, reforms can be assessed not only by their success during the government that implements them but by the degree to which they have been accepted and maintained by successive governments, particularly from the opposition.

Proponents of reform in Brazil insist that many reforms have not yet been implemented. Some even fear that future reforms will be abandoned, and that actual reforms could be reversed.[1] In Brazil, the issue of democracy appears to be resolved, but there is the age-old distrust of who the populace will choose to lead and whether that government would be one that would cater to populist demands or would further the reform agenda. The increased attention that alternative policies often receive highlights the importance of democracy and the need for governments elected via regular elections. This is true across the region, even as some of the commitment of elite and popu-

---

1.   The first quarter volume of the Inter-American Development Bank's Latin American Economic Policies tries to address "The Future of Reforms," and, in doing so, lists the concerns of the Washington Consensus, UNECLA, and the World Social Forum (IADB, 2002). The inclusion of different voices shows a significant movement in the IADB, also found among international financial institutions more generally, which is that the technical expertise of economists is no longer accepted without question and the recognition of the importance of dialogue with different academic and popular voices is essential to the success of a government's program, whatever it may be.

lar sectors to democratically elected leaders, and sometimes democracy itself, may fade (e.g., Ecuador, 1999, Peru, 2000, Venezuela 2002, among others).

Reforms in the electoral system have been significant and are the source of considerable pride among Brazilians, especially in light of the contested U.S. presidential elections of 2000.[1] Additionally, the once highly contested idea of reelection for executive officers (president, governor, and mayor) now seems to be accepted. However, there have been recent controversial changes and proposed amendments to the nature of party coalitions and how political parties can prepare their electoral lists. In fact, it can be said that political reform is one of the major reforms that was only partially considered and, in the view of many academics and politicians, much remains to be done (see Fleischer in this volume; also Power, 2000).

As Almeida argues in her conclusion in this volume, although there has been a considerable shift in terms of consensus over the state-led growth model and acceptance of some liberal ideas, the role of the state in the economy remains a fundamental and unsettled issue. The uncertainty over the role of the state and its commitment to efficiency-gaining measures and policies can lead to investor concerns, greater pressure on the *real*, and higher rates of interest on international capital markets. New laws which limit fiscal profligacy and an increasingly autonomous and credible Central Bank help.

Intergovernmental finances are especially important for the maintenance of federal fiscal balances and international creditability. Much of the improvement in the strength of federal finances has come as a result of careful political maneuvering by President Cardoso (see Montero in this volume). But there is concern that Cardoso's gains could be temporary—due to his personal efforts—and that they still may not be fully institutionalized. But, as Eliana Cardoso's contribution argues, significant reforms are necessary in terms of tax collection, intergovernmental finances, and overall fiscal burden.

The importance of a new regulatory model, one that necessarily differs from that of the state-led industrialization period, is critical. The old corporatist system corresponded to domestic and international conditions that no longer exist. The new system, however, must find a way to address political actors, new and old, whose political demands and methods of political contestation have shifted (see Gomes and Guimarães, Sandoval, and Pereira in this volume). It must not only find a way to accommodate and intermediate between interests groups, but it must do so in a way that is perceived as fair, and one that does not destroy the fundamental social bases of the state. As opposed to institutional and political reform, this is an area where policy shifts and reversals are possible. The chapters by Kingstone, Gomes and

---

1.   In fact, it is telling that few of the chapters in this book discuss democratization as an idea—since it is assumed—and instead focus on making the democratic state more efficient and equitable.

Guimarães, and Sandoval highlight how important groups, such as business and labor, can and should be involved in Brazilian political economy.

Reforms may also be on shaky ground in the area of social policy, although the general idea of targeting "at-risk" populations instead of broad-scale social policies is likely to remain unchanged. Sandoval's and Pereira's chapters analyze some of the most vocal opponents of the reform agenda, including those that have benefited from the new model, and the very new methods of interest articulation by non-state actors and the novel and traditional ways that the state has responded. But, there is still considerable disagreement over the direction of economic policy, particularly over the role of the state. Brazilian politicians have been very reluctant to liberalize completely and a stabilized economy may have weakened the appetite for further reform.

This volume is hardly conclusive and cannot address all of the reforms undertaken or ignored—and the consequences thereof—that have entered or should enter the Brazilian political arena. However, the book does collect leading authorities on political institutions, political economy, social policy, and economic reforms. Their analysis of the effects of the reform agenda in their specific areas of expertise gives a robust picture of the very significant accomplishments of the Cardoso administration.

Cardoso left the presidency of Brazil with Brazil in better shape than when he entered, a seemingly remarkably modest claim, but one that few other presidents in Brazil's recent history can claim. More than simply leaving Brazil in better shape than he found it, Cardoso has contributed to the further consolidation of democracy in Brazil, stabilization of the economy, and has engendered conditions for the long-term improvements of political, economic, and social conditions in Brazil. There is still much to be done, as many of the chapters in this book suggest, but a fundamental and strong base has been established in the last eight years. This base is likely to endure even if further reforms are not implemented, if current reforms remain unimplemented and if some reforms are reversed. But such a dire reversal is very unlikely due to the increased institutionalization of the Brazilian political process which has been made possible by the stability of the two Cardoso governments.

Part II
Reforms

CHAPTER 2	*Monetary and Fiscal Reforms*

Eliana Cardoso

Brazil experienced three important macroeconomic structural changes in the 1990s: the opening of trade at the beginning of the decade, the end of mega-inflation in 1994–1995, and the floating of the exchange rate in 1999. This chapter examines the fiscal and monetary policies that put an end to inflation and led to the floating of the exchange rate. It describes the institutional changes that underlie the new monetary regime of inflation targeting and discusses fiscal reforms that remain incomplete.

The End of Inflation

Between 1981 and 1994, Brazil's annual rate of inflation exceeded 100 percent in every year except 1986. As a result, containing chronic inflation became the focus of economic policy. This led to a spectacular series of failed stabilization plans involving six monetary reforms in ten years.[1] Yet despite the unanimous failure of these various reform efforts, megainflation did not destroy the Brazilian economy. Indexation, the adaptive policy response, became pervasive throughout the economy. Tax revenue did not fall significantly and remained high relative to other Latin American countries. Furthermore, Brazil's financial sectors and industrial businesses kept functioning well. Except during short periods, policymakers kept the exchange rate competitive, allowing the country to generate substantial trade surpluses until mid-1994.[2]

Brazil's capacity to accommodate inflation may partially explain why the government failed to engage in serious structural change. The behavior of

---

1. During the twentieth century, Brazil had eight monetary reforms that removed zeros from the previous currency and changed the name of the currency, as follows: *Mil-Réis* (1900–1942), *Cruzeiro* (1942–1966), *Cruzeiro Novo* (1967–1969), *Cruzeiro* (1970–1986), *Cruzado* (1986–1989), *Cruzado Novo* (1989–1990), *Cruzeiro* (1990–1993), *Cruzeiro Real* (1993–1994), and *Real* (1994–2000).

inflation in the late 1980s can be characterized as a ratchet pattern, with a series of heterodox policy interventions that lowered inflation rates for a few months, only to have inflation climb up again. The cycle began with the *Cruzado Plan*, which was initiated in February 1986 and lasted for sixteen months. Under this directive, prices were frozen, indexation in financial markets was prohibited, and after a wage increase, both wages and the nominal exchange rate were frozen as well. However, as the government lacked fiscal and monetary discipline, and was unable to arrest growing trade deficits, it was forced to dismantle price controls and change to an exchange rate regime using daily devaluations. Thus, in June of 1987 inflation returned and a new stabilization attempt was imposed—the *Bresser Plan*—which also relied on price freezes and a new wage indexation scheme. Later still in 1988, a standby agreement with the International Monetary Fund was approved but failed because of inadequate fiscal performance. Finally, in January 1989, the *Summer Plan* introduced yet another price and wage freeze, which was relaxed in April with a return to formal indexation. Thus, in the wake of a decade-long roller-coaster ride, inflation was close to 3,000 percent per year by early 1990.

In the face of inflation that could not be easily accommodated through indexation, the *Collor Plan* of March 1990 drastically cut liquidity. An arbitrary freeze was imposed for seventeen months on nearly two-thirds of the money supply (M4), broadly defined to include demand deposits, mutual funds, federal bonds, state and municipal bonds, saving deposits, and private bonds. Although Brazilians eventually managed to circumvent some of these controls, the financial freeze took over personal assets and was wildly unpopular. Fiscal policy was tightened, price controls were set in place, and indexation rules modified. Public debt was also cut because the official inflation correction of indexed debt (the monetary correction) was set below the actual inflation rate in March and April. The plan contained important components of structural reform, including trade liberalization and privatization of public enterprises, that were later sustained throughout the decade. In 1992, however, President Fernando Collor was ousted from power in a corruption scandal, and inflation hit 1,000 percent per year. Inflation would reach even higher rates soon after.

---

2.   The exceptions occurred in 1986, when the exchange rate was fixed, and in 1989 and early 1990, when inflation accelerated and the minidevaluations lagged behind as an overt policy effort to slow down inflation. But after 1994, partly as a result of liberalization, imports increased substantially. The average tariff rate fell from more than 30 percent in 1991 to 14 percent by the end of 1994. Both nominal and effective protection declined and became more uniform between 1991 and 1994, but part of this progress was lost in 1995 when tariffs were increased on imports of motor vehicles. The combination of liberalization and exchange rate appreciation was perilous. The trade balance, which for ten years had been in surplus, showed a deficit during the last two months of 1994 that was to persist in the following years, and contribute to a rising current account deficit.

By the time Collor left power, the resilience of the economy had been sapped. In an attempt to manage the crisis he left behind, a standby agreement with the IMF in January 1992 temporarily shifted the regime from heterodoxy to orthodoxy, with an emphasis on high real interest rates. But this approach was short lived. As nominal interest rates fell in 1993, gross domestic product (GDP) increased and inflation accelerated again. With inflation soon exceeding a staggering 2000 percent, the *Real Plan* was launched in December of 1993.[3]

The *Real Plan*

Under the *Real Plan*, stabilization went through three stages: a brief fiscal adjustment, monetary reform, and the use of the exchange rate as a nominal anchor. In its first stage, Brazil's Congress approved a fiscal adjustment plan in January 1994 that included cuts in current spending and the creation of the Emergency Social Fund. The fund, financed by redirecting federal revenues limiting the ability of states and municipalities to access credit, and recovering mandatory social security contributions, allowed the government to break some of the mandated links between revenues and expenditures. Twenty percent of revenues that had been earmarked for other purposes were freed. The resulting increase in flexibility led to an operational surplus in 1994.

The second component of the *Real Plan* entailed a temporary monetary reform measure and linked contracts, prices, wages, and the exchange rate to a single daily escalator and unit of account URV (*Unidade Real de Valor*, or Real Value Unit). The adjustment, which started on March 1, 1994, lasted four months. The Central Bank determined a daily parity between the *cruzeiro real* and the URV based on the current rate of inflation. Finally, as its third and final step, a new currency, the *real*, which converted contracts denominated in URVs into *reais* at a rate of one to one, was introduced on July 1, 1994.

The *Real Plan* brought inflation under control with remarkable speed. Following the introduction of the *real*, inflation fell from four digits in 1994 to two digits in 1995 and to less than 2 percent in 1998. Indeed, Cardoso's success in securing the right to run for reelection in 1998 drew on the popularity he derived from sustained price stability. Economic growth was also strong: GDP growth averaged 4 percent per year between 1994 and 1997, compared to flat or declining output in the prior years, as had happened in the first phases of the other exchange rate–based disinflation programs of the previous five years. The economic boom that began in 1994 did not, however, originate from a decline in real interest. In fact, real interest rates remained

---

3.   At the same time, the fall of international interest rates eased the external debt burden and led to an agreement with creditor banks, concluded in April 1994, involving an exchange of instruments that covered over US$50 billion in debt stocks and arrears.

TABLE 2-1. Indicators of Fiscal Performance, percent of GDP

Period	Nominal PSBR*	Operational PSBR	Primary PSBR	Real Interest Payments	Net Public Debt
1993	58.1	(0.2)	(2.7)	2.5	32.0
1994	43.8	(1.3)	(5.1)	3.8	28.1
1995	7.1	4.9	(0.4)	5.3	29.9
1996	5.9	3.7	0.1	3.6	33.3
1997	6.1	4.4	1.0	3.4	35.2
1998	7.9	7.5	0.0	7.5	43.4
1999	10.0	3.1	(3.2)	6.3	49.4
2000	4.6	0.0	(3.5)	3.5	49.6

Note: Borrowing Requirement (PSBR) equals total revenues less expenditures including all government levels, the Central Bank, and public enterprises, but excluding state and federal banks.
Source: Banco Central do Brasil.

high throughout the period. Instead, the Brazilian boom originated from the increase in real wages. Between 1993 and 1995, several wage adjustments took place, including increases in minimum wages and in government's wages and salaries. These gains in income were reflected in booming imports and durable goods consumption. High real interest rates drew in capital to finance growing imbalances, but they undermined fiscal balance.

Yet, despite the promising start, the fiscal adjustment achieved in 1994 was lost in subsequent years. The operational deficit, which includes real interest payments, moved from a surplus in 1994 to a deficit equal to 5 percent of GDP in 1995; it remained at around 4 percent of GDP in 1996 and 1997, and deteriorated further in 1998 and 1999 (see Table 2–1). The primary surplus, which excludes interest payments, declined in 1995, reflecting the significant increase in payroll outlays, and turned into a deficit in 1996. Factors that contributed to the primary imbalance included a 43 percent increase in pensions following the increase in the minimum wage in May 1995 and the significant growth of "other expenditures," particularly once the 1998 elections were approaching.[4] The combination of these factors resulted in a budget deficit that reached 10 percent of GDP in 1999.

Fiscal problems were further compounded by the emergence of substantial quasi-fiscal deficits in federal and state banks. For example, the federally owned Banco do Brasil (a traditional source of subsidized credit to agriculture) and the National Bank of Development (BNDES) introduced programs that subsidized credit to exporters in 1996. Partly in order to finance these programs, the treasury recapitalized Banco do Brasil with R$7.9 billion (over 1 percent of GDP). Such intergovernmental transfers contributed to an

---

4. "Other Expenditures" is an item of the central government budget that includes investment and other current expenditures ("Outras despesas de custeio e capital," known as OCC) to which the treasury allocates resources in proportion to congressional appropriations. It creates a bargaining arena between the national administration and politicians.

increase of total net public debt, from 30 percent of GDP in 1995 to 35 percent in 1996.

Furthermore, with the end of inflation, bad loans from state banks to state governments became a serious problem. In the case of BANESPA, a bank owned by the state of São Paulo, the federal government agreed to swap bonds of its own for the obligations of São Paulo to BANESPA for about R$33 billion. Although this did not directly increase the net federal debt—for its bonds were offset by state obligations—such measures to stabilize weak state banks further increased the federal government's vulnerability to capital shocks. The ratio of net public debt to GDP increased from 28 percent in 1995 to 44 percent in 1998, and jumped to 50 percent after the devaluation in January 1999.

Monetary Policy Is a Poor Substitute for Fiscal Reform

Stabilization under the *Real Plan* was supported by tight monetary policy, including an increase in reserve requirements. The required reserves-to-deposit ratio rose from an average of 26 percent during January–June 1994 to 64 percent during November 1994–April 1995. This increase in required reserves and the decline of inflation led to a substantial decline in the inflationary revenues of deposit banks.

With the rise in lending restrictions under the *Real Plan*, the share in total seigniorage seized by the Central Bank increased from an average of 60 percent in the first half of 1994 to 84 percent a year later. As a consequence, the share in GDP of seigniorage seized by deposit banks fell from 2 percent to close to zero and seigniorage collected by the Central Bank rose from 1.8 percent of GDP in 1993, the peak inflation year, to 3 percent in 1994, the year of the *Real Plan* (Cardoso, 1998).

This appropriation of seigniorage from the banking sector to the Central Bank helped to finance government spending as inflation ebbed, but it also put the banking sector at risk. A more balanced policy would not have transferred the revenues from money creation so drastically from deposit banks to the Central Bank, and thus would have avoided the increase in interest rate spreads and nonperforming loans. But as it was, the elements exposed the Brazilian banks' weaknesses, particularly those of public banks, further straining the fiscal resources needed for restructuring. Between mid-1994 and mid-1997, the Central Bank intervened in 51 banks and 140 other financial institutions. The failure of two big banks, Banco Econômico and Banco Nacional, prompted the creation of a program providing assistance to private banks known as PROER (Programa de Estímulo à Reestructuração e ao Sistema Financiero Nacional).

Brazil's success in bringing down inflation was also associated with real exchange rate appreciation. Between 1994 and 1998, the average real

FIGURE 2-1. *Real* Effective Exchange Rate, June 1994=100

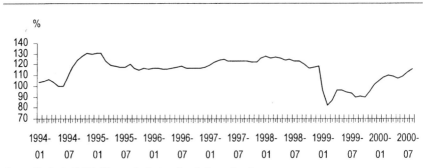

Source: Fundação Getúlio Vargas, *Conjuntura Econômica*, various issues.

exchange rate was 31 percent above the average of the prior fourteen years: the only comparable peaks occurred prior to the debt crisis and in the wake of the failed heterodox plans. The rapid appreciation under the *Real Plan* occurred at the end of 1994. Despite minor devaluations between 1995 and 1998, the real exchange rate at the end of 1998 was still as high as it was at the beginning of 1996 (see Figure 2–1).

There were no structural changes or anticipated growth to justify the large appreciation of the exchange rate. On the contrary, sustained long-run growth would have been inconsistent with the large current account deficits that were bound to prevail at the going real exchange rate. The behavior of the trade balance reinforces this observation. During 1995, Brazil's trade deficit increased during the first semester and started to decline during the second semester as the economy contracted. But a small recovery after June 1996 was enough to produce further deterioration of the trade deficit. The trade balance continued to deteriorate, producing a deficit of US$8.4 billion in 1997 and US$6.5 billion in 1998. Evidence of overvaluation was also apparent in the slow growth of exports. Between 1995 and 1998, the growth rate of exports in dollar terms was 4.2 percent per year compared to an average of 11.3 percent per year between 1991 and 1994.

The strong currency harmed the industrial sector and increased unemployment. The government reacted by creating subsidized credit to exporters through the National Development Bank (BNDES) and by approving legislation to exempt primary and semimanufactured exports from indirect taxes (manufactured goods were already exempt from indirect taxes). But neither was sufficient to offset the effects of overvaluation.

In order to sustain external equilibrium and reduce trade deficits as the real exchange rate appreciates, policymakers often use monetary policy to reduce aggregate demand. Such measures therefore seemed appropriate for Brazil. However, between June 1995 and December 1998, the passive real interest rate averaged 22 percent per year. High real interest rates make fiscal adjustment even more difficult because they increase public debt servicing. They also contribute to the deterioration of bank portfolios and increase the need for subsidies to recapitalize banks. The difference between domestic and foreign interest rates increases external borrowing and sustains real appreciation, providing apparent stability. As long as reserves and capital flows are available, the temptation to continue to use the exchange rate to keep inflation under control seems irresistible.

High Interest Rates and the Deterioration of Fundamentals

The *Real Plan*'s strategy to contain inflation by using monetary and exchange rate policies reduced domestic savings and created unsustainable current account deficits. These policies, in turn, led to a boom in capital flows that initially helped stabilization. Accumulating reserves fed by capital flows masked the severity of the current account deficits and the decline in private savings. As capital continued to enter Brazil, it sustained currency overvaluation and clouded policymakers' perception of the maturing crisis.

To avoid a monetary expansion induced by capital flows, inflows were partly sterilized. Sterilization created significant fiscal costs in financing high levels of reserve holdings, because of both the scale of the operations and the size of the interest differential vis-à-vis U.S. dollar rates (and rates in other reserve centers). The rise in monetary authorities' gross foreign assets in relation to the increase in the monetary base suggests that sterilization operations were large and costly in Brazil in the 1990s. In 1995, the stock of Central Bank securities and treasury securities outside the Central Bank grew 53 percent in real terms. Between 1994 and 1996, the ratio of the net debt of the public sector to GDP increased from 28.5 percent to 35 percent, as high real interest rates allowed a weakening of the fiscal stance for two years in a row. Net debt continued to grow in the following years, reaching 44 percent of GDP by 1998.

The lack of confidence in the regime's ability to sustain the exchange rate anchor and to meet its obligations was reflected in the increasing use of dollar-denominated and floating rate debt. Prior to the problems of 1998, most domestically denominated debt was set at fixed rates, and about 15 percent was dollar-indexed. By early 1999, 21 percent was dollar-denominated and 70 percent was indexed to the overnight interest rate. Moreover, maturities fell: the interest due on domestic debt in January 1999 alone exceeded 6 percent of GDP. These foreboding signs soon spelled disaster for Brazil.

The *Real* Collapses in Early 1999

As fundamentals deteriorated, investors lost confidence. While the 1997 Asian crisis caused a brief panic, the real jolt came with the Russian crisis in

August 1998. Brazil's foreign currency reserves fell by US$30 billion as the government struggled to defend the *real*.

The IMF moved quickly to set up a loan package, but domestic politics, including the timing of presidential and gubernatorial elections and the relationships between the central and state governments, delayed negotiations. Finally, in December 1998 Brazil signed a US$41.5 billion financial assistance package. Contributions were to come from the IMF (US$18 billion), the World Bank, the Inter-American Development Bank (US$4.5 billion each), and bilateral creditors (US$5 billion of which would be provided by the United States and US$9.5 billion by European governments).

The IMF program gave the financial sector time to reduce its exposure in Brazil. It was soon overtaken by events, however, as monetary policy failed to prevent a collapse of the exchange rate. Capital outflows, lack of fiscal progress, strong resistance by the domestic business community to the record high interest rates, and growing demands for correction of the overvalued exchange rate forced the government to adopt a new exchange rate regime. Thus, the *real* was let free to float on January 15, and by the end of February it had depreciated by more than 35 percent.

A Floating Exchange Rate and a New Monetary Regime

Although most economists would agree that the *real* was overvalued throughout the plan, there is no consensus on the size of the overvaluation. After its collapse, the average real exchange rate in the first quarter of 1999 was close to that which prevailed prior to the *Real Plan*. But it was not stable: between mid-January and the end of March, its value against the dollar fluctuated, reaching 2.2 to 1 before settling at a rate of 1.68 to 1 in early May 1999.

The most difficult problem was in setting monetary policy during the first few weeks following the collapse of the exchange rate, when financial market conditions and expectations were unsettled. Inflation can increase sharply after a speculative attack on the currency, as substantial depreciation causes a one-time adjustment in many prices. This temporary increase in inflation could then reduce real interest rates on debt denominated in domestic currency, and thus fuel capital flight. To offset this near-term effect, at least partially, it was appropriate for policymakers to raise nominal interest rates to avoid further depreciation and the danger of igniting a spiral of depreciation and inflation. At the same time, policymakers also had to pay attention to the debt denominated in foreign currency. The larger this debt is, the greater the impact of the devaluation on the debt/GDP ratio. In the case of Brazil, that ratio had reached 53 percent by January 1999.

The most difficult question was: by how much should the Central Bank tighten monetary policy to avoid the deadly devaluation-inflation-devaluation spiral? If it increased the interest rate too little too late, inflation would pick up and the economy would return to its history of persistent inflation. If it increased the interest rate too much, the resulting recession might be too severe, and inflation could decline ahead of interest rates, leading to higher real interest rates. The combination of recession and high real interest rates would increase the budget deficit and reduce confidence in the government's capacity to service its debt without resorting to money creation again. Moreover, the prospect of a severe recession can undermine confidence in the government's resolve to sustain tight monetary policy, and thus set off a new round of inflationary expectations.

The short-run task, then, was to negotiate a path of declining inflation and interest rates and avert another big decline of the exchange rate. By any standard, Brazil negotiated its way through the *real* crisis with extraordinary ease and speed. By May 1999, the *real* rose to US$1/R$1.67, compared to a low of US$1/R$2.21 in March. Short-term interest rates fell from 45 percent in March to just 23 by May 25, and inflation, measured by the national consumer index, declined from an annualized rate of 16 percent in March to 6 percent in April. Further progress was achieved in 2000.

What explains the rapid turnaround? Certainly a dose of good luck has to be acknowledged. Interest rates in the United States remained low. Agricultural output grew by 18 percent in the first quarter of 1999 thanks to a record harvest following good weather conditions. But central to the restoration of investor confidence was fiscal action and shrewd monetary policy. Awareness of the risk of a grave collapse among even intransigent legislators and governors helped: in February, the collapse of the *real* galvanized Congress into passing the partial pension reform legislation that it had rejected in 1998. Congress also approved an increase in a temporary tax on financial transactions. Measures were also introduced to rein in expenditures by state and local authorities. Thus by the end of the first quarter of 1999, a primary fiscal surplus at the central government of US$5.6 billion was achieved.

Monetary Policy Played a Critical Role

Following the inflationary shock of the mid-January devaluation, inflation immediately increased, pushing real interest rates down. The Central Bank reacted by increasing interest rates that turned into extraordinarily high real interest rates in March. As inflationary expectations fell, nominal interest rates were allowed to decline. This strategy successfully shifted the economy from a potentially explosive situation to a path of steadily declining inflation, allowing real interest rates to decline gradually.

The Central Bank demonstrated its commitment to restraining inflation through tight monetary policy, even as official forecasts pointed to a 4 percent contraction in GDP and unemployment was rising. This resolve restored confidence partially and by April, short-term capital was flooding back, attracted by the high yields in Brazil's financial markets.

Brazil's banking sector was also a factor in this recovery. PROER, the 1995–1998 program of assistance to private banks, had restored bank's balance sheets to a healthy position. Furthermore, since many banks had anticipated the devaluation in 1999, they had both positioned themselves to profit from it through currency-futures contracts and hedged by holding dollar-linked government bonds. As a result, the risk of a banking sector collapse did not threaten fiscal balance, as it had in Asia and Mexico.

Inflation Targeting Becomes the New Monetary Framework

The new exchange rate regime allowed the government to adopt a more balanced policy mix. It also imposed the need for a new monetary framework and a new nominal anchor, i.e., an intermediate monetary policy target that would serve to form expectations on future inflation.

Between 1995 and 1998, Brazilian monetary authorities managed the exchange rate variability tightly, using the exchange rate as an anchor until its collapse in January 1999. Having abandoned the exchange rate as nominal anchor, they then had to establish an alternative credible anchor. The choice was inflation targeting.

A successful implementation of a floating exchange rate and an inflation targeting regime requires a clear description of the objectives of monetary policy and an institutional design that grants the central bank the independence necessary to pursue these objectives. While an independent central bank does not need to have goal independence (i.e., the ability to set its own nominal target), it needs to have instrument independence. Under instrument or operational independence, the central bank is free to decide how to adjust its policy instruments (for instance, the short-term interest rate) in order to reach the nominal target.

Bogdanski et al. (2000) describes the process that led Brazil to the implementation of inflation targeting. After the forced floating of the *real* on January 15, 1999, most of the Central Bank's board of directors was replaced. The new board immediately recognized the need for a monetary anchor that would substitute the abandoned crawling peg and decided to adopt an inflation-targeting framework. However, two practical constraints hindered the implementation of inflation targeting: First, the Central Bank did not have operational independence and second, there was a lack of technical skills. In particular, the Central Bank did not have a good research department and very few staff members had any knowledge of how inflation targeting worked.

Nonetheless, the Central Bank convinced President Fernando Henrique Cardoso and his economic team that inflation targeting could work in Brazil. This led to a formal adoption of inflation targeting with a decree that granted the Central Bank "the responsibility to implement the policies necessary to achieve the target." At the same time, the Central Bank started building technical capacity by organizing an international seminar on inflation targeting (see Blejer et al., 2000). It also created a research department with a research area specifically designated to the study of inflation targeting and the development of models of the transmission mechanisms of monetary policy in Brazil.

Formally adopted in June 1999, the new policy framework faced difficult hurdles. The most important was to meet the stringent inflation targets that had been fixed (8 percent for 1999 and 6 percent for 2000). Brazil achieved the targets for both years. This was a remarkable accomplishment, especially given the initial technical difficulties posed by the implementation of the new policy framework and also by the large number of exogenous price shocks, and the growing crisis in Argentina. The reduction of tariffs after 1990 and the substantial progress that had been achieved in de-indexing the economy after 1994 facilitated the success in meeting the targets.

In addition to complying with the 6 percent inflation target for 2000, the authorities also succeeded in lowering market interest rates. Concerned with the fact that the high level of market interest rates was posing a major obstacle to Brazil's return to a path of sustained economic growth, the authorities began taking a series of measures to lower market rates and increase the supply of credit. In September 1999, for instance, reserve requirements for demand deposits and time deposits were lowered from 75 percent to 65 percent and from 20 percent to 10 percent, respectively. Subsequently during 2000, additional reductions in the reserve requirements on demand deposits were implemented, first to 55 percent in March, and then to 45 percent in early June. Also in that same year, the long-term interest rate charged by the National Economic and Social Development Bank (BNDES) was lowered from 12 percent early in the year to 9.75 percent in October. Finally, in November 2000, the Central Bank took additional measures aimed at the creation of a system of credit derivatives, the improvement of guarantee instruments in credit operations, and the reduction of the costs of financial transactions.

The success of the flotation of the *real* brought real interest rates down between 1999 and 2001 to half the levels between 1995 and 1998, and assuming continuity of policy, one can forecast further reductions of interest rates. The bad news is that lending rates and bank spreads continue to be very high. In 2001, interest rates reached an annual average of 44 percent for business loans and 73 percent for personal loans. As the inflation rate remained below 8 percent, it is clear that long-term loans at these rates cannot be sustained. High reserve requirements, high taxation levels, and the cost of nonperforming loans affect bank spreads between interest rates on deposits and interest rates on loans.

Fiscal Balance and Expenditures

The end of inflation made Brazil's fiscal problems more transparent. Economists think of extreme inflation as an unstable process, the instability reinforced by the Tanzi effect—a decline in real tax revenues as inflation rises. However, empirical evidence suggests that a powerful effect runs in the other direction through declining real spending levels—the Patinkin effect (Cardoso, 1998).

Observed aggregate budget data on nominal, operational, and primary deficits contain very little information about the true fiscal position of the public sector when inflation exceeds 500 percent per year. The Tanzi effect predicts that real tax revenues decline as inflation rises because collection lags inflation, and thus the budget deficit is higher at higher inflation rates. But there is also a reverse Tanzi effect—the Patinkin effect. If the Patinkin effect dominates at high inflation rates, real expenditures are lower than they would be if there were no inflation, and real expenditures tend to increase when inflation disappears. Thus, the fiscal adjustment needed once inflation disappears is usually underestimated. Several factors explain this phenomenon:

- Real interest rates decline with increasing inflation rates and usually rise following stabilization. This rise in real interest rates contributes to the increase in real government expenditures once inflation disappears.

- During periods of high inflation, local governments' payments of salaries and wages lag inflation. When inflation exceeds 1,000 percent per year, this delay produces a substantial decline in real expenditures. When inflation disappears, delaying payments no longer reduces real expenditures.

- Although governments have learned to lessen gaps in tax collection and index delayed tax payments to inflation, they still program expenditures with a forecast for inflation that is usually lower than observed inflation. As a consequence, realized real expenditures are much lower than programmed expenditures. When inflation disappears, actual expenditures will be closer to their programmed levels.

- The inflationary revenue of state banks can finance credit subsidies that are not recorded. This revenue disappears when inflation disappears. Furthermore, if inflation has been concealing banks's weaknesses, and these weaknesses are accentuated by the rise in real interest rates that follows stabilization, the government will have to use fiscal revenues to rescue banks, and recorded real expenditures will increase with stabilization.

- Because inflation reduces real expenditures but not real taxes when governments fully index taxes, inflation can be used to accommodate conflicting spending demands from different government levels. Thus inflation produces operational budget deficits consistent with the amount of real seigniorage that the government needs to finance the deficit.

One should note, however, that the Patinkin effect could only partially explain the resurgence of large fiscal deficits after inflation disappeared with the *Real Plan*. Of course, high real interest rates—a factor in the Patinkin effect—did undermine fiscal efforts. But problems inherent in the constitution of 1988, the failure to rein in excessive pension payments, and increased expenditures during the 1998 election year lay at the core of the fiscal fragility in the second half of the 1990s.

Fiscal Effort in 1999 to 2001

Despite a series of important measures, the Brazilian economy still needs further actions on the fiscal front. This section highlights pressing issues. Although it does not discuss all the areas that could be improved, it indicates that a stronger fiscal stance would help inspire confidence among investors and mitigate the impact of external financial shocks.

In 2000 and 2001, despite the Argentinean government's efforts to assuage rumors that it would be forced to abandon its eight-year-old fixed exchange rate that pegged the peso one-for-one against the dollar, markets were once again shaken by contagion. This posed a serious threat to Brazil, as it remains vulnerable to external shocks: the current account deficit is large and external finance remains vital to service external liabilities accumulated during the past five years.

In addition to external vulnerability, public sector borrowing requirements are large due to accumulated interest obligations on domestic debt, and there is a risk that interest rates could turn out to be too high to allow for a declining debt/GDP ratio. Government will have to pursue a tighter fiscal policy to contain the risk of the impact of renewed increases in interest rates on fiscal balance.

Thus, the 3.5 percent primary surplus projected for 2001 is not overkill if one considers yet other factors that can easily put Brazil's fragile fiscal balance in jeopardy. The threats come not only from any increase in interest rates or devaluation, but also from a drop of subnational government's fiscal performance and from unexpected off-budget liabilities that could arise from bank failures, the risk of new rulings on pensions and wages, or public enterprise losses.[5]

Fiscal adjustment in Brazil has to take place on the expenditure front, considering that past adjustments largely involved increases in the tax burden rather than decreases in expenditures. Further increases in the tax burden must be ruled out to avoid further declines in competitiveness. But rigidities in government's expenditures that undermine the effectiveness of budget institutions in achieving fiscal discipline will pose major challenges to a balanced budget. The expenditures are rigid largely because they obey constitutional mandates reflecting, in turn, a political choice that largely materialized in the 1988 constitution. The 1988 Charter established a mandate to increase social expenditures, transfers to subnational governments, and benefits to the civil service.

These rigidities surface whether one classifies expenditures according to sector destination (e.g., health, education) or by functional use. At the end of the 1990s, for example, under a functional partition of expenditures (salaries, retirement benefits, interest, etc.), constitutional expenditure mandates covered over 80 percent of the federal budget and about 70 percent of the total government budget. From the sectoral perspective, social expenditures in the public sector, strongly protected by the constitution, comprised more than 60 percent of the budget.

Personnel expenditures at the federal level (payments to active staff, retirees or their survivors) reached an all-time high in 1995–1998. At the federal level, savings can be achieved by attrition (replacing only a fraction of those who retire) or by control of wage growth. Wage control was substantial in 1995–1996, after the strong real wage increases during stabilization, and in 1999, with the implementation of the Government's Fiscal Stability Plan.

Reducing the burden of retirement benefits in the public sector also remains a key fiscal need. Other areas of expenditure, such as debt service, are less subject to cuts. More reductions in other costs and investments are possible, but they may not be sustainable. Cuts in administration and supplies, while possible, are of limited scope; they amount to about 7 percent of total expenditures.

Policymakers have also begun to address the inflexibility of expenditures in different ways. The Fiscal Stabilization Fund, which expired in 1999 and was extended with the passage of a new constitutional amendment (the Desvinculação das Receitas da União) established a 20 percent fraction of earmarked federal expenditures to be freely allocated. Some progress on social

---

5.   In recent years, recognition of off-budget liabilities has included items such as: issuance of securities to finance R$8 billion capitalization of Banco do Brasil; reduced investments from the Monetary Reserve Fund to cover judicial decisions on the liquidation of banks Comind and Auxiliar; difference between nominal bid price and market value of government debt used in payment for the privatized assets; recognition of debts to Itaipu and Eletronorte; recognition of debts and assets with Development Funds into net debt statistics; debts emerging from subsidies on oil products; issuance of securities to pay for agricultural sector debts to banks; accumulated subsidy on indexation of mortgage portfolio in Fundo de Compensação de Variações Salariais (this is perhaps the largest item, with an accumulated value of about R$20 billion, and some US$36 billion to come from future maturities).

security reform was achieved to increase contribution time, reduce retirement time, reduce benefits, and raise effective contributions. Administrative reform has removed the full tenure granted to civil servants in 1988.

The truth is that there is no way out for Brazil except to continue the implementation of administrative reforms (that will help overcome the wage bill rigidity) and social security reforms (that will help overcome the retirement benefit rigidities). Overall, the problem at the federal level is more one of high compensations and structure than of absolute numbers. In the case of subnational governments, employment reductions will be more important than wage reductions and generous retirement benefit provisions will have to be cut.

The pension system that covers workers in the private sector is also under financial imbalance. A recent constitutional reform eliminated the private sector's 100 percent replacement formula from the constitution and thus opened the way for improving the actuarial balance through additional legislation. This additional legislation, enacted in November 1999, has come in the form of progressively lengthening the number of years used to calculate the salary base that determines benefits to existing employees. The reform could produce a positive fiscal balance of the private sector system by 2003 which would last for several years, after which demographics should bring the system into deficit again.

The adjustments in retirement contributions by public employees would contribute to sustainability, but do not come anywhere near the amount needed to cover benefit costs in an actuarial sense. Clearly, more adjustments in pension parameters or taxes will need to take place.

Taxes, Intergovernmental Finance, Efficiency, and Tax Reform

Brazil's tax/GDP ratio of 30 percent is high by developing country standards, but well below the size of the tax burden in countries such as France, Germany, and Italy, where public revenue is around 45–55 percent of GDP. Brazil's share in GDP of government revenue is similar to that in the United States and Japan and it is the highest in Latin America, where the tax burden is around 15 percent in Argentina and 18 percent in Mexico. The level of taxes is about right but the structure of taxes is not. The federal government was compelled to introduce new taxes to avoid revenue sharing of traditional taxes with subnational governments and to meet the expenditure mandates that were not delegated to those governments along with the increased revenue sharing. Reform of the taxation system could contribute to increase the efficiency of the economy and thus to increase confidence in the Brazilian economy.

TABLE 2-2. Taxes and Contributions, late 1990s

Taxes and Contributions	Base	Value in 1997 (R$)	% in Relevant Variable	Destination
Federal Taxes				
Income Tax	Personal and Business Income	35.6	4.6% of GDP	Federal: 53%; States: 21.5%; Municipalities: 22.5%; Development Funds: 3%
Import Tariffs	CIF Imports	5.1	8.3% of Imports	Federal
Industrial Products (IPI)	Industrial Value Added	16.6	9.8% of Manufacturing GDP	Federal: 43%; States: 21.5%; Municipalities: 22.5%; Dev. Funds: 3%; Export Fund: 10%
Financial Operations (IOF)	Loans, Insurance, Foreign Investment	3.8	6.7% of Financial GDP	Federal
Rural Land	Land Values	0.2		Federal: 50%; Local: 50%
Fees	Various	0.3		Federal
Federal Contributions				
Social Security	Private Wage Bill	44.1	20.1% of Non-Government Wages	Social Security Benefits
COFINS (Social Security Contrib.)	Gross Revenues	18.3	2.4% of GDP	Social Security Benefits
CPMF (Financial Turnover Tax)	Check Debits	6.9	12.1% of Financial GDP	Health
CSLL (Net Profit Contrib.)	Pre-Tax Corporate Income	7.2	2% of Operational Surplus	
PIS/PASEP (Social Integration Program)	Gross Revenues	7.3	0.9% of GDP	FAT: Deposits at Federal Financial Institutions
Federal Employee	Federal Wage Bill	2.6	6.1% of Federal Taxes	
Contributions		0.6	Wages	Payment of Federal Pensions
Other Social Contributions	Various			
FGTS Economic	Wage Bill	12.9	5.9% of Non-Government Wages	Severance Benefits, Housing
Contributions	Various	0.9		
Education Salaries	Wage Bill	2.8	0.8 of Wages	FNDE (National Fund for the Development of Education)
State Taxes	Value Added	59.8	7.7% of GDP	States: 60%; Local: 25%; FUNDEF: 15%
Value Added (ICMS)	Vehicle Value	3.8		States: 50%; Local: 50%
Vehicle (IPVA)	Inheritance Value	0.3		States

TABLE 2-2. Taxes and Contributions, late 1990s

Taxes and Contributions	Base	Value in 1997 (R$)	% in Relevant Variable	Destination
Inheritance (ITCD) Social Security Contributions	Wage Bill	1.5	1.9% of State Government wages	States
Municipal Taxes				
Urban Property (IPTU)	Assessed Value	3.1	2.6 of Rental Income	Municipalities
Transfer of Fixed Assets (ITBI)	Value Asset	0.8		Municipalities
Services (ISS)	Value Added	4.4	0.9% of Services GDP	Municipalities
Fees	Various	2.0		Municipalities
Other	Various	0.1		Municipalities

Source: Mauricio Carrizosa, 2000, "Brazil Structural Reform for Fiscal Sustainability," *World Bank Report* No. 19593 (Washington, D.C.: The World Bank).

The Brazilian constitution assigns specific taxing authority to each level of government. Table 2–2 lists the main taxes and contributions, indicates their base, value, and destination, and calculates the share of that value in a relevant aggregate. Table 2–3 shows the relative importance of different taxes in total revenue during the 1990s.

The most important federal tax is the income tax, with rates of 15 percent and 27.5 percent on individual income and of 10 percent and 25 percent on business profits, depending on the level of income and profits. Income tax revenue in 1997 was 4.6 percent of GDP and 14.7 percent of public sector taxes.

At the state level, the principal source of revenue has been ICMS, the value-added tax on goods. Revenues from ICMS amounted to approximately 7.7 percent of GDP in 1997. Tax rates are 17 percent on most intrastate trade and 25 percent on luxuries. Municipal governments collect taxes on urban property (land and buildings), on asset transfers, and on services (the ISS, which is the most important source of municipal government own-source revenue).

Intergovernmental Transfers

The constitution requires the federal and state governments to share significant fractions of their revenue with lower levels of government. For example, the federal government is required to transfer almost half of its revenue from taxes on income to subnational governments and regional development funds; these revenue-sharing funds are divided approximately equally between state and municipal governments.

The Federal Indirect Tax on Industrial Products (IPI) is shared with state governments and the state governments themselves must again share with the municipalities. The state governments must also transfer to the municipalities 50 percent of the revenue that they collect from taxes on vehicles, and 25 percent of the revenue that they collect from their main revenue source, the ICMS. The federal government also shares half of the rural property tax with municipalities.

States in turn share their revenue from IPI transfers, the ICMS revenue, and half of the vehicle tax revenue with their municipalities.

As a result of these transferable and the nontransferable taxes, the federal government collects about 66 percent of all taxes and keeps about 56 percent, with the main beneficiaries of the transfer process being the municipalities. Municipalities collect about 5 percent of total taxes but can use about 17 percent of total tax revenues as a result of the transfers.

In addition to the systematic intergovernmental transfers mandated by the revenue-sharing formulas spelled out in the constitution, there are other, less regulated transfers between different levels of government. The central government has assisted some state governments by having the federal treasury absorb nonperforming state government debt. These bailouts of subnational governments are of substantial magnitude. It is anticipated, however, that the situation will improve with the new law of fiscal responsibility detailed below.

The Law of Fiscal Responsibility

Brazil approved a Fiscal Responsibility Bill that came into force in May 2000. It sets limits to federal, state, and local governments debt stock, indebtedness, and personnel expenditure. It also reaffirms the constitutional "golden rule" provision: gross borrowing cannot exceed capital expenditures. In addition to the federally issued numerical limits on debt and the operating balance restrictions, governments should set individual targets with regard to expenditures, revenues, fiscal balances, and debt. The targets would in effect introduce fiscal planning into the key fiscal policy documents including the multiannual plans and budget directives laws. Noncompliance with the numerical limits and balance constraints would trigger financial constraints (no new credit operations and restrictions on intergovernmental grants) and mandatory corrective actions. Noncompliance with individual targets would trigger automatic expenditure cuts.

The new law bans the federal government from bailing out debt-ridden states and municipalities, and bans politicians from leaving their successors a stack of unpaid bills. The targets and corrective measures are legally binding and noncomplying officials are subject to prosecution—they could be banned from office or even jailed.

The Current Tax Structure

In the second half of the 1990s, Brazil completed a reform that improved direct taxation. A new reform is needed to improve the structure of its indirect taxes and reduce tax distortions due to the existence of important taxes with cascading effects.

The social security system absorbs about 35 percent of total public sector expenditures but social security contributions account for only 20 percent of total revenues. The federal government has created cascading taxes and labor taxes to help finance the federal social security budget. Federal taxes earmarked to social security expenditures increased from 34 percent of total taxes in 1991 to 39 percent in 1997.

Aside from the taxes on individual and business income, the federal government imposes a series of taxes on the gross receipts of different types of businesses:

- The tax on financial operations (IOF) is levied at various rates on loans and other financial operations (life and accident insurance premium are taxed at a 2 percent rate; premium for insurance of goods is taxed at a 4 percent rate; some transactions involving the exchange of currencies are taxed at a rate of 25 percent, while others are exempt).
- The COFINS for social security is levied at a rate of 3 percent on the gross receipts of firms that sell goods and services.
- Businesses are also subject to a tax on liquid assets (CSLL), applied at a rate of 18 percent to financial enterprises and 12 percent for other businesses.
- The PIS is assessed on the gross receipts of businesses, at a rate of 0.65 percent for nonfinancial enterprises and 0.75 percent for financial institutions.

The legislation for the taxes listed above does not exempt sales to other businesses from taxation. Thus, these taxes are different from retail sales or value-added taxes. Because they are levied on total receipts and not on value-added, the cumulative impact of taxes on prior stages of the production process determines the effective burden on any activity. The result is a system with effective rates of taxation that vary widely and arbitrarily across sectors and impose a high cost on economic efficiency. The CPMF (a tax on transactions) is also a cascading tax.

At the subnational level, the two principal taxes of state and municipal governments, the ICMS and the ISS, are not broad-based taxes. Both exempt large areas of economic activity and create uneven fiscal disincentives. The ICMS is also difficult to administer at the subnational level because, like a value-added tax, it requires special treatment for goods crossing jurisdictional boundaries.

The mismatch between service provision and taxation by the ICMS and the ISS distorts choices of location by private sector businesses. Service sector activities have incentives to flee municipalities with high ISS tax rates,

TABLE 2-3. Tax Structure, 1991–1998, percent of total taxes and contributions

Year	'90	'91	'92	'93	'94	'95	'96	'97	'98
FEDERAL	**67.30**	**66.29**	**67.66**	**71.79**	**69.45**	**67.29**	**66.82**	**68.05**	**69.34**
Fiscal Budget	**30.32**	**27.72**	**28.72**	**30.25**	**29.02**	**27.71**	**26.23**	**25.76**	**27.71**
Income Tax	15.83	14.45	15.27	15.46	13.81	16.2	16.05	15.38	17.74
Individual	1.17	0.61	0.57	0.83	0.93	1.08	1.05	1.05	1.05
Business	5.42	3.39	5.36	4	4.19	4.71	5.52	4.86	4.48
Withholding	9.23	10.45	9.34	10.64	8.69	10.41	9.48	9.47	12.21
Industrial Products Tax	8.36	8.85	9.24	9.48	7.39	6.99	6.78	6.61	5.98
Financial Operations Tax	4.64	2.46	2.47	3.14	2.33	1.67	1.26	1.5	1.31
International Trade Tax	1.37	1.74	1.58	1.73	1.75	2.55	1.88	2.03	2.42
Land Tax	0.01	0.08	0.01	0.03	0.01	0.05	0.09	0.1	0.08
Checking Debits Tax	0	0	0	0.29	3.59	0.08	0	0	0
Federal Fees	0.12	0.14	0.15	0.14	0.14	0.17	0.18	0.14	0.18
Social Security Budget	**30.07**	**31.25**	**31.68**	**34.74**	**33.13**	**31.78**	**32.85**	**34.64**	**33.23**
Social Security Contributions	17.56	18.66	18.47	21.07	16.85	16.74	17.9	17.56	17.34
COFINS	5.28	5.35	3.92	5.19	8.37	7.63	7.61	7.29	6.57
CPMF	0	0	0	0	0	0	0	2.75	3.02
CSLL	1.87	1.14	2.84	2.99	3.16	2.92	2.75	2.87	2.43
PIS/PASEP	3.94	4.25	4.21	4.42	3.67	3.07	3.16	2.89	2.65
Public Employee Contributions	0.36	0.48	0.27	0.32	0.75	1.09	1.14	1.03	0.92
Other Contributions	1.07	1.38	1.97	0.74	0.32	0.32	0.28	0.25	0.31
Other	**6.91**	**7.32**	**7.26**	**6.79**	**7.3**	**7.8**	**7.73**	**7.66**	**8.41**
FGTS	5.06	5.32	5.11	4.88	4.77	5.09	5.17	5.14	6.24
Economic Contributions	0.33	0.51	0.62	0.41	0.38	0.44	0.39	0.36	0.35
Salary-Education	0.73	0.65	0.66	0.5	1.2	1.24	1.22	1.1	0.91
Various Contributions	0.78	0.83	0.87	1	0.95	1.04	0.94	1.05	0.91
STATES	**29.62**	**28.97**	**28.5**	**25.19**	**27.17**	**28.04**	**28.34**	**27.34**	**26.39**
ICMS	27.76	27.26	26.72	23.76	25.02	24.57	24.69	23.7	22.63
IPVA	0.62	0.33	0.54	0.5	0.58	1.28	1.38	1.53	1.65
ITCD	0.06	0.02	0.07	0.07	0.07	0.09	0.09	0.11	0.12

TABLE 2-3. Tax Structure, 1991–1998, percent of total taxes and contributions

Fees	0.34	0.48	0.45	0.31	0.37	0.54	0.55	0.54	0.52
Public Employee Contributions	0.46	0.62	0.35	0.42	0.98	1.42	1.48	1.34	1.35
Other	0.37	0.27	0.37	0.12	0.14	0.14	0.14	0.14	0.12
COUNTIES (*Municípios*)	**3.08**	**4.74**	**3.84**	**3.03**	**3.38**	**4.67**	**4.84**	**4.61**	**4.27**
ISS	1.11	1.33	1.23	1.35	1.44	1.73	1.93	1.8	1.68
IPTU	0.78	1.81	1.23	0.58	0.71	1.44	1.49	1.44	1.32
ITBI	0.23	0.53	0.36	0.23	0.29	0.34	0.33	0.33	0.29
Fees	0.54	0.76	0.71	0.49	0.59	0.86	0.88	0.85	0.78
Public Employee Contributions	0.05	0.07	0.04	0.04	0.1	0.15	0.16	0.14	0.14
Other Taxes	0.38	0.24	0.27	0.33	0.25	0.16	0.06	0.05	0.05
TOTAL	**100**	**100**	**100**	**100**	**100**	**100**	**100**	**100**	**100**
Total as % of GDP	**30.51**	**25.22**	**25.86**	**25.73**	**29.46**	**29.74**	**28.96**	**29.00**	**29.84**

Source: Mauricio Carrizosa, 2000, "Brazil Structural Reform for Fiscal Sustainability," *World Bank Report* No. 19593 (Washington, D.C.: The World Bank).

leaving behind a population with public service demands that cannot be financed. The relative ease with which new municipalities are formed underscores this problem. An area with a high concentration of activities that bear high ISS burdens can withdraw from the existing municipal jurisdiction to form a new one in which it is no longer necessary to pay heavy taxes to support public service provision for others. Similarly, some activities have a fiscal incentive to locate in states where ICMS tax rates are low. Households that benefit from public services have a fiscal incentive to locate in areas where the public service provision is generous. A state or municipality that finances a high level of public services through taxation will tend to drive away those activities that produce substantial net fiscal contributions.

On the other hand, the response of the private sector to taxation creates incentives for state and municipal governments to adjust their fiscal policies accordingly. These policy responses on the part of subnational governments tend to mitigate the impact of their policies on choice of location, but they can also lead to poor levels of public service provision. Efficient provision of public services is undermined when governments do not have appropriate revenue instruments at their disposal with which to finance them.

In summary, the structure of taxes in Brazil faces many problems. Cascading taxes by the federal government undermine competitiveness, and tax evasion places most of the burden of taxation on the formal business segment. Taxes on imports remain high, despite strong trade liberalization in the early 1990s, and taxes on wages discourage employment and foster informality. The states have used the ICMS as a means of predatory competition among states rather than a source to meet the demand for state public services. Based on these phenomena, it is inevitable to conclude that reform of the tax system is a priority.

After five years of debates in Congress, a substitute proposal is still waiting to be voted on. It would create a broad federal and state value-added tax in place of the IPI, ICMS, and ISS. The social contributions, COFINS, PIS/PASEP, and *Salário-Educação*, would be changed into a single noncumulative contribution. Municipalities would be allowed to collect a retail tax in place of the ISS.

Although many feel that the reform of Brazil's tax system can no longer be postponed, the federal government is concerned about the impact of eliminating cascading taxes on revenues.[6] These concerns are important. The federal government collected 3.6 percent of GDP in the three cascading taxes (CPMF, CSLL, and PIS/PASEP). Despite their economic shortcomings, cascading taxes are effective tax collectors, managing to tax those who evade by hiding income or value added. If they were to be removed from the government's revenue instruments, they would need to be offset by decreasing expenditures or by increasing other taxes.

Conclusion

In 2000, Brazil's recovery gathered momentum despite the hike of petroleum prices and the mounting economic uncertainty in Argentina. Output and employment increased and led to higher than expected primary budget surpluses. Inflation and interest rates continued to decline. The *real* devalued by 7 percent in nominal terms during the year, with the bulk of the devaluation concentrated in the second half of the year, when the economic situation in Argentina deteriorated. As happened in 1999, the renewed weakening of the *real* immediately impacted the stock of debt, since the share of dollar-linked debt obligations remained high at more than 20 percent of public debt. The negative impact of devaluation more than offset the reduction of interest rates, thereby causing interest payments to increase. The rise in the primary surplus approximately equaled the increase in interest charges. The final result was a nominal deficit equivalent to 4.6 percent of GDP in 2000.

In July 2000, the Central Bank began a series of interest rate reductions that lasted until January 2001. But in February and April 2001, it raised interest rates again, citing fears of inflation jumps from heavy pressures on the exchange rate.

---

6.   See Afonso and Mello (2000) for a detailed and substantive discussion of the proposal now in Congress. See also Giambiagi, 2000.

During 2001, the weakening of the *real* had a variety of causes including the fall in global stock markets (that triggered a shift away from emerging market securities), the contagion effects from the crisis in Argentina, a domestic energy crisis, a political crisis, and corruption scandals. The conflict between Jader Barbalho, president of the Senate, and Antônio Carlos Magalhães, the most powerful senator, erupted in January 2001 and paralyzed a Congress that did not approve major legislation during the first semester of 2001.

External shocks and a domestic energy crisis made for an inflation rate in excess of the target set for 2001 and dampened the positive growth outlook. But by the end of the year, the correlation between the sovereign spreads on the debts of Brazil and Argentina had fallen substantially, indicating a decoupling between market expectations for the two countries. At the same time the energy crisis receded and Brazil's prospects for 2002 improved.

Stopping the formation of inflationary expectations forced the Central Bank to raise domestic interest rates in 2001. High interest rates threaten economic recovery and put fiscal balance at risk unless government can produce higher primary surpluses. To do that in a sustainable fashion, it must approve and implement the social security reform.

Social security reform will be difficult to achieve. The civil service and private employee social security systems are actuarially unbalanced and a solution will require deeper reforms than those already in place. The most salient problem resides in too small contributions made by civil servants (and often made for short periods of time), compared with the size of the pensions received. These payments represent an especially heavy burden in states such as São Paulo, Rio de Janeiro, and Rio Grande do Sul.

Other priorities remain the approval of the tax reform proposal and the reduction of cascading taxes (taxes that burden gross production—not value added—at several stages of the production chain).

The economy will remain vulnerable until further progress on fiscal reform permits the reduction of the debt/GDP ratio. Fiscal legislation, including the Fiscal Responsibility Law, is working on imposing controls and ensuring that spending plans are sustainable. If the next government continues to generate large primary surpluses, this will encourage currency stability and bring interest rates down. These factors would in turn reduce nominal deficits and the debt/GDP ratio.

CHAPTER 3

Privatization: Reform through Negotiation

Maria Hermínia Tavares de Almeida

The privatization of public firms is the most successful aspect of the ongoing process of state reform in Brazil. In fewer than ten years a significant part of the once burgeoning Brazilian public sector has been turned over to private hands. From 1991 to 2001, sixty-eight enterprises owned by the federal government have been privatized, including almost all public steel, chemical, petrochemical, and fertilizer companies, Brazil's largest mining corporation, the railway system, and several electric enterprises. The entire telecommunications system was auctioned between 1998 and 2001. Some important privatization also occurred at the state level. As of the end of 2001, the federal program reached US$37.705 billion, including debts transferred to the new owners (see also Table 3–5). This sum reaches US$68.623 billion when the telecommunications sector is included.

Brazil's experience challenges the conventional wisdom, found in recent academic literature on economic reform, that successful reform requires executive autonomy in order to conceive and enforce reform strategies apt to circumvent vested interests. This chapter argues that this is not necessarily true. In Brazil, in spite of the fact that there was and is no such a thing as an autonomous reformist executive, privatization of state-owned firms went forth. It was—and still is—a rather negotiated process of reform, embedded in an institutional setting that multiplies veto points and veto players. Consequently, successful reform policies depended on the interplay of the interests for or against privatization, conditioned by the institutional framework, and especially on the predominant ideas about the role and extension of the public sector among the relevant veto players.

In the first section, I briefly discuss the generally accepted interpretation of the necessary conditions for successful economic reform and present the analytical framework of this chapter. The second section summarizes basic facts about the Brazilian public sector and the evolution and results, thus far, of the privatization of state-owned enterprises. In the third section, I discuss the politics of privatization policy, showing the veto capacities it endows each relevant actor in the decision-making process as much as its implementation. Finally, I discuss the importance of the change in prevalent ideas about the state's economic role.

Conditions for Reform

The literature on economic reform has considered executive insulation and autonomy to be the main conditions for starting and pursuing economic reform in developing countries. According to this view, the executive capacity—especially the presidential and state technocratic abilities—to design and put forward strategies of change, above and beyond pressures from vested interests, is the independent variable that explains successful market-oriented reform (Haggard and Kaufman, 1995: 156–159). This view asserts that centralization of authority in the executive is essential to cope with three types of political hurdles: collective action dilemmas, distributive conflicts, and problems related to decision makers discounting the future. On the one hand, economic reforms are public goods, whose production faces collective action dilemmas (Olson, 1965). On the other hand, since the cost of reforms tends to be concentrated and immediate, while their benefits are diffuse and postponed, those who oppose change are more likely to organize themselves to pursue their aims than those who will benefit from it in the future. Finally, since politicians are vote-maximizers, even when believing they will benefit from the process in the future, they prefer low electoral cost strategies in the short run.

In the same vein, Torre (1994) distinguishes between the autonomy necessary to the reform process takeoff, and the embedded autonomy (Evans, 1995) necessary to continue the effort for a longer period. Executive insulation from conservative interests is seen as an unavoidable condition for inaugurating reforms. Here the central actor is the president, supported by a competent and loyal technocratic staff. His *virtù* is seen as crucial in order to change the governmental agenda and take steps toward a new balance between state and market. Nevertheless, once started, the continuity of the reform process would depend on the executive's ability to combine independence with coalition building, gathering together the interests that benefit from change.[1]

Recent analysis also paid attention to structural conditions that favored market-oriented reforms. Deep economic crisis during the 1980s is seen as a powerful inducement to the adoption of a reformist agenda (Nelson, 1993; Whitehead, 1993; Waterbury, 1993). Yet, autonomous executive capacity for designing policy change is always thought to be the fundamental ingredient. According to mainstream literature, economic crisis renders visible the impossibility of state-led growth under the new circumstances and also creates the conditions for executive autonomy (Torre, 1997; Waterbury, 1993).[2] Permanent institutional arrangements and constitutional provisions may also increase the presidency's discretionary powers to start and protect reformist policies against shortsighted political pressures (Haggard and Kaufman, 1995: 163–165).

There is no conceptual problem with the idea of executive autonomy: a government is autonomous if it "has its own goals and the institutional capacity to make decisions and enforce them" (Przeworski, 1995: 77). Yet, it is by no means clear what embedded autonomy really means and to what extent it differs from normal conditions for government existence in stable democracies. Unless we suppose that the state is nothing else but the executive committee of prevailing interests, every government, if it is not on the verge of collapse, shows some capacity of autonomous initiative and relies on some sort of political coalition.

However, executive autonomy, embedded or not, has not been a feature of the Brazilian political system in the last twenty years. Quite the contrary, the long transition to democracy—and democratization itself—brought about a loss of presidential capacity for independent decision making.[3]

---

1.   Haggard and Kaufman state, "However, a strong executive is not a reliable substitute for organized party support that can provide cohesive legislative and electoral support backing for the government's policy course. The building of such coalitions can even be undermined if strong or insulated executives lack the incentive to negotiate broader acceptance of their policy agenda. Particularly where parties are weak and legislative majorities unstable, executives risk increasing isolation and difficulty in sustaining reform" (Haggard and Kaufman, 1995: 165).
2.   Waterbury (1993: 158), for instance, asserts that the adoption of market-oriented reforms "is not so much a function of crumbling blocking coalitions as it is of economic crisis that disarms the defenders of the status quo and numbs the populace at large to the specific hardships engendered by specific reforms. This combination of privileged interests beggaring their neighbors in the quest to preserve specific entitlements and the underprivileged consumed by the challenge of day-to-day survival affords the leaders of the phase two reforms an opportunity to force through change even in the absence of organized political support."
3.   Sallum Jr. and Kugelmas (1993: 294) pointed out that, "when inflation soars dramatically . . . the Presidency emerges powerful, imposing itself to the other centers of power and to society through decrees and, after 1988, provisional measures. In all cases, the illusion of a imperial Presidency was ephemeral, dissipated as it was by the resurgence of high inflation. With the *Collor Plan*, the illusion was stronger, but not less deceiving, because Fernando Collor, besides showing himself as the country's redeemer from economic disorder, benefited from the legitimacy bestowed upon him by the popular vote that made him President of the Republic . . . Even so, with the exception of his initial period in power, his leading capacity eroded itself fast. His efforts in order to revive the imperial Presidency were undermined by the barriers put forth by other republican powers." A different appraisal, which underlines the importance of Collor's presidential autonomy for the launching of the reform process, can be found in Torre (1994).

In Brazil, the absence of autonomous executive initiative did not hinder the takeoff of economic reforms, nor did it mean that the executive forfeited its important role in defining the reformist agenda.[4] Nevertheless, it seemed to account for a moderate and negotiated process of change.[5] Consequently, we need an analytical framework that takes into consideration not only the actors, with their economic ideas and perceptions of their own interests, but also the institutions that define the conditions under which those actors must compete and negotiate.

Tsebelis (1995) and Immergut (1995) presented a (neo)institutionalist approach to comparative analysis of policy change in terms of veto players whose power is institutionally embedded. This chapter follows their analytical suggestion, emphasizing institutional veto players and ideas about reform that set the framework for defining their preferences as much as those of relevant actors not endowed with institutional veto powers but capable of exerting pressure on those who have.[6]

Yet, both authors seem to mold their discussion of the conditions of reform processes to the production of new legislation. They do not seem to pay due attention to its implementation. On the contrary, I consider that privatization of state-owned firms, as any other reform policy, is a two-step process. The first is the creation of the legal framework for policy change; the second is the implementation of the new policy. Reform processes can also be aborted at this second step. On the other hand, the structure of veto points is different in both moments as are the veto players. In the legislative realm the veto players are: the executive, the Congress, and the political parties inside it. Interest groups may influence the decisions through their relations to some of the players, but do not have institutional veto capacity.

Congruence among different veto players, as well as their internal cohesion, is crucial and effective. Congruence regarding the reform agenda makes changes easier, while internal cohesion may ease change or strengthen the veto capacities of each player. Therefore, both may have different consequences on the probabilities of successful transformation. At the moment of implementation the different actors in the executive are important veto players: ministries, governmental agencies, the president. The judiciary may be another. Meanwhile, strategically placed interest groups may delay policy implementation. Here coherence among different players, especially between

---

4.   To say that the executive lacks autonomy is not the same as to hold that it lacks powerful resources. As it will be seen later, the Brazilian presidency retains significant constitutional political privileges and power resources, even in economic affairs.
5.   Elsewhere, I tried to discuss the factors that conditioned market-oriented reforms in Brazil (Almeida, 1996a). See also Sola (1994: 235–279).
6.   According to his definition, "veto players are individual or collective actors whose agreement (by majority rule in the case of collective actors) is required for a change in the status quo" (Tsebelis, 1995).

the executive and the judiciary, is important. Nevertheless, internal cohesion of all relevant players is essential.

From Control to Privatization

Public firms played a central role in the state-led import-substitution process of industrialization in Brazil.[7] From the 1930s onward, government's direct participation in the production of goods and provision of public utilities grew steadily, as capitalist modernization dramatically changed the country's economic structure. Table 3–1 presents a measure of the public firms' relative importance before the privatization process took momentum.

TABLE 3-1. Public Sector Share of Capital Formation, 1947–1987

Period	State Firms*	Gov't. budget	Public Sector	Private Sector	Total
1947–1955	2.9	23.2	26.1	73.9	100
1956–1964	9.3	23.9	33.1	66.9	100
1965–1973	18.7	23.7	42.4	57.6	100
1974–1979	22.1	14.7	36.9	63.1	100
1980–1987	19.4	15.2	34.6	65.4	100

* Over 1966–1979, includes only the federal large state firms in steel, mining, petrochemicals, telecommunication, electricity, and railroads.
Source: state firms data from Werneck (1987; 99) for 1947–1965; Trebat (1983: 122) for 1966–1979, and Dinsmoor (1990: 126), Moreira (1995: 193), IBGE (Instituto Brasileiro de Geografia e Estatística, Brazilian Institute of Geography and Statistics.

Since the 1940s, the creation of public firms had been an important tool for promoting and steering industrialization, under the state-led model of growth that prevailed in Brazil for almost fifty years. Barros de Castro (1993) emphasized the importance of public firms for long-term development planning in the absence of a stable and professional bureaucracy capable of ensuring the continuity of industrialization policies. Huge public mining, steel, electric, and oil corporations were created between 1943 and 1964. During twenty years of military rule (1964–1984), especially in the 1970s, the expansion of public firms gained momentum. Their growth was spurred by an institutional framework that promoted the concentration of resources and decision-making capacity at the federal level and, simultaneously, freed the so-called mixed economy enterprises from government controls, endowing them with great autonomy to make decisions concerning investment and prices (Martins, 1985: 43).[8] Ambiguous legislation, issued from 1967 to 1978, allowed those corporations to thwart the Tribunal de Contas's overview of their expenditures (Pessanha, 1997: 132–135). Although individual

---

7.   In Brazil, there are two kinds of state-owned firms: a) the public enterprise, whose shares belong 100 percent to the state and b) the mixed economy enterprise where the government holds at least 51 percent of the shares. The expansion of direct state participation in the production of goods and provision of services occurred basically through the creation of the later form. This chapter deals with both species.
8.   Basic rules for public enterprises and mixed economy enterprises were established by Decree 200, of February 1967, that instituted administrative reform.

enterprises were supposed to be regulated by sectoral bodies, they later lacked the independence and leverage to do their jobs adequately. State-owned firms were frequently more powerful than their regulators. As a matter of fact, there was no centralized control over the aggregate of state-owned firms. Multiple agencies—ministries, councils, sectoral holdings, with different capacities and different levels of efficiency—had regulatory and control functions.[9] The central government kept only one important instrument of control: the power to appoint firms' chairmen and directors. Either way, by the end of the 1970s, the decentralized state's productive sector was a "black box," unknown even to the federal government, to the extent that the executive was not able to figure out their assets and liabilities. Asymmetrical information was the crucial weapon of the bureaucracies of the public firms in keeping their principal, the central government, at bay. Neither the executive nor the Congress had adequate devices to exert efficient control.

The government's relations with public enterprises changed from the end of the 1970s on. Changes in the international economy, after the second oil shock, put economic adjustment on the national government's agenda. Control over state-owned firms became part of the macroeconomic policies conceived to curb inflationary pressures. Therefore, a set of institutions was designed to cope with this particular principal-agent problem.

The first step toward reversing the previous pattern of relations between the government and its companies was the creation of the Secretary for the Control of Public Enterprises (SEST) in 1979 under General Figueiredo's administration. It was under the authority of the Planning Secretary and its purpose was to establish stringent control over the expenditures of state-owned firms. The SEST was part of a broader effort aiming at a consolidated budget of the federal public sector, including not only the federal administration but also the treasury's direct transfers to the monetary authorities and decentralized state-owned firms. The SEST was to define the global expenditures budget of all kinds of state-owned corporations, establishing global and case by case limits to investment and current expenses as well as restricting their access to foreign and domestic credit, treasury funds, primary stock, financial markets, and to their own retained profits (Werneck, 1987:14).[10] The goals of centralized control were clearly stated by its first director:

> The forecasted global expenditures of state-owned firms for 1980 is twice the budget of the Federal government. . . . The acknowledgment of the consolidated figures was crucial for the government to understand definitely that controlling

9. See Werneck (1987: 15), and Trebat (1983).
10. SEST had the following responsibilities: a) to define the global expenditures budget; b) to establish a ceiling on expenditures with oil and its derivatives; c) to establish a ceiling to borrowing in national and foreign currencies; d) to establish a ceiling to imports expenditure.

public firms' expenditures is an essential part of a successful policy to fight inflation and control the balance of payments.[11]

Since the overall purpose was to increase the efficiency of government's short-term macroeconomic policies, no consideration was given to policies aimed at rationalizing the operation of public firms and enhancing their efficiency. As a matter of fact, according to conventional wisdom prevailing in Brazil, state-owned enterprises had no significant efficiency problems. They were thought to be as efficient as private firms of the same size and complexity, since they supposedly followed private entrepreneurial standards.

The SEST was not the only mechanism through which the federal government tried to subdue the powerful and once autonomous public corporations. During the 1980s, as inflation soared dramatically, federal authorities resorted frequently to public price and tariff controls as an anti-inflationary device. They also attempted, not always successfully, to rationalize and limit wage increases in the state-owned enterprises.[12] The decade witnessed a tug-of-war between the government, which strove to curb the powerful public firms, and the firms themselves, obstinate in circumventing control.[13] The results were not clear cut, but by the end of the 1980s the *estatais* were undoubtedly submitted to constraints unheard of at the beginning of the decade.

Efforts to impose government authority over public firms make Brazilian policies diverge from the reform sequence shown in Waterbury's comparative study of privatization in four developing countries. In the cases he analyzed, moderate reform, granting some autonomy to state-owned firms, was the first response to economic strains due to external shocks in the 1970s and early 1980s, and preceded the shift toward privatization (Waterbury, 1993: 135–159). In Brazil the sequence was autonomy, then control, and finally privatization.

Although privatization of public corporations only became a central governmental policy in 1990, the Figueiredo administration (1979–1984) marked a turning point in the historical trend of the public sector's direct participation in the production of goods and provision of services. The previous expansion of state-owned firms came to a halt. In 1981, shortly after the creation of SEST, the federal government issued a decree establishing the Comissão Especial de Desestatização (Special Commission for Destatization), with the purpose of "limiting the creation of new state-owned enterprises, stopping the activities of or transferring to the private sector the public

---

11. Cf. Kliass (1994: 185).
12. During the military rule a special council, the CNPS (National Council for Wage Policy), had the power to regulate wages in public firms. After redemocratization, it was replaced by the CISE (Interministerial Council for Wages in the state sector).
13. For a good account of this process in the oil industry see the interesting study on Petrobrás by Alveal (1993: 143–208).

firms whose public control was no longer necessary or justified."[14,15] The word privatization was not even mentioned, but the idea that some kinds of public firms could turn to private hands entered the agenda of the government and the elites. The commission was a sign that federal authorities were responsive to increasing pressures from entrepreneurial organizations and the media, against what was said to be an excessive growth of productive public sector under President Ernesto Geisel (1974–1978).

In 1985, the new democratic regime established the Privatization Program and replaced the Special Commission with the Interministerial Council for Privatization.[16] The program opened up the possibility of selling some categories of public enterprises: those, previously private firms, that fell under control of the Banco Nacional de Desenvolvimento Econômico e Social (BNDES) due to unpaid debts; subsidiaries no longer thought to be necessary to accomplish the main firm goals; and those operating in sectors where enough private capacity made state participation unnecessary. Individual firms would be included in the program by presidential decree.

In 1988, a new presidential decree created the *Programa Federal de Desestatização* (Federal Program of Destatization), presided by the Federal Council of Destatization.[17] The decree broadened the scope of the program in order to include all state-owned enterprises except the public monopolies mentioned by the constitution, allowed for the use of foreign debt titles in the privatization process, and increased the power of the Ministry of Planning in the decisions concerning the inclusion or exclusion of individual firms.

In spite of all the legislative initiatives, concrete results were dismal. During the last military government and the first democratic administration, privatization, not yet a central policy issue, only meant the devolution of state-controlled private firms to their former owners and the sale of a few subsidiaries of public companies; nothing that could resemble a large-scale program of privatization. Goals and results were modest, but they showed that the era of public sector expansion was over.

The break-even point took place in 1990, when privatization became an essential part of a whole program of market-oriented economic reforms put forward by President Collor de Mello (1990–1992). Law 8.031/90 created the *Programa Nacional de Destatização* (PND, National Divestiture Program). The law established an initial list of firms to be privatized, put the program under the National Development Bank's (BNDES) management, and gave the executive the authority to add or exclude firms from the list. Complementary legislation defined privatization currencies, allowing for the use of sev-

14. Decree 86.215, of July 15, 1981.
15. Decree 86.215, of July 15, 1981.
16. Decree 91.991, November 28, 1985.
17. Decree 95.886, March 29, 1988.

TABLE 3-2. PND Results by Presidential Term, in US$ millions

Period	Number of Firms (a)	Revenues in Cash (b)	Sales Total (c)	Percent Revenues in Cash (b/c)	Debts Transferred (d)	Total (c+d)
1991–1992 (Collor)	18	49	4,015	1.2%	1,356	5,371
1993–1994 (Franco)	15	1,590	4,593	34.6%	1,910	6,503
1995–1998 (Cardoso I)	30	9,110	11,003	82.8%	5,935	16,938
1999–2000* (Cardoso II)	3	8,640	8,893	99.3%	-	8,893
TOTAL	68	19,384	28,504	68%	9,201	37,705

* Includes privatization of BANESPA, public offers of Petrobrás shares, auctions according to Decree n. 1.068, and Gerasul's shares sold to employees.
* Telecommunications privatization's revenues not included.
Source: BNDES.

eral kinds of federal debt certificates acquired by financial markets in order to buy shares of auctioned enterprises.[18] The Collor administration began the privatization of public steel, petrochemical, and fertilizer firms. After his resignation, the program continued, albeit reluctantly, under former vice president, then successor, Itamar Franco (1993–1994).[19] The process gained momentum in the following administration, led by Fernando Henrique Cardoso (1995–1998). The new president introduced important institutional changes.[20] Law 8.031 was reshaped, and constitutional reform in 1995–1996 allowed previous state monopolies in telecommunications, electricity, coastal and domestic navigation, gas, and oil to be included in the privatization program. Legislation creating regulatory agencies to supervise privatized companies in telecommunications, oil, and electricity sectors was also approved by the Congress. During Cardoso's second term in office (1999–2002) privatization continued, although at a much more moderate pace. As a matter of fact, the privatization of federal electricity firms came to a halt due to political pressures and, above all, to divergent views about the best privatization model to adopt within the parties of Cardoso's coalition.

Besides increasing the number of privatized firms, the Cardoso administration enlarged cash revenues, as Table 3–2 shows. The rationale of the privatization policy, especially under Cardoso, seems to have been getting the highest possible price, although in the telecommunications program there was also an explicit effort to avoid property concentration and to create com-

18. The privatization currencies were: Debêntures da Siderbrás (SIBR); Certificados de Privatização (CP); Obrigações do Fundo Nacional de Desenvolvimento (OFND); Créditos Vencidos Renegociados—securitizados—DISEC; Títulos da Dívida Agrária (TDA); Títulos da Dívida Externa (DIVEX); Letras Hipotecárias da Caixa Econômica Federal (CEF); Notas do Tesouro Nacional, série M (NTN-M).
19. For an interesting discussion of the period 1985–1994 see Velasco Jr. (1997a).
20. Velasco Jr. (1997b) considers the Cardoso administration a turning point in the privatization policy, which became part of a broader project of state reform.

TABLE 3-3. Privatization of Telecommunications, 1998–2001, US$ millions

Sectors	Auction Results	Transferred Debts	Total
Federal companies	$19,237	$2,125	$21,362
Wireline and long distance services	11,970	2,125	14,095
Mobile phones (A Band)	6,974		6,974
Sales to employees	293		293
Concessions	9,556		9,556
Mobile phones (B Band)	7,613		7,613
Mobile phones (D Band)	1,334		1,334
Mobile phones (E Band)	482		482
Competing wireline and long distance companies (mirror companies)	128		128
Total	$28,793	$2,125	$30,918

Source: BNDES.

petition in each of the service areas. The PND did not include the telecommunications sector that was auctioned under a special program of privatization that included wireline, long distance, and mobile systems and that had embedded rules providing for the existence of competing companies in each type of service. The results to date can be seen in Table 3–3.

Explaining Negotiated Reform: Institutions, Agents, and Strategies

During an entire decade, policies regarding public firms, issued either by the last authoritarian or by the first democratic governments, were made through presidential decree. The Congress did not have a say in the creation of SEST or on the content of the three different programs meant to advance privatization in the 1980s. This practice changed with the 1988 constitution. The executive lost the possibility of legislating by decree and the Congress and the Supreme Court acquired new powers.

The Brazilian presidential system now endows the executive, the Congress, and the judiciary with constitutional veto capacities. Executive faculties are enhanced by significant legislative powers, such as exclusive initiative in specific matters, veto power over legislation approved by the Congress, and the possibility of issuing *Medidas Provisórias* (MPs), "provisional measures."[21,22] The Congress retrieved powers lost during the authoritarian regime and the judiciary had its own powers greatly enlarged.

21. They include the organization of Armed Forces, any law regarding taxes, budget, public administration, civil service regulations, creation and changes in the attributions of ministries, and other public administrative organizations.
22. *Medidas Provisórias* differ from presidential decrees.

Privatization policy took place in two different settings: one where the rules were defined, and the other where divestiture of each enterprise was accomplished. Privatization demanded a definition of the institutional framework, the set of norms that assigned responsibilities, specified which companies should be included in the program, laid out the adequate procedures for the sales, the currencies to be accepted, and the government agency that should preside over the process. The two processes partly overlapped, since rulemaking continued long after the first sales of public enterprises. Despite the coexistence, they occurred in different institutional and political settings, with different structures of veto points as well as the number and the kind of veto players.

Definition of the rules involved the executive and the legislature, both endowed with constitutional veto powers, that varied according to the type of rule at stake.

The structure of veto points changed according to the nature of the executive's proposal.[23] There are a different number of veto points—and, therefore, increasing degrees of difficulty—to get approval for a new rule proposed by the executive, whether it is sent for Congressional deliberation as a Provisional Measure (MP), an ordinary bill, or a constitutional amendment proposal. Provisional Measures are the easiest way for the executive to have its proposals approved; they reduce veto points, since they must be voted on by a joint session of House and Senate; they increase the costs of rejection borne by representatives, since they take effect the moment they are issued; and they force their way in the congressional agenda, since they must be appraised for a short period. Finally, MPs allow the executive considerable room to maneuver when their prospect of approval is dismal, as long as they can be reissued with small changes. Ordinary bills or "law projects" can face up to three veto points. They must be discussed and approved separately in both the House and the Senate, and if they are amended by the second chamber they must return to the first. Finally, constitutional amendments must be approved in both houses, twice in the Chamber and twice in the Senate, with three-fifths of the votes in each case.

Successful results, as far as privatization was concerned, depended on the degree of convergence between both government branches, or at least between the executive and the majority of the legislature. Interest groups that favored or opposed privatization had no means to act other than exerting pressure on both actors. There is no doubt that privatization policy was conceived and proposed by the executive, even though it previously had the initiative of controlling state-owned firms as shown in Table 3–4.[24]

---

23. I am grateful to Fabiano Guilherme dos Santos for drawing my attention to these differences.

TABLE 3-4. Privatization Bills, by original proponent, 1990–1997

Proponent	Approved	Rejected	Total
Executive	24*	6	30
Legislative	2	98	100
Total	26	104	130

* Includes eleven *Medidas Provisórias*.
Source: Maurício Moya, 1998. *As privatizações e o poder legislativo no Brasil*. Relatório final de Iniciação Científica. São Paulo, Brazil: Universidade de São Paulo, Dept. Political Science.

A significant part of the executive's initiatives came as *Medidas Provisórias*, which went into immediate effect and needed to be urgently appraised by the Congress. Law 8.031, which created the PND, was paradigmatic. Originally it was part of the package of MPs issued by Collor de Mello to fight inflation. But even after being amended and approved by Congress, it was changed significantly several times through MPs issued by Cardoso's administration before eventually becoming a new law approved by the Congress.[25] The importance of MPs in shaping the privatization policy is clear after 1989: they amounted to 42 percent of all legislative initiatives issued with that purpose.

The executive's overwhelming legislative lead is only part of the story. More important is assessing the actual participation of the legislature in shaping privatization's legal framework. Table 3–5 gives a quantitative idea of the intensity of congressional engagement in the process.

The pattern of congressional intervention is clear. First, it did not introduce any change in six out of the twelve legislative proposals for providing additional credit to firms in process of privatization. In all other cases, except for one, there was no congressional participation with regards to the financial arrangements necessary to prepare the sale of enterprises included in the program. Second, Congress did not interfere significantly in the definition of rules regarding the currencies accepted in the privatization. On the other hand, it discussed and introduced moderate changes in projects that defined the program guidelines and the regulatory agency for oil enterprises. It altered key points of the bills regulating port activities, concession of public utilities, and the creation of electricity and telecommunications regulatory agencies. In brief, Congress did not interfere in the financial issues of the privatization model, but it was quite active in shaping the framework for public utilities' concessions and regulations.

As shown elsewhere (Almeida and Moya, 1997), the presidency took congressional preference into account when establishing the list and the order of corporations to be privatized. Privatization began in areas where an early and

---

24. During the 1980s, executive decrees tried to control state-owned enterprises and return the firms under the control of BNDES to private hands.
25. Law 9.491/97.

TABLE 3-5. Congressional Participation in Changing Proposals*

Typeof Change	Executive	Legislative	Total
No change (0)	12	0	12
Minimal change (1)	6	0	6
Moderate change (2)	3	0	3
Important change (3)	2	2	4
No information	1	0	1
Total	24	2	26

*Only legislation already approved and sanctioned by the presidency.
0 = no amendments approved, nor parts suppressed through DVS (separated voting).
1 = fewer than 5 amendments approved and/or less than 10 parts suppressed through DVS.
2 = 5 to 15 amendments approved and/or 10 to 30 parts suppressed through DVS.
3 = more than 15 amendments approved and/or more than 30 parts suppressed through DVS.
Source: Maurício Moya, 1998. *As privatizações e o poder legislativo no Brasil.* Relatório final de
Iniciação Científica. São Paulo, Brazil: Universidade de São Paulo, Dept. Political Science.

firm majority of legislators favored its transfer to private hands: steel, chemical, fertilizer, and petrochemical firms.[26] A constitutional amendment to
allow for the privatization of coastal navigation, gas, iron-ore mining, telecommunications, and electricity came after privatization policy had won
some degree of legitimacy. Although the state monopoly on oil was broken,
Petrobrás, the largest Brazilian company and the icon of state-led development, has not been included in the privatization program thus far.

Interest groups were not absent from the debate on the establishment of
privatization's legal framework and sometimes exerted pressure on legislators related to specific points. Few entrepreneurial associations favorable to
the selling of public firms were active in the congressional debate regarding
the rules for the concession of public utilities to private groups and the creation of the electricity service's regulatory agency.[27] Public sector worker and
employees unions, usually opposed to privatization, were generally absent
except in the case of the constitutional amendment intended to allow for the
privatization of state monopolies, especially during the congressional discussion on ports.[28]

Battles against privatization were fought when the program was set in
motion. Opposition to divestiture included left-wing political parties, and
workers from public firms and employee unions belonging to the Central
Única de Trabalhadores (CUT) labor confederation.[29] Unions loyal to the
CUT's rival, Força Sindical, supported privatization, especially after Law

---

26. Preference for privatization in Congress showed a very consistent and ideologically
coherent distribution pattern: it decreased from right to left of the parties continuum. Nevertheless, support for privatization of steel, chemical, petrochemical, and fertilizers corporations, as well as coastal navigation was higher than for ports, telecommunications,
electricity—which, in its turn, was higher than for iron mining and oil (Almeida and Moya,
1997).
27. Data from Mancuso (1999).
28. I discuss unions' behavior in detail in Almeida (1997).
29. Central Única de Trabalhadores, the biggest Brazilian peak association.

TABLE 3-6. Legal Suits against Privatization, 1992–1997

Industry	Number of Firms Privatized	Number of Cases
Steel	8	92
Chemical and Petrochemical	14	105
Fertilizers	4*	35
Electricity	6	35
Railway	1	19
Mining	1	148
Bank	1	4
Other	3	22
TOTAL	38	460

*Includes one firm excluded from the privatization program and another whose auction was cancelled.
Source: Vanessa Oliveira, 1998. O Judiciário e as privatizações. Relatório Final de Iniciação Cientifica. São Paulo, Brazil: Universidade de São Paulo, Dept. Political Science.

8.031 guaranteed state enterprises' workers and employees the offer of a variable percentage of the auctioned shares.[30] Opposition adopted two strategies to block actual privatization: public protest and appeal to the courts. Violent street rallies, near the stock market building where the sales took place, occurred during almost every important privatization auction. Although important to publicly show discontent, demonstrations failed to hinder privatization.

The appeal to the courts was the main strategy chosen to block the process, by appealing to judiciary veto powers. Decentralization of the judiciary system and the various legal instruments for appealing to courts granted to the citizenry by the 1988 constitution, made resorting to the courts a very promising way of blocking governmental action. Table 3–6 shows the number of legal appeals the industrial branch made between 1991 and 1997. Opposition parties and unions also appealed to the Supreme Court in 1991 in order to revoke the PND on grounds of its alleged conflict with the constitution.[31]

Different cases presented at different regional courts all over the country sometimes delayed privatization auctions. Nevertheless, as of the writing of this chapter, not one single sale was reversed by judicial sentence. Only one firm was excluded from the privatization roll and another had its auction suspended. Also, the Supreme Court has not overruled one single sale on the grounds of its alleged incompatibility with the constitution. Decentralization and lack of coherence among different regional courts have transformed

---

30. Ferraz (2000) shows the importance of selling privatizing firms' shares to workers as means to curb union opposition.
31. There were three ADIN (ação direta de inconstitucionalidade, or direct actions of unconstitutionality) and eight other types of appeals against the PND.

divestiture in a judicial battle. Nevertheless, the convergence between executive's policy and the Supreme Court interpretation of the constitution allowed privatization to continue.

Congruence among major institutional veto players—the executive, the legislative majority, and the Supreme Court—explains the success of privatization compared to other issues of the Brazilian government's reform agenda, such as reform of the social security and tax system. Both still face great political difficulties. But this congruence itself must be explained.

Breaking the Statist Consensus

State-led development was a huge success story in Brazil. It provided industrialization, long-term sustained growth, and modernization, as well as high spatial and social mobility, despite great social inequalities. Public enterprises were a decisive tool of long-term strategies of economic growth and economic change. As such, they were highly praised by the elites as much as by the populace. They became national symbols as the material proof of Brazil's aptitude to transform itself from an agrarian society into a highly urbanized one in a couple of generations. For decades, an almost unanimous consensus sustained state interventionism and its multiple manifestations, public corporations among them. Usual arguments about their inefficiency—due, on one side, to the vicious triangle of no-profit, no-competitiveness, and soft budget constraints (Kornai, 1981); and, on the other, to self-serving managers and insatiable unions—were seldom brought about. Except for a right-wing liberal minority, there was a widespread, highly positive evaluation of public firms' performance and of their role in promoting rapid industrialization. Breaking this consensus took a long and gradual process as well as the crisis of the authoritarian rule and the transition to democracy in the late 1970s and the 1980s.

The demise of the predominant statist consensus was a two-level process of change: first, in the way national opinion and organized groups in society envisaged the public sector; second, in decision makers' economic understandings of the proper role of the state and its companies.[32] The first sign of discontent with the growth of public corporations was private entrepreneurs' "Campaign for Destatization," around 1976–1977. While its authors' motivations and goals varied, the campaign inaugurated an open discussion on the acceptable limits of direct state participation in the productive sector.[33] Entrepreneurs' protests were followed by other manifestations by different social

---

32. I use statist consensus in a broad sense as approval for an active role of government in the economic process. As Bielchowsky (1988) has shown, there was a huge array of different positions, corresponding to groups and organizations that accepted the idea of state-led development although diverging about the intensity, forms, and means of state intervention.
33. For a good discussion see Cruz (1996).

groups against the military government. Although their agenda and demands differed widely, their opposition to authoritarian rule took the form of a common claim for freeing society from excessive state intervention and control. The idea that such intervention could be excessive and damaging was the first small crack in the statist ideological building.[34]

Authoritarianism, which left the executive branch's discretionary powers unchecked, was blamed for such excesses as the uncontrolled expansion of state-owned firms and of autonomous rent-seeking bureaucracies. For the left and center-left antiauthoritarian opposition, democracy meant the promise of establishing a new virtuous cycle of state-led growth under the aegis of an empowered civil society. Political programs of all opposition parties— PMDB (Party of the Brazilian Democratic Movement), PDT (Democratic Labor Party), PT, and the small communist and socialist organizations— praised the *estatais* and believed in the continuation of state-led development income distribution.[35]

The positive image of governmental intervention in the economy eroded gradually in the second half of the 1980s, during the turbulent years of democratization and high inflation combined with stop-and-go economic growth. Several experiences contributed in changing the social perception of the public sector. First, heterodox anti-inflationary exchange-rate, price-, and wage-control policies meant the exacerbation of government intrusion into the private economy. The protests of entrepreneurs' interest associations against price-control policies increasingly became a libel against state interventionism at large, and a defense of economic liberalization and of privatization of public firms. Labor unions joined them in the opposition to stabilization programs that imposed wage control, although not in their praise for privatization.[36]

On the other hand, in spite of the fact that social services expanded under the new democracy, public administration and public service flaws, like inefficiency, clientelism, and corruption, were more openly exposed by the media, contributing to enhance an already existent negative picture of the workings of the government machine. If Brazil's public administration never enjoyed good fame, public enterprises, once considered symbols of efficiency and good management, became increasingly discredited. Political parties interfering in the appointment of their boards of directors, as well as real or supposed excessive benefits granted to their employees by self-interested managers were said to jeopardize firms' economic performance.[37] The actual importance of these issues is irrelevant here. The fact is that by the end of the

---

34. On this see Weffort (1988: 511–515).
35. For the founding programs of Brazilian parties see Kinzo (1993).
36. For an account of business and labor responses to stabilization programs see Almeida (1996a) and Diniz (1988).

1980s, public support for state-owned firms had shrunk in tandem with a diffuse sympathy for anti-interventionist political rhetoric in large sectors of Brazilian society.

Changes in the perception of the state's adequate economic role were also deep at the level of policymakers. Those changes did not come about due to the rise of technical elite groups with different economic ideas as in Mexico (Heredia, 1993; Centeno, 1994), but due to learning from either domestic or international experience.[38] Domestic practice was one of the failures of heterodox monetary stabilization programs and of coping with recurrent fiscal crises. Privatization entered economic policymakers' agenda mainly as a tool to reduce public indebtedness. Secondarily, privatization was thought to allow for new investments that government could not provide to public firms. Some of the state-owned enterprises' managers came to accept privatization as they experienced, during the 1980s, increasing bureaucratic control and difficulties to get new investments.[39] On the other hand, permanent negotiation with international organizations during the troubled 1980s, such as the IMF and the World Bank, created several opportunities for discussing the market-oriented reform agenda they proposed as an overall solution for indebted developing countries. Conditionalities did not work as such, but they were important instruments in persuading technocratic elites.[40]

The demise of the statist consensus did not give way to a new hegemonic view on the balance between state and markets. Today, the debate over the proper role of the state is a central political divide in Brazil. On one side, state-led growth is still a powerful vision for parties, social organizations, and movements that oppose the reform coalition and its policies. On the other, those who push market-oriented reforms forward reject the neoliberal credo

---

37. The continued decline of public firms' performance was the subject of extensive debate. Critics of privatization stress: a) government policies that stimulated public firms to get loans in the international markets in the 1970s; b) controls established after 1979; and c) the subordination of public firms to short-term macroeconomic goals. Nevertheless, there are those who also acknowledge the negative effect of political appointments and unions' predatory activism (Barros de Castro, 1993).
38. Technical elite groups in charge of economic policies were replaced eight times between 1979 and 1994, six under democratic regime. Differences in institutional origins as much as academic background were significant. Nevertheless, they all roughly shared the belief in active government at least during a great part of the 1980s. On the role of international organizations and of learning for the spread of privatization see Ikenberry (1990).
39. Bureaucratic obstacles to public firms management were brought about in our research interviews with former managers and one former Minister of Transports and now member of the House of Representatives (research interviews numbers 1, 2, and 4).
40. Privatization was introduced in the agreements between Brazil and the IMF in 1988, but has never been a strong conditionality. Nevertheless, frequent participation in seminars and international meetings promoted by international organizations was considered by a former Minister of Economy quite important for changing his ideas about privatization and other market-oriented reforms (research interview number 7). On this see Jamil Chade. 1997. *O FMI e as privatizações no Brasil*, 'Iniciação Científica' Fellowship Final Report.Universidade de São Paulo, Dept. Political Science, São Paulo, Brazil.

and see themselves as pragmatic reformers in search of a new paradigm of active government.[41]

The politics of privatization is embedded in this struggle between conflicting visions on the relations between the state and the economy. Its path is a mirror image of the gradual process through which state intervention turned into a contested issue.

---

41. Bresser-Pereira (1993) calls it the "fiscal crisis approach."

CHAPTER 4

Social Policy Reform

Sônia Draibe

There have been two substantial modifications of the Brazilian system of social protection over the last twenty years, carried out in two distinct cycles of social policy reform. The first took place in the 1980s within the context of redemocratization and economic instability. The second began in the second half of the 1990s, under the aegis of a complex agenda of stabilization, institutional reform, and the consolidation of democracy.

Starting in the closing years of the 1970s, redemocratization imbued the social policy arena with the reformist agenda of a democratic transition process (Draibe, 1998). The processing of this agenda—consecrated in the 1988 constitution—introduced several significant changes in social policies, such as the emphasis on the principle of social rights, the affirmation of universal access to basic social programs, and, in the case of social security, a relative slackening of the contribution link as the backbone of the system, combined with the fixing of minimum sums for benefits. Nevertheless, its implementation has been consistently partial and modest, probably due to countermovements and signals emanating as much from economic restrictions as from the corporativist distortions of organized interests.

Since the mid-1990s, a new social agenda ushered in another reform cycle, now informed by the broader and more complex context of economic adjustment, completion of institutional reforms, and the democratic consolidation process. The hallmark of this new stage has been a tense reconciling of macroeconomic objectives geared to securing stabilization and social reform targets theoretically designed to achieve greater efficiency and equity.

Observing the two periods or cycles, one cannot but be struck by the modest achievement of the changes and innovations wrought. If one retains a strong concept of reform—meaning the effective alteration of the basic principles and organizational structure of social policy institutions—it is possible

71

to conclude that only health policy and welfare programs have undergone proper reform. Social security reform, undertaken in 1998, was partial and it did not modify the system's principles. In education, major changes have been almost entirely restricted to elementary schooling. Areas such as housing, basic sanitation, and public transportation have been virtually excluded from the recent reform agenda.

However, one cannot deny the importance and cumulative impact of the innumerable alterations made to the social protection system as a whole and in some of its specific sectors. Beyond increases in social spending, even during the economic adjustment period, the modifications had affected the organizational and institutional levels of social policy over all.

Brazil enters the new century with poor social indicators, including an intolerable level of income inequality, a high level of poverty, and low average years of schooling. But it is also true that its social protection system is better equipped and enabled to face these difficulties, mostly due to the great efforts and strides made toward institutional improvement over the last twenty years.

In this chapter, I try to reconstitute part of this reformist effort, as well as to register some of the results already achieved. I focus on the social policy areas of education, health, social security, and poverty alleviation. These are key areas to address, taking into account the goals of more equitable development and broader opportunities.

Educational Reform

Brazil has more than fifty million students registered in all levels of its educational system, as shown by the enrollment figures for the public and private sector in 2000 in Table 4–1. The national educational system is predominantly public at the primary and secondary levels, and mostly private in higher education.

The Brazilian educational system is divided into three levels: *Primary Education*, including students 7–14 years of age and lasting eight years, is divided into two cycles: 1st–4th grade and 5th–8th grade; *Secondary Education*, lasts three years and serves students 15–17 years of age;[1] *Higher Education* is divided into two levels: undergraduate, from four to six years, and graduate, master's, and Ph.D. programs. It also includes specialization, postgraduate, and postdoctoral programs.

Primary education is compulsory and free. Secondary education is similarly free, but not mandatory, although a constitutional mandate directs the state to establish its compulsory status. Early education (nursery and pre-

---

1. In this chapter, I use the official nomenclature—primary and secondary education levels—but also the old denomination, primary and secondary schooling.

TABLE 4-1. School Enrollment, by sector and level, 2000

Educational Level	Public Sector	Private Sector	Total
Early Education	4,341,868	1,670,392	6,012,260
(Nursery)	(582,258)	(334,626)	(916,884)
(Pre School)	(3,332,173)	(1,089,159)	(4,421,332)
(Literacy)	(427,437)	(246,607)	(674,044)
Primary Education	32,528,707	3,189,241	35,717,948
Secondary Education	7,039,529	1,153,419	8,192,948
Higher Education	887,026	1,807,219	2,694,245
TOTAL	44,797,130	7,820,271	52,617,401

Source: MEC/INEP/SEEC. Sinopse Estatística da Educação Básica, 2000; and MEC/INEP/SECC. Números da Educação no Brasil. Grandes Números do Ensino Superior-Graduação 2000.

school), although not required for system entrance, serves the age-group below seven. Young and adult citizens who did not finish regular schooling may take supplementary examinations to obtain their degrees (*ensino suple-tivo*).

With regard to the participation of the different levels of government in public school services, state and municipal governments are responsible for providing primary and secondary schooling. Municipal governments are also responsible for providing preschool education, as show in Figure 4–1.

The federal government, states, and municipalities also share educational funding. In fact, public financing of education relies squarely on tax revenues constitutionally allocated for education, and on the education-wage (*salário-educação*), a compulsory contribution of 2.5 percent of firms' payrolls collected by the federal government. A constitutional norm (Calmon Amendment, 1983) mandates that 18 percent of federal tax revenues and 25 percent of state and municipal revenues, including government transfers, must be allocated to the development and maintenance of primary schooling.

The educational system exemplifies the competitive nature of Brazilian federalism, as the states and municipalities compete in providing educational services at the primary and secondary levels.[2] We must recall that Brazil is currently organized into twenty-six states, a Federal District (Capital District), and 5,561 municipalities. Consequently, although subject to national

---

2. Legislation is unclear concerning the division of functions between the three levels of government. Basic legislation stipulates that the Union, through the Ministry of Education, MEC, and the National Council of Education, is responsible for the coordination of the design of National Education Plans; the provision of financial and technical assistance to the states, municipalities and the Federal District (Brasília); the maintenance, administration, and development of its own technical and higher-education systems; and the supervision of the network of private universities. Within their jurisdiction, states and municipalities are responsible for similar functions through state and municipal secretariats of Education and state and municipal Councils of Education. Municipal Councils may also discharge functions delegated by State Councils. Finally, functions may be delegated and partnerships established, through collaborative agreements, between levels of government, and between those levels and the private sectors.

FIGURE 4-1. Enrollment at Public Schools, by government level, percent

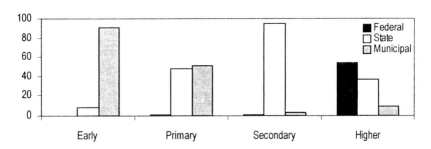

Source: MEC/INEP/SEEC. *Sinopse da Educação Básica, 2000*, and MEC/INEP/SEEC. *Números da Educação no Brasil. Grandes Números do Ensino Superior-Graduação 2000*, Brasil.

legislation and norms, the educational system was, historically, extremely fragmented and heterogeneous in its organization, content, and performance.

Paradoxically, despite this decentralized structure, the regulatory and economic powers of the federal government are considerable, making state and municipal administrations highly dependent, particularly in the smaller municipalities and in the poorer regions of the country. In other words, until recently, the political power of the central government over states and municipalities was very strong through the negotiation of educational funds. Universal norms that defined the amounts of transferable resources were only recently established. This is one of the innovations implemented through the federal government's ongoing policy of decentralization.

With respect to participatory aspects, it is important to emphasize that the country lacks a strong tradition of active school communities and associations. Parent-teacher associations, school councils, municipal councils of education, and other types of associations—with social, advisory, and decision-making functions—are stipulated in legislation, but their implementation is only beginning.

In the 1990s, the decentralization of educational policy—in both the federative and functional decentralization sense—has become one of the main tenets governing the reorganization of the system, though concrete steps in this direction have only been made since the mid-1990s.

Public spending on education is greatest at the primary level and higher education receives the second largest share. From the federative perspective, states and municipalities spend the largest part of their resources on primary and secondary education, while Union expenditures are concentrated in higher education, as shown in Table 4–2.

Table 4–2 also shows the marked decentralization of Brazilian educational spending, even before the education reform of the mid-1990s. While

TABLE 4-2. Public Spending in Education, 1996, percent

Level of Education	Government Level (Government level = 100%)				Government Level (Education level = 100%)			
	Federal	State	Municipal	Total	Federal	State	Municipal	Total
Early	0.0	0.6	18.5	5.6	0.0	5.2	94.8	100
Primary	11.2	77.7	71.8	58.6	5.1	59.7	35.3	100
Secondary	9.4	9.7	7.8	9.0	27.3	48.0	24.6	100
Higher	79.4	12.0	1.9	26.8	77.9	20.1	2.0	100
Total	100	100	100	100	20.2	49.1	30.8	100

Source: Rodriguez and Herrán, 2000.

the Union contributes approximately 20 percent of total public expenditure in education, states and municipalities account for 49 and 31 percent of consolidated total educational government expenditures respectively. Even federal transfers to subnational governments for education represent only 12 percent of total government expenditures (Afonso, 1996: 12). Public spending on education was estimated to be about 5.1 percent of GDP in 1995 (Almeida, 2001). About US$709 is spent on individual students at the primary level, and US$1,502 at the secondary level.

An Inadequate Educational System

Beginning in the mid-1980s, and intensifying in the early 1990s, severe criticism highlighted the insufficient educational coverage at all levels of schooling, the poor quality of teaching, and the sizable gap between new demands for workforce qualifications and the educational content of school curricula. Moreover, the sharp differences within the educational system are reflected in the inequality of access, disparities of educational coverage and performance among genders, social groups, classes, regions, and municipal and state public school networks. Some figures can illustrate the educational situation.

In 1991, the Brazilian rate of illiteracy was still 21.3 percent, and adults had completed, on average, fewer than five years of schooling. At the same time, access to primary education, covering the 7–14 age group, reached 83 percent (1994). But in the case of secondary education, coverage was below 20 percent, one of the lowest among Latin American countries. The cause is striking: low secondary-school coverage was not due to the insufficient availability of schools, but was rather the result of the low quality of primary education. In fact, repetition and drop-out rates were about 50 percent, meaning that only one in every two pupils who began was able to complete the eight years of primary schooling, and a large number of students attended classes out of step with their age group (on average the age gap was more than four years).

The consequences in terms of the inefficiencies in the school system were tremendous: estimates for 1998 indicated that only two in every three students who began could expect to complete the eighth grade. Those pupils who were successful took an average of fourteen years to complete the eight years of primary school, and twenty-three years to complete the eleven years of both primary and secondary school (Rodriguez and Herrán, 2000: 13–15).

Another related problem, pointed out by the majority of educational diagnoses, was teacher qualification. The difficulty was less quantitative—for the student/teacher ratio was about 22.3:1 at the primary level in 1994—than qualitative. At the primary level, 80 percent of teachers were certified, half of them with secondary-school training and half with college degrees. At the secondary level, 74 percent of teachers had college degrees. The major problem was most likely the absence of teacher training programs, with the exception of four or five states.

Related to this was the low level of teachers' wages at the primary level, and the enormous variation in salaries. Most analyses of the educational situation during the first half of the 1990s pointed to the perverse relation—really a vicious circle—between low wages and the low qualification of teachers. Solving this problem was one of the great concerns of the 1995 educational reform group.

Problems of equality cut across the educational system. Regarding income, it is important to remember that, from the 1970s to the present, the middle class had already enrolled its children in private schools in search of higher quality education. Consequently, the majority of students in public schools came from low-income families.

Regional inequalities are even greater than income inequalities. From 1989 to 1992, some efficiency indicators such as grade repetition and dropout rates in elementary education revealed that interregional differences were decreasing, as rates in the north and northeast neared the national mean. However, qualitative indicators, such as teachers' certification or student performance in national exams, reveal the great differences that still polarize the northeastern and northern regions, on one side, and the southeastern and southern regions, on the other.

Finally, qualitative differences between state and municipal schools have been notorious and have increased over time. Besides regional differences, state schooling systems historically offered higher-quality teaching, while municipal schools presented worse conditions. Empirical evidence shows a pattern of high/low quality in schools, in which positive or favorable conditions existed in state schools, large schools, and schools of large municipali-

TABLE 4-3. Educational Reform Strategy, 1995

Area to be Changed	Content/Guidelines
Funding/spending	Redistribution of funds to benefit primary schooling Decentralization of spending Reinforcement of progressive and distributive impact of funds Recovery of regional balance in resources allocation
Organizational structure/decision-making	Decentralization Deconcentration of funds and posts
Public-private relations	Parent participation Partnerships with civil society
Didactic-pedagogical aspect	Modernization of syllabi Diversification of careers Creation of national teacher training systems
Introduction of new programs	Cash program to poor families to support primary education
Monitoring and quality control	Creation of an integrated national educational assessment scheme

ties, whereas negative or less favorable conditions existed in the municipal schools, small and medium-sized schools, and those located in small municipalities with fewer resources (Draibe, 1999).

Reforming Education

By the mid-1980s, a great part of the diagnosis concerning the education sector's greatest problems and challenges, predominantly in the primary and secondary levels, had already been identified with reasonable accuracy. In addition, in the second half of the decade, some states and municipalities had begun to experience a variety of institutional changes and innovations in their own educational systems, with largely positive results. However, at the national level, educational policy reform was one of the tardiest of the social reforms. Although the modern reformist agenda first appeared during the democratization period, the first innovation measures were defined and implemented only during the second reformist cycle, in the second half of the 1990s.

Defined and begun in 1995, in the first year of President Fernando Henrique Cardoso's first mandate, the educational reform strategy was founded on a set of relatively integrated lines of action and fronts. Table 4–3 displays those dimensions of the overall educational system that were principally affected and the contents or guidelines of the changes.

Elements at all levels of the educational system are in a state of flux. Primary education registers the most profound and complete changes, including resource decentralization, municipalization of basic enrollments, modernization of curricular contents, and investment in teaching quality.

Given the objectives and limits of this chapter, I chose to address two sets of reform measures undertaken by the federal government's Education Ministry between 1995 and 1998. The first set is the radical decentralization of federal resources and programs that support state and municipal primary schools. The second refers to changes in the educational finance law. In addition to the intrinsic importance of each of these measures, both sets allow us to examine the important and varied impacts of education reform over the country's federated structure.

Decentralizing Federal Education Programs. The transfer of financial disbursement power to states, municipalities, and schools has been a guideline of virtually all federal programs designed to promote primary education. Between 1995 and 1997, besides completing the decentralization of the School Meals Program (PNAE), the Ministry of Education introduced two new decentralized programs, the Program for the Maintenance and Development of Teaching (PMDE) and the Distance Education "TV Escola" Program. The first one transfers funds annually to municipal and state public elementary schools to facilitate disbursement of small items of day-to-day expenditures and for the physical maintenance of school buildings. The second, aimed at continued teacher training, is a daily television broadcast of pedagogical films that are recorded by schools and teachers.

Recent studies and surveys have recorded the positive results of decentralization in terms of efficiency and effectiveness, registering improvement in coverage and regularity of services. In the three documented experiences, evidence also shows that the decentralized programs reinforce school autonomy and encourage more active participation of the school community—both teachers and parents—in the management of schools. Owing to regional differences and to discrepancies within the school networks themselves, effects on the quality of teaching are as of yet unsatisfactory.

New Law for Funding Primary Education. The most radical educational reform measure was FUNDEF—*Fundo de Manutenção e Desenvolvimento do Ensino Fundamental e de Valorização do Magistério* (Fund for the Development and Maintenance of Basic Education and Teacher Development), which changed the distribution of educational resources in favor of primary schooling.[3]

Under the new scheme, 60 percent of all the funds constitutionally allocated to education by state and municipal governments—or 15 percent of available revenues and fiscal transfers—are pooled in each state in a fund for distribution to the state itself or to municipal districts. The sums distributed

---

3.   FUNDEF was created by Constitutional Amendment 14, September 1996, and regulated by the Law 9.424, December 1996, but its implementation only began in January 1998.

TABLE 4-4. Elementary Education: Promotion, Repetition, Dropout, and Age-Grade Gap Rates, 1995/1996 vs. 1999/2000

Promotion Rate		Repetition Rate		Drop-out Rate		Age-Grade Gap Rate	
1995-1996	1999-2000	1995-1996	1999-2000	1995-1996	1999-2000	1995-1996	1999-2000
64.5	73.6	30.2	21.6	5.3	4.8	47	41.7

must be proportional to the number of primary schoolchildren actually attending school in the respective school networks, on the basis of approximately US$150 per child per year. Likewise, under the new scheme at least 60 percent of the total resources in the fund must be spent on improving the pay of primary school teachers, the suggested minimum salary being equivalent to per capita annual expenditure on pupils. It falls on the federal government to compensate for states that fail to attain the minimum expenditure level owing to lack of resources. Evidently, social control was also a concern of the new law.

The Results of Reform Efforts: Certainly, the improvement of some educational indicators is related to several innovations and reforms, some of which are described in this chapter. Indeed, it is impossible to determine a causal link between those indicators and the changes introduced in the past years, as we know, educational performance results from interrelated factors. Some changes in the educational situation correspond to long-term tendencies, rather than recent circumstantial innovations. Keeping in mind this methodological advice, we can detect some positive long-term educational changes.

High rates of growth in enrollment confirm that primary education is becoming universal, with attendance rising to more than 97 percent in the 7–14 year age group in 2000. At the secondary level, the increase in the coverage of the 15–17 years age group is more impressive, growing from 17.6 to 32.6 percent between 1991 and 1999. However, it is still lower than the average for other Latin American countries.

The illiteracy rate among people aged fifteen years or more likewise fell sharply from 21.3 to 13.3 percent, between 1991 and 1999, but regional differences continue to be glaring, with the backward northeast region still recording illiteracy rates as high as 30 percent. Between 1990 and 1999, the average length of schooling among adults aged fifteen or older rose from 3.6 to 5.7 years, but it was still lower than countries at the same level of economic development. Improvements in the efficiency of the education system between 1995 and 2000 were also impressive. Table 4–4 shows a significant increase in the promotion rate, while repetition and dropout rates are falling.

Changes supposedly more directly related to the FUNDEF can be detected through other indicators. Briefly, the available information points to the following results.

Increased coverage of primary schooling: Between 1997 and 1998, enrollment increased 6 percent and the coverage rate rose from 93 to 95.8 percent. The enrollment increase was strongest in municipal schools and schools in the northeast and north.

Regional redistributive effects: Global transfer of funds relating to FUNDEF in 1998 totaled R$13.3 billion, approximately US$7.3 billion, or 1.5 percent of Brazilian GDP, 61.6 percent for states and 38.4 percent for municipalities. The redistributive effects and the reduction of regional inequalities are clear: eight states in the northeast and north—the two regions previously registering the lowest levels of spending per student—received net resources from FUNDEF.

Increased average spending per student: The increase in per capita spending on schoolchildren was approximately 22.7 percent nationwide, but it was considerably more pronounced (90 percent) in the northeast. In all, 49 percent of Brazil's municipalities providing 34 percent of seats available in elementary schools, increased annual spending per pupil. In 1997, average annual spending per pupil in these municipalities was R$167, and increased 129 percent to reach R$375 in 1998.

Between 1998 and 2000, annual spending per pupil grew 48.5 percent nationwide, 117.5 percent in the northeast, 90 percent in the north, and 20 percent in the centerwest regions. Without FUNDEF, and with the same growth in enrollments, spending would have only increased 6 percent (Semeguini, 2001).

Improvement in teachers' salaries: The nationwide average increase was 13 percent between 1997 and 1998, while in municipal schools in the northeast the increase was about 49 percent.[4] Between mid-1997 and mid-2000, the average teacher's salary had increased 29.5 percent nationwide, 54 percent in the northeast and 35 percent in the north.

Improvements in Teachers' Qualifications: Between 1997 and 2000, the number of unqualified public school teachers was reduced by 46 percent, while the proportion of teachers who completed secondary education rose 10.6 percent, and the proportion with higher education rose 12 percent.

Certainly, the most impressive impact of the reform was the municipalization of primary schooling. The new law's strong, built-in incentive for decentralization to municipalities cannot be ignored: it was expected that large and medium municipalities would lose resources if they did not spend

---

4.   The improvement in salaries was truly remarkable in some municipal districts: 270 percent in Girau de Ponciano (Alagoas); 195 percent in Boa Viagem (Ceará); 180 percent in Coroatá (Maranhão); 175 percent in Itabaiana (Sergipe); 165 percent in Redenção (Ceará); 150 percent in Santo Antônio de Jesus (Bahia) and Barras (Piauí); 131 percent in Araci (Bahia); 125 percent in Anápolis (Goiás); and from 85 percent to 110 percent in Marapanim (Paraíba), Ceará-Mirim and Macaíba (Rio Grande do Norte).

FIGURE 4-2. Enrollment at Elementary Level, states and municipalities, 1970–2001

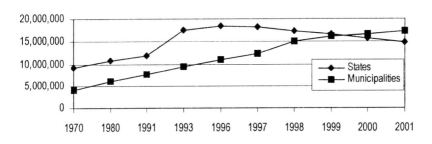

Source: MEC. *Censos Escolares, 1970–1994*, MEC. *Educação no Brasil, 1995–2001*.

15 percent of their revenues in elementary education. Small municipalities would increase revenues if they expanded elementary-education enrollment. Differently, as already stated, states such as São Paulo and municipalities that already have much higher levels of per capita expenditures would stop receiving federal resources for elementary education. In the northeast, on the other hand, states would tend to lose federal resources in favor of municipalities, as the former spent the largest proportions of public provision in elementary education.

The results, in terms of enrollment distribution between states and municipalities confirm these expected effects, as shown in Figure 4–2.

The figures show a trend toward the reversal in state and municipal participation in public enrollment between 1970 and 2001. States' participation fell from 70 to 46 percent, while municipalities' increased from 30 to 54 percent. The effect of the reform is clear: the growth of municipal participation, slow until 1997, accelerated between 1998 and 2001, immediately after the implementation of the new funding law.

Considering the whole set of educational measures, however, it has only been at the elementary level that a number of breakthroughs can be credited to education reform (quantitative progress and impact on redistribution and equity, as already registered):

- Improved universalization of primary education, greater coverage in secondary education, and greater regional and individual redistribution of spending;
- Qualitative progress: improved syllabus content and educational procedures, political-institutional achievements, in terms of increased credibility of educational policy and authorities;
- A broader coalition in support of changes in the field and the democratization of information;
- Improved assessment systems and control of educational results, improvement in the quantity, quality, and speed of educational data and statistics, introduction and extension of educational assessment schemes at all three levels of education.

Nevertheless, there is still plenty of room for improvement. As already stated, secondary and higher education still lack properly structured, coherent reform projects. At the secondary level, despite recent growth in enrollment, coverage is still glaringly insufficient. Secondary schooling still lacks resources for funding in the present and for expansion in the future.

Health Policy Reform

Until the 1980s, Brazil's health policy operated within a highly fragmented institutional framework in which the dichotomy between prevention and curing prevailed.

The public sector was divided between preventive/collective medicine (administered by the Ministry of Health, State Health Secretariats, and the secretariats of some large and medium-size municipalities) and prophylactic/individual treatment provided by the social security system. State and municipal authorities in large and medium-size municipal districts also provided hospital facilities. In this health care model, urban medicine based in hospitals and geared toward curing predominated, to the detriment of basic, preventive health actions, especially where the rural population was concerned. Private medical institutions collaborated with the public health system in the provision of public health services, the former supplying 70 percent of all the medical services contracted by the public sector and, since the late 1980s, accounting for more than 30 percent of the entire health market.

A powerful social movement supporting health care reform developed in the late 1970s, guided by the following main principles: decentralization, focusing on the states and increasing the role of municipal authorities; integration of the managing authority in each tier of administration; and participation of civil society to ensure social control and systemic integration of preventive and prophylactic actions.

The reform, wrought during Brazil's redemocratization, was consecrated in the 1988 constitution as the Unified Health System (SUS), and organized according to these main principles: concerning the health care model, as a system of free demand and universal access to all types of services regardless of complexity; in organizational terms, as a system based on principles of decentralization, municipalization, observance of hierarchy, regionalization, integration and unified command; and, in terms of resources, funding by a mix of resources derived from social security contributions and fiscal revenues. The new health system was implemented in 1988, but until the mid-1990s its decentralization process was slow and the SUS had progressively fewer resources. A series of measures unveiled in 1995 and 1996 has gradually changed the face of the SUS.

The unstable SUS financing system led to the creation of a specific source of funding passed by Congress in 1996 in the form of a tax on checks, the Provisional Financial Transactions Contribution (CPMF). In 1996 the system of decentralization and engagement was simplified to comprise just two types of management: "Full Basic Assistance"—involving a lesser degree of autonomy—and "Full Municipal System" (or state system in the case of states)—under which municipal authorities assume full responsibility for the administration of health. By the end of 1998, 5,136 municipalities (93 percent of Brazil's 5,506 municipalities) had already adhered, 4,665 to the Full Basic Assistance scheme and 471 to the Full Municipal System.

A new system of transferring funds to state and municipal administrations (Basic Assistance) was introduced in 1997, transferring a base rate of approximately US$8.80 per inhabitant per year to cover the cost of basic health actions. The mechanism raised the level of spending for many municipalities, especially those not spending a sum equivalent to the base rate on health. The Basic Pharmacy, on the other hand, distributes medicines to approximately 4,000 municipal districts with fewer than 21,000 inhabitants, providing coverage for about 33 million people at a rate of R$2 per inhabitant per year.

The strongest programmatic and conceptual innovation is certainly that relating to the Family Health Program and, within it, to the Community Health Agents Program. The Family Health Program (PSF) features a strategy for implementing community care. It seeks to redirect basic assistance, strengthening local health systems, ultimately promoting change in the current health care model. Today, fifty million people are already covered by this system. The Community Health Agents Program (PACS—*Programa de Agentes Comunitários de Saúde*) trains and mobilizes people from within the local community to carry out basic health and educational actions among poor families, particularly in rural areas. Two major innovations in this program deserve special mention as they represent, if not an advance, at least a correction of SUS deficiencies: territorial restriction of clientele and the decision to elect the family unit as the unit of reference.

Probably one of the most decisive initiatives in the new cycle of change in health policy involves the modernization of the codes, regulatory systems, and public controls on private-sector provision of medical and sanitary services. The broad-ranging, strong, and diversified health market was traditionally governed by a loose, old-fashioned system of norms and institutions incapable of disciplining the market and safeguarding consumers' rights. The new law regulating private health insurance passed by Congress in 1998 is a watershed. Among its innovations are the extension of risk coverage to the treatment of chronic-degenerative diseases, in addition to the requirement that insurers provide financial compensation when the patients make use of public health services.

Public Health Spending: Trends and Challenges

The legacy of health care reform, initiated in the 1980s, is a system of enormous dimensions, organized according to the principles of universality and free care. In consequence, the potential clientele of the SUS is the entire Brazilian population, about 170 million people. Research suggests, however, that forty million people are covered by the private sector, which would reduce the still massive number of SUS clientele to 130 million people. Given this figure, it is not surprising that resources and management issues are the most difficult challenges this system faces.

In some measure, recent spending behavior endorses the expansion of the system. Recent spending patterns reveal two clear trends: increased spending and, in terms of structure, the rising share of subnational administrations in total public expenditure on health, as is shown in Table 4–5.

TABLE 4-5. Health Spending, in US$ billions

Year	Federal Absolute	Federal %	State Absolute	State %	Municipal Absolute	Municipal %	Total Absolute	Total %
1989	12.3	82.0	1.3	8.7	1.4	9.3	15.0	100
1992	7.2	72.0	1.5	15.0	1.3	13.0	10.0	100
1995	14.9	60.6	5.5	22.4	4.2	17.0	24.6	100
1998 *	16.7	66.8	4.5	18.0	3.8	15.2	25.0	100

Source: Medici, 1999 (*) estimates based on budgets.

There have also been major changes in the makeup of public spending on health, reflecting the overall adjustment in the public sector. Indeed, the evolution of itemized federal public expenditure during the period of stability (1994–1996) shows a sharp decline in spending on personnel, an almost imperceptible and shrinking share of investment, and a rise in spending to amortize debt. These figures, however, are accompanied by an undeniable effort to sustain the level of spending on medical assistance and substantial growth in negotiated transferences to state and municipal administrations.

The Brazilian government has been insistently criticized for allocating insufficient funds to health, though there have been substantial increases in public funds allocated to this sector. As a result, the drive to eliminate inefficiency has been a permanent concern in the implementation of the SUS. The government's determination to sustain and increase funding in such a critical area throughout a period of severe fiscal adjustment and deep recession undoubtedly makes the Brazilian case both interesting and important.

In spite of the great institutional effort to improve the Brazilian health system, many difficulties and challenges remain, in particular the insufficiency and poor quality of services provided.

In regard to the design and dynamics of health policy, the problems mentioned undeniably stem from serious limitations and constraints. The SUS health care model is based on unfettered demand, and thus lacks principles for limiting clientele and for determining the only recently outlined "front door" for access to the system. Insufficient investment leads to the incomplete installation of intermediate and basic service networks, which tends to overload and impair the efficiency of the hospital system, and, finally, the low effectivity due to the perverse combination of the high costs of the system as a whole and the utterly insufficient levels of pay for staff and services.

Social Security and Welfare Reforms

Only at the end of 1998 did Brazil's social security system undergo substantial—even then, only partial—reform. A number of adjustments and alterations were, however, made during the first round of reforms and in the early 1990s. Certain characteristics of the system make it possible to identify the factors that are progressively making it unworkable.

The social security system provides welfare services for approximately 32 million beneficiaries at a cost of about 11 percent of GDP—roughly half the consolidated outlay on social spending for the three tiers of government.

The private segment of social security, managed by the National Social Security Institute (Instituto Nacional da Seguridade Social, INSS), operates on a pay-as-you-go system with defined contributions. As it advanced into the 1980s, besides differing significantly from the social security system for civil servants (including military personnel), two other major features set it apart: glaringly unequal protection for urban and rural workers and relatively complete coverage for risks in urban areas with the exception of unemployment security, introduced in 1988.

By way of contrast, the social security regimes for civil servants were distinguished by the following features: the absence of any actuarial rule or link between the level of contribution and the benefits received; unequal rules, contributions, and benefits among the three tiers of government, among the different careers within the civil service and among the departments of the direct administration and the associate government agencies of the respective governments; and a system of rights and privileges that facilitated early retirement on full pay or on even higher income.

The general regime is based on payroll-associated contributions: employees pay 8 to 11 percent of their salary, depending on their income bracket, while employers contribute 21 to 23 percent of the payroll, the percentage varying according to the risk of the labor activity involved. The role of the state is confined to covering the system's administrative and personnel costs and, at the federal level, paying the pensions of federal civil servants. The social security systems for civil servants vary considerably: each tier of government has its own retirement and pensions scheme to which civil servants contribute at different rates.

In terms of benefits, it is worth recalling that it was only after the 1988 constitution that urban and rural workers began to receive equal treatment. Another salient feature is the variation and inequality of the sums paid for different types of retirement: due to permanent disability, age, length of service (proportional to the number of years of employment), and special retirement. Between 1974 and 1994, the system included a type of "social pension" (lifelong monthly income) for destitute elderly adults and invalids not eligible for retirement or other pensions.[5,6,7,8]

Civil servants, on the other hand, besides being entitled to the same types of retirement pensions, could receive privileged benefits as follows: they retire on full salary as of the date of retirement, plus 20 percent in the case of federal civil servants, their benefits thus being subject to no upper limit; they have retirement pensions indexed to the salaries of regular civil servants, their income being adjusted whenever civil service salaries are raised.

Partly because of this state of affairs, the civil service social security system has gradually come to be financed solely from fiscal resources, losing the link between contributions and benefits. In the 1990s, it was these civil service regimes that sank into financial bankruptcy.[9]

The growth of the Brazilian welfare system was rapid, particularly in terms of the number of contributors to the general regime. In 1970, there were 7.6 million; in 1980, there were 23 million; and by 1990, the figure had risen to 32 million contributors. The growth curve for beneficiaries was not excessively sharp until the 1980s, when it climbed steeply, the total number rising from 9 million in 1980 to about 13 million in 1990 and more than 16 million in 1996. Among the fastest growing groups of beneficiaries were rural workers. In 1991, there were no more than 4 million, but by 1994 they already exceeded 6 million.

---

5.   Until 1988 the minimum ages for retirement on full pension were seventy for men and sixty-five for women; from then on they were lowered to sixty-five and sixty, respectively.
6.   Thirty-five years in the case of men and thirty for women. Very few countries retain this type of benefit.
7.   Teachers can retire after thirty years on the job (men) and twenty-five years (women).
8.   In 1993 this benefit was replaced by the "old person's benefit," equivalent to one minimum wage granted after means testing to poor senior citizens whose per capita family income does not exceed the minimum wage by more than 25 percent.
9.   In 1998, the states of Rio de Janeiro, Rio Grande do Sul, Piauí, Espírito Santo, and Alagoas spent, respectively, 36 percent, 35 percent, 35 percent, 34 percent, and 30 percent of their total revenue on this item.

Such growth, though, should also be examined from the standpoint of structural factors contributing to the financial imbalance of the social welfare system. There is the system's relation with the labor market, more specifically the traditionally low coverage of the economically active population. The main explanation for this is the sheer size of the informal labor market in Brazil. In 1995, for example, while 47.4 percent of the economically idle population contributed to the social security system, 52.6 percent were non-contributors. At present, this proportion is 42 and 58 percent respectively. This negative relation with the labor market is certainly one of the main causes of the financial imbalance in the social welfare system today.

Other structural factors that explain the current imbalance stem from recent demographic transition trends and the consequent aging of the population. Besides the growing proportion of people aged sixty or over in the total population, life expectancy is also increasing, as is the number of years beneficiaries actually make use of retirement pensions—a matter of direct interest to the welfare system.[10] Consequently, dependency rate on the welfare system, which stood at 3.18 in 1980, has shrunk to 2.5 contributors per beneficiary—a rate close to that for countries with populations whose average age is much higher.

In the second half of the 1990s, the financial imbalance of the Brazilian Social Security system had already reached the proportion of 3.7 percent of GDP.

Reforming Social Security

Reformers in the 1980s pursued three objectives in the social security system: to universalize the system and make it more evenhanded; to correct the main internal distortions; and to diversify sources of funding so as to protect the system from the most acute fluctuations in the economy.

The following innovations and modifications introduced by the 1988 constitution deserve special mention: establishing the concept of social security (encompassing social welfare, assistance, and health) as the basis of the system; diminishing the inequalities between urban and rural beneficiaries; setting a base rate for welfare benefits (one minimum wage), thus slackening the direct link between contributions and benefits; introducing the principle of selectiveness with a view to enhancing the protection of lower-income segments among beneficiaries; defining the payrolls as the exclusive basis for social security contributions, and diversifying sources for other areas of social security (health and assistance). These measures were implemented

10. Demographic projections show that Brazil's elderly population (i.e. those aged sixty-five years or more) will total 8.7 million in the year 2000 and by 2020 will have grown to about eighteen million.

between 1988 and 1993, and were accompanied by a significant increase in spending.

As the second cycle of reform got under way between 1992 and 1993, parliamentary circles endeavored to establish a consensual reform bill. It was only in 1995, however, that the government finally tabled its new welfare reform bill. However, the negotiated reform was partial. It modified some important characteristics of the system, mainly the elimination of retirement for length of service, proportional and cumulative retirement, suppressed the special civil service regimes (except military personnel), and included the states and municipalities regimes.

It is virtually a consensus that the reform undertaken to date is incomplete and would only contribute to reduce the social security financial deficit in the short term. To a certain extent, this limitation reflects poorly designed political strategies on the part of both the government and the various groups opposed to reform.

For the government and for an important part of public opinion, social security reform did not create a solution to the crucial problems of this system, mainly those concerned with the civil servant states and municipalities regimes. Another challenge, not touched by previous reforms, is the lack of protection for the great mass of informal sector workers. A new wave of changes will most likely be part of the next government's agenda.

Welfare and Antipoverty Measures
The last decade of 1990 to 2000 saw substantial change in the way social assistance and antipoverty programs were administered. The difference is especially sharp if one considers the legacy of the previous period: an uncoordinated mass of programs heavily concentrated in the federal administration; fragmented, discontinuous action; glaring ineffectiveness in terms of the results obtained and the impact produced among the target population; and, above all, the strongly clientelistic approach adopted in implementing such programs.

However, legislative measures may have restricted major alterations in this field in the two reform cycles, and change is forging ahead in a gradual, cumulative manner. The effects are felt above all in terms of key concepts and policymaking.

Among the strategic options shaping current action in this field, the following deserve special attention: the emphasis on social rights as the normative underpinning for programs; the preference for programs that enhance the target group's autonomy; the combination of universal and target programs, not the polarization of both; the liaison with civil society viewed as an efficient strategy for combating poverty; the decision-making mechanisms that foster participation; the more efficient, decentralized, and transparent management standards; and finally, the introduction of innovative procedures in the implementation of programs, affecting particularly the selection process of beneficiaries and the monitoring and evaluation process.

The central social assistance policy reform occurred in the first reformist cycle, its terms being defined in the 1988 new constitution and completed in 1993, when the Social Assistance Law (LOAS—*Lei Orgânica da Assistência Social*) was passed. With regard to policy on poverty, the Solidary Community Program has been active in the poorest communities since 1995.

A strong innovation was introduced in the second reformist cycle, with the implementation of several in-cash programs targeted at poor families. In 2002, almost 2 percent of GDP was destined for these kinds of social programs, the more visible of them being the School Grant (*Bolsa Escola*), destined to poor families with children between 6 and 15 years of age. The set of in-cash programs, besides being a shift in Brazilian tradition to offer social services instead of grants to poor families, seems to respond to a government strategy to create a social safety net to fight poverty.

Many welfare programs, from the oldest to the newest, have rendered positive local results, as demonstrated by numerous research studies. However, we have no evidence about their effectiveness in reducing inequality or eliminating poverty at the national level.

Conclusion

International policymakers are often caught in the difficult dilemma between the new global political economy and the new politics of the welfare state (Pierson, 1998; Castles, 1999; Green-Pedersen, 1999). In the case of Latin America, it is said that governments, under international financial pressure and with great independence, have taken the radical option of economic and fiscal adjustment, producing as consequence the dismantling of the embryonic welfare states previously created in some countries of the region (Draibe, Azeredo, and Guimarães, 1995).

However, analysis of the recent trends in the social policy reform process in Brazil does not show the dismantling of the national social policy system. In fact, the collected evidence shows that there has been a gradual shift in Brazilian social protection standards over the past twenty years, promoted by at least three new features: decentralization, the emergence of new parameters for allocating resources, and the redefinition of public-private relations in the funding and provision of social goods and services. An additional feature sets the Brazilian case apart from other social reform experiments: public social spending has increased despite concomitant fiscal adjustment even when, on many occasions, contingencies and cutbacks have seriously hampered the implementation of social policies.

TABLE 4-6. Changes in Social Policy Arena

Target of Change	Emergent Elements
Conceptualizing policy standards	Civil rights as the basis for policy
Criteria of justice	Statement that basic programs (elementary education; health) are universal and free of charge Stress on selectiveness and improvement of focus criteria Greater progressiveness in spending
Policy/management style	Reduction of clientelistic practices
Public/private funding	Introduction of private sector participation
Provision	Strengthening of third sector partnerships
Type of programs implemented	Introduction and/or boosting of monetary transference programs Introduction of "productive"-type programs—training and popular credit
Institutional set-up shaping policies, financing, and decision making	Decentralization of decision making and resources Federative delegation of powers
Supervision and control	Expansion and institutionalization of social participation

The reform of Brazil's social programs is not yet complete, and there is considerable room for improvement in terms of efficiency and equity. The modest results obtained to date belie the intensity of change that, despite the lack of broad-sweeping reforms, has been altering the shape of social programs since the 1980s, making significant alterations to the profile of the distorted, centralized welfare state the country inherited from the military regime. Table 4–6 identifies key trends in Brazil's social policy arena and the main lines of action affected by the changes introduced during the two reform cycles described above.

Indeed, the last fifteen years have witnessed a large number of changes and shifts in a variety of programs, affecting everything from basic design to funding, organization, modus operandi, and the approach to management. As we have underscored in this study, the results across the board in social areas confirm significant change in objectives, approaches, and guidelines, even though not all the policy outlines have been sufficiently redesigned.

It would therefore be no exaggeration to state that a gradual shift or reformation in Brazilian social protection services began over the past two decades. Not all the tenets of the emerging standards are yet discernible. And the recentness of these modifications prevents distinguishing between permanent elements and other more circumstantial features related to the guidelines adopted by governments and specific administrations. Even so, at least three of the new features described in this study seem to be creating more lasting changes in the sphere of the national social policy system: decentralization, the new parameters for allocating resources, and the redefinition of public-private relations in the funding and provision of social goods and services.

I have already given details of how these trends translate into each policy area. However, two salient features tend to set the Brazilian case apart from other experiments in social reform. One is that public social spending has increased despite concomitant fiscal adjustment, even when on many occasions contingencies and cutbacks have seriously hampered the implementation of social policies.

The other is that the reform movement has developed in two cycles with distinct, if not contradictory, approaches and objectives that partially overlap. This has undoubtedly fostered the search for more complex, innovative options than those envisaged by the simplistic neoliberal prescription of the 1980s. The final shape of the new social protection system now emerging from this process will in all likelihood reflect the peculiarities of the current situation and the options derived from it.

CHAPTER 5

Agrarian Reform

Anthony Pereira

The prominence of agrarian reform as a political issue was one of the great surprises of the government of Fernando Henrique Cardoso's presidency (1995–2002). Mobilization for reform was widespread and intense, the extent of the government's land redistribution program was far higher than that of any of the preceding postmilitary governments, and agrarian reform occupied a prominent place in the government's rhetoric about its accomplishments. The reform went beyond what most political observers anticipated at the time of Cardoso's election, and exceeded what the president himself seems to have expected. Agrarian reform also became a symbol of and a focal point in the battle between supporters of the government's economic policies and their opponents.

How is one to explain and interpret this surprising outcome? What does the government's agrarian reform represent for Brazil's politics and economy? One answer to the latter question is that the increase in land redistribution represents a major economic and political reform. In this view, the Cardoso government, reflecting the president's progressive past as a scholar and social critic, broke with past policies. By granting small producers a more secure place in the agricultural sector, and by recognizing, negotiating with, and partly accommodating the landless, the Cardoso government has democratized economic and social policy in the countryside. An alternative interpretation would stress the continuity of the Cardoso government's policies with the past. In this interpretation, a look behind and beyond land redistribution reveals policies that disproportionately benefit a small number of large politically powerful producers and a series of opportunities to benefit the rural poor that were missed.

This chapter argues that the second interpretation is more accurate than the first. It proceeds in four steps. First, it examines some claims about past policies, and the Cardoso government's impact upon them. Second, it looks at the situation that the Cardoso government inherited, and the trends in agriculture and land use that preceded the government's ascension to power. Third, it examines the course of agrarian reform since 1995, looking beyond the statistics on land redistribution to examine the issues of land titling, agricultural credit, taxation, payments for expropriated land, and rural violence. In the final section, I suggest that the Cardoso government did not fundamentally alter the development model or the pattern of policies in agriculture.

It might be objected that the analysis of Brazil's agrarian reform offered here misleadingly treats a whole series of complicated processes that vary enormously by region and over time as a single phenomenon. However, it is possible to recognize the complexity and variability of the reform process, as I do here, and at the same time seek some preliminary generalizations about its overall trends and consequences. Without such a possibility, it would become untenable to write of a host of important and complex processes that interest social scientists, such as industrialization, urbanization, democratization, and the like. I also maintain that the most productive way to gauge the success or failure of Brazil's agrarian reform is in terms of its impact on long-term trends in rural political economy. Clearly, the analyst attempting such an assessment must make his or her expectations clear, and reasonable people can differ as to what such expectations should be.

Prior Policies of Conservative "Modernization"

Brazil's state policies have traditionally followed a pattern well summarized by Sorj: "the state takes responsibility for the onus, the bonus is distributed among the dominant classes, and the crumbs left over are for the subaltern groups" (Sorj, 1998: 28). The oligarchic and patronage-based features of these policies have their roots in the agrarian past. Land in Brazil has traditionally been not merely a factor of production but a reward for service and proximity to power, as well as a foundation for the accumulation and maintenance of more power and privilege. This power includes the ability of large landowners to direct the legal and coercive apparatus of the State in their region. It also entails landlord control over and obligations to subaltern populations. The original division of the colonial *capitanias* among a handful of *amigos do rei* (friends of the king) reflects this reality (Gonçalo, 2001: 23). In Brazil, unlike the United States, the State's exclusionary tendencies were not substantially mitigated in later stages of development by frontier policies that granted land to the landless. Whereas the Homestead Act of 1862 in the United States granted frontier land to anyone willing to settle it, Brazil's 1850 Land Law (*Lei da Terra*) prohibited the acquisition of public land by any means other than purchase, thus putting an end to previous rights to gain land through occupancy (*posse*) (Viotti da Costa, 2000: 78–79).

Brazilian policies in agriculture in more recent years can best be characterized as the promotion of conservative "modernization." Unlike Latin American countries such as Mexico and Bolivia, Brazil has never had a political rupture that weakened the landed oligarchy and allowed large-scale redistribution of land to those who cultivate it. In addition, Brazil's rural workers have never fully enjoyed the benefits of the Vargas-era Consolidated Labor Laws (*Consolidação das Leis do Trabalho*, or CLT), unlike urban workers. The brief period of mobilization around land and rural labor issues in the late 1950s and early 1960s, which saw the emergence of the Peasant Leagues and rural trade unions, was ended forcefully by the military coup d'état in 1964. Subsequently, the military regime of 1964–1985 imposed policies that essentially took land redistribution in already settled areas off the political agenda. Government policies of subsidized credit (mainly for large producers), tax breaks, price supports, and other incentives promoted the development of large, highly capitalized, mechanized farms and ranches, many of them producing for the export market. This conservative "modernization" created an exodus from the countryside, as sharecroppers, tenants, and small farmers lost access to land, and rural workers lost jobs (Pereira, 1997). At the same time that land concentration was taking place, new, previously unused lands were also passing into private hands. Leite calculates that the private sector acquired, by purchase and government grants, some 31.8 million hectares of previously public land in the 1970s alone (Leite, 1999: 173); this phenomenon was especially marked in the west and north of the country. To minimize potential social unrest in the face of these policies, the military regime initiated programs of rural social assistance (pensions and health programs) and colonization, mostly in the Amazon region.

The Cardoso government is seen by some observers as making a historic break with these policies of conservative modernization in agriculture. This view places Cardoso in the mold of previous presidents, such as Getúlio Vargas (1930–1945; 1950–1954) and Juscelino Kubitschek (1955–1960), who were credited with creating a new order in Brazilian politics (for example, see Roett, 1999; Sorj, 1998; and Gordon, 2001: 125–130). The prominent Brazilian rural sociologist José de Souza Martins is probably the best-known proponent of this view (Martins, 1999; 2000). Martins sees the Cardoso government's agrarian reform as the culmination of one process and a dramatic break with another. It is the capstone of a process that began under Getúlio Vargas to undo the absolute dominion given to private property in land by the 1850 Land Law, and to reassert the public and social character of landholding.[1] On the other hand, it also represents a long-awaited supersedence of the oligarchic, personalistic, and patronage-based pattern of Brazilian politics in the countryside that prevailed even under democratic regimes. Martins sees President Cardoso's PSDB (Partido da Social Democracia Brasileira or Brazilian Social Democracy Party) as an antioligarchical political party with enough force to push Brazil toward political modernity in the rural areas (Martins, 1999: 117).[2]

Martins sees in land reform four fundamental changes in Brazil's society and state. First, unproductive or underproductive large estates (*latifúndios*) have become capitalized and modernized, submitting themselves to the logic of capitalist reproduction and integrating with financial and industrial capital. Second, family farmers have finally won guarantees to a place in the economy and society. Third, the state has become more representative, institutionalized, pluralized, and democratic. Finally, the state has replaced repression with law and negotiation in the countryside, submitting erstwhile *latifundiários* to the rational-legal control of public authority (Martins, 1999: 119, 121, 125). In his enthusiasm, Martins redefines the government's opponents on the land reform issue—the MST (Movimento dos Sem Terra, or Landless Workers's Movement), the Catholic Church's CPT (Comissão Pastoral da Terra, or Pastoral Land Commission), and the Workers' Party—as its real allies in this historic transformation (Martins, 1999: 120).[3]

Later in this chapter, I argue that there is some wishful thinking in this portrait of rural Brazil and the Cardoso government's policies toward it.[4] While certain of the trends that Martins points to have occurred, policies in land and agriculture do not, across the board, reflect the kind of wholesale innovation described by Martins. However, before considering this evidence, it is necessary to examine the general tendencies in land and agricultural policies before the Cardoso government came to power, and how the Cardoso agrarian reform related to them.

Trends in Agriculture and Land

With the election of a civilian president in 1985, land redistribution returned to the political agenda due mainly to pressure from below. President José

---

1. This process includes the constitutional allocation of subsoil mineral rights to the national state rather than individual landowners, and the right of the state to expropriate land not fulfilling a "social function." From an Anglo-American liberal perspective, of course, such assertions of the state over individual rights are anathema.
2. Martins does admit that the PSDB allied itself with an oligarchical party, the PFL (Partido Frente Liberal, or Liberal Front Party), and that the decentralization of land reform discussed below might well lead to the reform's domination by large landowners in some regions.
3. These three entities are the most active forces in opposition to the government on the land reform issue, although they are by no means always fully in agreement on every detail.
4. Ondetti (2001a: 15) argues that most specialists on agrarian reform do not share Martins' views. I report them in detail here because they do, I believe, reflect the attitudes of many people who are in and who support the present government in Brazil.

TABLE 5-1. Beneficiaries of Land Reform, 1985–2001, government figures

Government	Beneficiaries Claimed	Promised Beneficiaries	Annual Average
Sarney ('85–'90)	83,000	1,400,000	16,600
Collor ('90–'92)	30,000		15,000
Franco ('92–'94)	18,000		9,000
Cardoso I ('95–'98)	287,000	280,000	71,750
Cardoso II ('95–'01)	585,683		83,669

Source: Ondetti 2001a for data in the first four rows. Data in the bottom row (Cardoso II) come from "Crédito Ainda Desafia Reforma, Diz Governo" in *Folha de S. Paulo*, January 6, 2002, p. A-8. The data from 2001 cover the period up to November of that year.

Sarney (1985–1990) promised a massive land redistribution program through the mechanism of expropriating unproductive estates. Very little of this reform was actually carried out, either by Sarney's government or by those of his successors, Presidents Collor de Mello (1990–1992) and Itamar Franco (1992–1994) (see Table 5–1). At the same time, partly as a result of the debt crisis, government subsidies to agriculture dropped precipitously. Agricultural credit, for example, declined from US$27 billion in 1986 to only US$6 billion in 1996, as measured in 1996 U.S. dollars (Leite, 1999: 162). Price supports were also reduced (Leite, 1999: 164).

This sharp cut in government support reflects a more market-driven approach to agriculture, enacted at first through sheer necessity, and later as a conscious strategy. This "sink or swim" strategy led to the demise of many small farms, and contributed to the dismissal of many farmworkers. To offset the potential for conflict and resistance generated by such policies, the government began to increase its spending on rural social security and welfare (*previdência social*) (Leite, 1999: 169), as it did on social programs in general (see the chapter by Sônia Draibe in this volume).

On one level, government policy in agriculture was successful. By the mid-1990s, Brazil's agricultural sector was clearly one of the most dynamic and productive in the developing world. Its productivity (value added per agriculture worker) doubled between 1979–1981 and 1996–1998, becoming almost twice that of Mexico's in the latter period (World Bank, 2001). Still the world's leading producer and exporter of coffee, Brazil has expanded into new agricultural markets, acquiring the largest herd of cattle in the world, and becoming the second-largest producer of soya and sugar cane. The country supplies 85 percent of the world market for orange juice concentrate and exports tobacco, cocoa, cotton, butter, beef, and corn (Brogan, 2000: 185).

Brazil's potential for even greater agricultural production is high. It still has a land frontier, and analysts estimate that the area devoted to crops in 1999—around 112.5 million acres—could easily be doubled (Economist

Intelligence Unit, 1999: 1). It is still experiencing growth in capital intensity and mechanization, and its importance to the Brazilian economy is higher than agriculture in the richest countries. While agriculture accounts for only about 9 percent of gross domestic product, it is responsible for around 35 percent of exports and 23 percent of the economically active population.[5] Furthermore, agriculture is internationally competitive and highly "globalized": 16.4 percent of all agricultural production was exported in 1995 (Leite, 1999: 160), almost twice the rate of the economy as a whole. These exports generate a significant, positive trade balance in the sector (Graziano Neto, 1998: 168–169) that amounted to US$19 billion in 2001.[6] This strong performance has also been achieved with far fewer subsidies than prevail in the United States and the European Union. According to one scholar, for example, Brazilian agricultural subsidies, which benefit about two million farmers, are only one-third of what the U.S. government spends on only 250,000 farmers.[7]

Brazilian agriculture is not just a success in overseas markets, but at home as well. Brazil's food production index has risen from 69.5 in 1979–1981 to 125.7 in 1996–1998 (World Bank, 2001: 288).[8] In 2001 the Brazilian government forecast a record crop of 91.6 million tons of grain, a 10 percent increase over the 83 million tons produced in 2000 (Rinelli, 2001: 4). The continuing problem of hunger in Brazil is thus the consequence of lack of sufficient income on the part of the poor, not an inadequate supply of food from Brazil's farms and ranches.

However, behind the glittering trajectory of Brazilian agriculture lies what historian Kenneth Maxwell calls "the other Brazil" (Maxwell, 1999/2000). Fully one-third of the rural population, according to the government's own 1990 data, lives below the poverty line (World Bank, 2001: 280). With one of the most unequal distributions of land in the world, the Brazilian countryside has been the site, not only of the creation of great fortunes, but of social devastation reminiscent of the enclosure of common lands in early

---

5.   Chris Brogan (2000) "Brazil" in *Nations of the World: A Political, Economic and Business Handbook*. New York: Grey House Publishing, first edition: 185. Agriculture accounts for 28 percent of male and 14 percent of female employment; (Brogan, 2000/184). The figure for the share of agriculture in GDP is value added as a percentage of GDP in 1999 and comes from World Bank 2001: 296.
6.   Fleischer reports that "Brazil's agribusiness sector posted a US$19 billion trade surplus in 2001, with exports of US$23.9 billion and imports of US$4.9 billion. This was a 28 percent increase from the US$14.8 surplus posted in 2000." From David Fleischer (2002b) *Brazil Focus Weekly Report,* January 5–11, p. 7.
7.   From comments by Marcus Sawaya Jank, a professor from the University of São Paulo, at a panel discussion entitled "Sustainable Development and Rural Poverty: A Brazilian Perspective" held at the Woodrow Wilson Center, Washington D.C., May 24, 2001. The U.S. government's support for agriculture looks likely to continue; in October of 2001, the lower house of Congress passed a bill authorizing US$170 billion in crop subsidies to agriculture over the next ten years. From "House Approves $170 Billion Farm Bill" in *The Times-Picayune* (New Orleans), October 6, 2001, p. A-3.
8.   In calculating the index, 1989–1991 = 100.

modern Europe or the out-migration of displaced small holders in the U.S. Dust Bowl during the Great Depression. This devastation has been created, in part, because the policies promoting the "modernization" of agriculture have placed a premium on narrow criteria of success: the creation of a large, exportable surplus of agricultural goods. Other considerations, such as maximizing rural employment, intensifying the cultivation of the land, and the desire of small farmers to continue to remain independent small producers, have been neglected.[9] Furthermore, social relations have changed in the countryside. Large landowners have jettisoned traditional bonds of obligation to the rural poor, who used to be their tenants, sharecroppers, and/or dependents or clients. This sense of noblesse oblige had at one time been a key component of the rural social order, but it has been eroded as large landowners used their privileged connection to the State to transform themselves into entrepreneurs of the new agribusiness. In many regions' face-to-face contacts between large landowners and the rural poor have become a thing of the past.

Conducted in December–January of 1996–1997, a major survey of 159,778 people resettled on land under the federal government's agrarian reform program from the period before 1960 until 1996 reveals the extent of deprivation faced by many rural dwellers. Thirty percent of those surveyed were illiterate, while less than 14 percent had received more than four years of primary school education (Schmidt, Marinho, and Couto Rosa, 1998: 24, 65). Sixty-four percent of those surveyed had no training or skills in the labor market other than their knowledge of farming (the survey used the terms agricultor/camponês), and 87 percent farmed their land themselves, without being in a cooperative or part of a larger enterprise. Well over half of these farmers said that they received "no" or "precarious" technical assistance from the government. The average household income of these smallholders was R$722 per year, or about the same amount in U.S. dollars at the exchange rate that prevailed at that time, while only a small minority lived in houses with running water or sewage.[10] Mainly growing basic staples such as corn, manioc, beans, sweet potatoes, and rice, only 5 percent of these struggling farmers had the benefit of irrigation, while in most regions even fewer had access to farm machinery or motorized vehicles. Their access to education

---

9.   Contrary to the common prejudice, large farms are not necessarily more efficient than small and medium-sized ones. When it comes to economic efficiency, measured by comparing output to inputs of land, labor, and capital, small and medium farms often out-perform large ones; in the area of pecuniary efficiency, measured by the advantages of vertical integration, tax breaks, and subsidies, large farms do better. In Angus Wright's words, "This then explains why less 'economically efficient' large farms prevail over small ones. And, of course, what this means is that their advantages are pre-eminently political and at least subject to policy reform." Personal communication with Professor Angus Wright, California State University at Sacramento, April 11, 2002.
10.   At the time of writing (April 2002), the U.S. dollar exchanged for roughly 2.35 Brazilian *reais*.

and health services were tenuous or nonexistent, and many of them reported serious health problems such as intestinal parasites (15 percent) and malaria (8 percent) (Schmidt, Marinho, and Couto Rosa, 1998: 55–112).[11]

Brazil's poorest farmers thus have a precarious toehold in the new agrarian order. Below them in the rural social order are the landless. These former small farmers, rural workers, and even urban workers face dim prospects in urban labor markets, where unemployment has risen in recent years. While the new rural Brazil boasts of vast farms and ranches run by prosperous owners with cell phones and pickup trucks, small armies of the dispossessed move, sometimes unseen, within it, migrating in search of seasonal jobs, shelter, and—the biggest hope of many—land. Despite the difficult conditions of life for small farmers, many of the landless seem to prefer this option to any existing alternatives.

The official system of representation in Brazilian agriculture has not been fully able to represent those losing access to land in the new agrarian economy. The National Agrarian Confederation (Confederação Nacional Agrária) is the official, state-recognized entity representing agricultural employers, while CONTAG (Confederação Nacional de Trabalhadores da Agricultura, or National Confederation of Agricultural Workers) is its counterpart on the labor side. While CONTAG does speak out on the issue of landlessness and agrarian reform, and its member unions do sometimes organize land occupations (Sigaud, 2000), its organizational structure makes it a more effective representative of small family farmers and wage workers than of the landless. This was a factor in the emergence of the MST, the principal critic of the government in the area of land reform (Pereira, 1999). The MST, which began its activity in the early 1980s, claims to speak for the estimated 4.8 million landless families in the country, and organizes marches, the occupation (or, as others say, the invasion) of unused public and private land, and, more recently, the occupation of government offices. It demands the radical deconcentration of land ownership via widespread distribution of land from large landowners to the dispossessed. It has attempted to prod the national conscience and speak for those excluded from the benefits of the modern economy (Pereira, 1999: 115, 119). The MST and its demand for agrarian reform, in turn, has been opposed by the UDR (União Democrática Ruralista, or Democratic Rural Union), an organization of large landowners opposed to land reform that emerged after 1985 (Sorj, 1998: 29; Payne, 2000). It is these last two organizations, both of which lie outside the official system of repre-

---

11. These data are a snapshot intended to illustrate the prevalence of rural poverty that existed at the beginning of President Cardoso's presidency. They are not intended to establish a relationship between Cardoso's policies and trends in rural poverty. For such an analysis, time-series data from the period 1995–2002 would have to be examined.

sentation, that have garnered most of the headlines in the struggle over agrarian reform in Brazil.

The Cardoso government therefore inherited an agricultural sector that was generating enormous wealth and misery at the same time, a dualistic process that was in turn creating a crisis of representation in the countryside. Despite the market-oriented reforms of the 1980s and 1990s, Brazilian agriculture, like agriculture everywhere, was still strongly dependent on the State. At its inauguration, the Cardoso government faced basic choices about what kinds of policies to enact, and whom to negotiate with.

State Policies in Agriculture and Land (or FHC vs. MST)

Both supporters and opponents of the Cardoso government's land reform policies saw the struggle over land in epochal terms. For the government, the reforms reflected candidate Cardoso's observation that "Brazil is not any longer an underdeveloped country. It is an unjust country" (Cardoso, 1994: 9). In this view, the State's responsibility was to maintain and stimulate a modern agricultural sector that finally produces for the best interests of the larger society, while using welfare programs, including land reform, to ameliorate the worst social effects of agricultural modernization and provide some relief to a conflict-ridden countryside. Raul Jungmann declared in 2001 that Brazil's land reform was "perhaps the biggest ever realized in an atmosphere of democratic stability and respect for institutions," and President Cardoso equated it with "a veritable peaceful revolution in the countryside."[12]

For opponents of the reforms, on the other hand, the Cardoso government perpetuated a fraud about its accomplishments, at the same time colluding with retrograde elements of the old social order, thus perpetuating oligarchic domination in the guise of "modernization." In the words of the president of the CPT in 2002, Dom Tomás Balduíno, "From the point of view of propaganda, it [the government] has achieved success. There is no lack of numbers, which are presented in accordance with their own criteria. The reality is totally different."[13] In this section, I will evaluate some of the claims and counterclaims of opponents and supporters of the government reform efforts.

Candidate Cardoso promised to settle 280,000 landless families on land by the end of his four-year term (Cardoso, 1994: 103). But once elected, Cardoso did not seem to make agrarian reform a priority. The government's overriding concern was to ensure the success of the anti-inflation plan, the

---

12. The Jungmann quote is from "Crédito Ainda Desafia Reforma, Diz Governo" in *Folha de São Paulo*, January 6, 2001, p. A-8, while the quote from President Cardoso is from Mac Margolis (2002) "A Plot of Their Own" in *Newsweek International Online* [http://www.msnbc.com/news], accessed on 02/06/02.
13. Quoted in "Crédito Ainda Desafia Reforma, Diz Governo" in the *Folha de São Paulo*, January 6, 2001, p. A-8.

Real Plan, initiated prior to the election in July of 1994. The government's basic attitude toward agriculture seemed to be that, regardless of the dubious conditions under which many large landowners had obtained their lands, and the benighted history of the *latifúndio* in general, the sector had been professionalized and modernized to such an extent that it would be counterproductive to threaten it with too heavy an emphasis on land reform (Graziano Neto, 1998: 168). Agriculture was one of Brazil's most competitive sectors; it could generate exports, anchor the *Real Plan*, provide cheap food to the cities, and survive any process of deepening of regional integration that the government decided to undertake.

On the other hand, the Cardoso government tended to regard groups pressing for land reform with skepticism and sometimes alarm. It saw the demand for land reform as an archaic and primitive "agrarian redistributivism" that advocates land expropriation and redistribution as a solution to Brazil's past and present problems (Souza, 1997: 80; Martins, 1999), based on an outdated ideology that criticizes a system of unproductive *latifúndios* that no longer exists, mistakenly assumes that only the ownership of the means of production (rather than the training, skills, and human capital of individuals) determines the distribution of income, and reflects a romantic reification of a traditional peasantry that was largely passing out of history (Sorj, 1998).[14] In the government's view, programs of land reform would primarily be for purposes of social welfare rather than agricultural production. Programs designed to fundamentally alter the structure of production and include more small farmers within it were foolhardy and pushed against the global trend toward the concentration of land and increasing capital-intensity in agriculture. For this reason, President Cardoso dismissed advocates of land reform for making a "nineteenth-century demand."

In making this remark, the president seemed to assume that the landless, or at least their leaders, were fighting for land out of some romantic, mystical attachment to the soil, or mere ideological bias. However, it seems more plausible to believe that the landless were quite pragmatic, and struggled for land because of a lack of viable alternatives. Many of them are relatively unschooled, unskilled, older workers, whose employment prospects in the Brazilian economy are bleak. A study of land occupiers by the Brazilian Intelligence Agency ABIN (Agência Brasileira de Inteligência) revealed that some 40 percent had at one time worked in cities (Gonçalo, 2000: 5), indicat-

---

14. Sorj makes the valuable point that unlike the Peasant Leagues and other "peasant" social movements of the late 1950s and early 1960s, the MST and its offshoots do not defend rural cultivators's traditional use-rights to land, but instead organize the rural and often urban poor from all over the country, leading them in land occupations on carefully selected properties in areas where many occupiers have never lived before. Thus, while MST leaders see themselves as the inheritors of the mantle of the Peasant Leagues, they are a very different kind of organization. See Sorj, 1998.

ing that at one time they were willing at least to try to find a place in urban labor markets. In the advanced capitalist countries, many rural dwellers welcomed the opportunities created by industrialization, and there is no reason to believe that Brazilians are fundamentally different from Europeans and North Americans in this regard. However, the Brazilian economy is not creating enough industrial jobs to absorb the landless.

President Cardoso's stance also ignored the possibility that smallholder agriculture could be more fully integrated into the productive structure of the country. Policies to redirect subsidies from larger to smaller farmers, and to increase infrastructural, technical, marketing, and financial support to labor-intensive small farms could be appropriate, and not "backward," in an emerging market economy such as Brazil's. Such policies could also have dynamic effects on the domestic market, as their redistributive effects would increase demand in the countryside. Yet the government did not seem to seriously contemplate such a strategy, and kept the old model of agricultural modernization largely intact. I argue that this was largely for political rather than economic reasons.

The Achilles' heel of the Cardoso strategy, at least in political terms, was that it could not offer a significant portion of the rural population a place in the new, "globalized" economic order. (In this sense, Cardoso's social democracy differs markedly from European social democracy of the early twentieth century, which did have a project for the rural poor.) The Cardoso government's early policy position seemed to consign several generations of the rural poor to social, economic, and political oblivion. The president frankly admitted that his policies could not include everyone in a lengthy interview with a journalist from *Folha de São Paulo* conducted in 1996. Declaring that his government favored the most advanced capitalist sectors of the economy, rather than the traditional "monopolistic and bureaucratic capitalism" or the "corporatists" (*corporativistas*) of the old patrimonial state, he added "I am also not going to say that it [my government] is of the excluded, because it cannot be. . . . Certain sectors are not part of this dynamic segment of the economy. And then what? (*E daí?*). . . . I don't know how many excluded there will be" (Cardoso, 1996: 6). After reflecting, he added that the excluded might number somewhere around sixteen million people!

Under these conditions, the organizing efforts of the MST and its multiple offshoots bore rapid fruit, partially filling the void left by the decline of the organized labor movement under the Cardoso government (see the chapter by Salvador Sandoval in this volume). Tens of thousands of landless people occupied unused private and sometimes public land (mostly in already settled areas rather than frontier, previously unfarmed land) in hundreds of encampments around the country; an estimated 60,000 people were in such encamp-

TABLE 5-2. Beneficiaries of Land Redistribution and Land Occupations, 1995–2001, government and MST figures

Year	Government	MST	Land Occupations
1995	42,912	33,312	
1996	62,044	19,800	397
1997	81,944	60,425	502
1998	101,094	76,027	446
1999	85,226	25,831	455
2000	128,986	NA	226
2001	83,477	NA	146

Source: "Crédito Desafia Reforma, Diz Governo" in *Folha de S. Paulo*, January 6, 2002, p. A-8. Data on land invasions come from the same article, and are attributed to the Ouvidoria Agraria Nacional and newspaper. The data from 2001 cover the period up to November of that year.

ments in early 2000 (Ondetti, 2001b; see also Table 5–2). The pressure on the government from these encampments was considerable; however, what seemed to trigger a change in the administration's attitude to agrarian reform were massacres of the landless in 1995 and especially in 1996. Ondetti argues persuasively that the rhythm of land expropriations closely follows the outcry that accompanied the massacres of ten landless people in Corumbiara in Rondônia on August 9, 1995, and the massacre of nineteen landless (and the wounding of sixty-nine) in Eldorado de Carajás, Pará on April 17, 1996 (Hammond, 2001; Ondetti, 2001a). In the wake of these atrocities, committed by military police forces ostensibly controlled by state governments, the federal government accelerated land expropriations and increased the number of people resettled on land. The MST, in turn, utilized the media spotlight that it found itself in to organize more land occupations and other actions, including a highly publicized march to Brasília in April of 1997.

According to the government's figures, from 1995 to 1998, roughly 287,000 landless families received land under the land reform program (Ondetti, 2001a: 11). This exceeds the 280,000 families that Cardoso promised to give land to in the 1994 presidential campaign. According to the official data, in seven years, the Cardoso government benefited 585,683 landless families, or more than four times as many as the 131,000 families listed as beneficiaries under its three predecessors (José Sarney, Fernando Collor, and Itamar Franco) combined (Ondetti, 2001a: 4–13) (see Table 5–1). According to government data, roughly twenty million hectares, mostly consisting of unused private holdings, were acquired for redistribution under the land reform program.

The MST disputed the Cardoso government's claims (see Table 5–2). It said (as of mid-2000) that the correct figures are 160,000 families settled on some eight million hectares. This discrepancy is due in part to the fact that the MST did not count squatters who were already on land before receiving legal title from the government, or beneficiaries who entered the land redistribution system before the advent of the Cardoso government.[15] The MST also referred to data that show that from 1995 to 2000, 400,000 small farmers lost land and 1.2 million rural workers lost jobs (Gonçalo, 2001: 4).[16] Furthermore, critics of the agrarian reform also cited partial surveys that found that within two years of receiving their plots, around a quarter of the beneficiaries of land reform abandoned them, due to an inability to service loans and other reasons.[17]

The MST further argued that despite the Cardoso government's policies, unproductive lands were still plentiful. The agrarian atlas (Atlas Fundiário Brasileiro) put out by the Ministry of Agrarian Policy (Ministério de Política Fundiária), for example, shows that only 28 percent of Brazil's cultivable land is being used in some productive activity, while 62 percent of it remains unproductive (Borin, 1997: 25). The MST even disputed the right of the Cardoso administration to call its policies agrarian reform, because in its view the reform does not change the productive structure of agriculture, and is therefore merely *assistencialist* (welfarist, or representing a form of social assistance, rather than offering the landless a viable place in the productive system).

The government rebutted such attacks by claiming that public support for agrarian reform, if not the methods of the MST, were due largely to the urban population's stereotypical attitude to landowners as semifeudal *latifundiários* (Graziano Neto, 1998: 168). President Cardoso complained that TV Globo's 1996 telenovela *O Rei do Gado* (Cattle King)—which portrayed grassroots members of the MST, if not the movement's leaders, in a sympathetic light—put pressure on his government to redistribute more land (Pompeu de Toledo, 1998: 324), even though such policies were of questionable economic value. The government position was that land reform was unlikely to increase output or raise rural incomes in what is a highly productive agricultural economy. Land redistribution should therefore not be a priority; it was better to tax unproductive land and encourage tenancy and crop-sharing arrangements to increase employment and alleviate poverty (Souza, 1997: 80).

In its conflict with the MST, the government emphasized the occasional violence of the landless themselves, and the apparent lack of commitment of some of the MST leaders to Brazil's currently existing version of democracy.[18] The government and its supporters sometimes characterized the MST

15. "Por Quê a Reforma Agrária no Brasil" in *Sem Terra* Number 1, July 2000, p. 2. Leite 1999: 173 lists beneficiaries as 42,827 families in 1995, then 61,674, 81,944, 34,978 (as of June 10, 1988) in 1996, 1997, and 1998.
16. These data come from the Escola de Economia da USP. The MST claims that some 900,000 smallholders lost access to land in this period, see the article cited above.
17. Mac Margolis (2002) "A Plot of Their Own" in *Newsweek* International Online [http://www.msnbc.com/news], accessed on 02/06/02.

as a political party rather than a social movement, alleging that the MST's broad attacks on the government's economic policies proved that it used land reform as a means to demoralize the government rather than as an end in itself.[19] They further argued that the government's measures to decentralize land reform and create a "market assisted" land reform program, with the help of the World Bank, that complements land expropriation by Instituto Nacional de Colonização e Reforma Agrária (National Institute of Colonization and Agrarian Reform, or INCRA) through the purchases of unproductive land, were opposed by the MST on purely ideological grounds.[20]

As an actor in a democracy, the MST's leaders, like the Cardoso government, had a blind spot. This was their attitude toward the agrarian structure. Some MST leaders seemed to regard any landholder with property above a certain size to be a *latifundiário*, regardless of whether the property is productive or unproductive. MST leader Stédile, for example, said in one interview that the maximum size of rural properties should be 1,000 hectares. It is not clear how such a radical deconcentration of landholding can take place under conditions of democracy and legal continuity, i.e., a nonrevolutionary situation. However, such a declaration should not be interpreted as representing the view of all members of the movement. Furthermore, the MST (and not just it; around half of all land occupations are led by other groups) did expose a weakness in the Cardoso government's approach to economic development, the social question, and the issue of political reform. The movement raised serious questions about the direction of Brazilian society in general, and not just the fate of agrarian reform.

The debate between the government and the MST exposed the cruel dilemmas that the Cardoso government faced. The government based its agri-

---

18. It seems to me that rather too much has been made of the MST leaders' ideological propensities. The MST's CD (*Arte em Movimento*) does contain songs extolling Che Guevara, Cuban socialism, and the like, but in a democracy ideas alone should not be seen as "subversive." There is at least one spiritist in the Cardoso cabinet, and people with semi-fascist views among the general public, but what should really matter are the actions of the MST and their effects. Democracy should be able to accommodate a wide variety of quaint and even bizarre opinions, and too much emphasis on ideological conformity smacks of the days of national security under the military regime.
19. It is interesting that both President Cardoso and the MST claim the late USP sociologist Florestan Fernandes as an ideological predecessor. Each side could claim to be the heir of different aspects of Fernandes' Marxism. Cardoso shares his former professor's teleological belief in the necessity of reaching the highest stage of a particular form of capitalism before moving on to the next. The MST, which refers to Fernandes on its Web page, shares the sociologist's interest (also notably articulated by the historian Caio Prado Junior) in creating an economy oriented primarily to the national market.
20. The MST's Stédile has responded in pragmatic terms. He claims that, given the government's budget of R$1 billion for the market-assisted land reform program, and an average cost of R$20,000 for each family settled, the program would only be able to settle about another 50,000 families on the land. From Stédile and Fernandes, 1999: 141. The MST also complains that the program is more generous to landowners and banks than the landless. For an initial assessment of the possibilities of market-assisted land reform, see Pereira, 1999.

cultural policies on agribusiness, but could not adequately address the needs of the rural dispossessed. It redistributed land, but accelerating land redistribution only led to more occupations. At the same time, almost as many people seemed to have left the land as were resettled on it. The government questioned the economic viability of land redistribution, but the public continued to support it. This public support, characterized by some of the government's allies as based on ignorance, was at least as likely to have been based on personal or familial acquaintance with the injustice and violence of the social order in the countryside; after all, the great waves of migration that transformed Brazil into an urban country occurred only in the last three decades, and many urban Brazilians retain links to the land.[21] It is all the more impressive because, despite the popularity of *O Rei do Gado*, analysis of the Brazilian media suggests that television news coverage of the landless movement has been generally negative (Porto, 2001: 21–24; Hammond, 2001).

However, the essential aspect of agrarian reform being explored here is to what extent it represents a major reform of preexisting policies. In this regard, land redistribution itself is less important than a series of other, related measures. These reforms include price stability brought by the 1994 *Real Plan*, which has reduced speculation in land as a hedge against inflation, thus lowering land prices and leading to rationalization of the use of land as a factor of production. Second, a gun control law was passed in 1997 to curb rural violence, especially by landowners wishing to evict land occupiers. In 1996, the government enacted a judicial reform to send members of the military police who commit intentional homicide to jury trials held in civilian courts. There have also been policies to decentralize land reform, and to supplement land expropriation with "market assisted" initiatives that buy unused land from owners. The most important reforms, however, are the increase in the rate of progressive taxation on unproductive land, and laws facilitating land expropriation and defending the rights of land occupiers. These will be described further below.

In December of 1996 the National Congress approved legislation concerning the rural tax *Imposto Territorial Rural* (ITR) and the procedure for land expropriation (rito sumário de desapropriação de terras). The landowners' lobby in Congress succeeded in reducing the rate of tax on productive land, but the government increased the rate of tax on unproductive land. The top rate for the largest estates rose from 4.5 percent to 20 percent (Cardoso, Fernando Henrique, 1997: 83). The modification of the land expropriation

---

21. Barreira records the words of a poem about a *pistoleiro* from the *literature de cordel* that reflects popular conceptions about the rule of large landowners: "Of Miranda [the *pistoleiro*] one has shame/because he is the product/of a violent world/and a corrupt system." [*De Miranda tem se é pena/porque ele é um produto/de um mundo violento/de um sistema corrupto.*] Poem by Otávio Menezes, *A prisão de pistoleiro Miranda*, quoted in Barreira, 1998: 124.

procedure allows the rapid expropriation and distribution of unproductive land and the subsequent negotiation of its price. At the same time, Congress also passed a law that brings in the Public Ministry (Ministério Público) in situations of land conflict (Sorj, 1998: 38). This legislation was introduced by the *Núcleo Agrário* of the Workers's Party (PT) and said that in any expulsion order (processo de despejo) a procedure has to be followed in which Public Ministry has to be present and a judge hears both sides before making a decision (Stédile and Fernandes, 1999: 116).

These legal changes, for many analysts, represent "another step in the integration and disciplining of the rural areas within the political-administrative structures of the Brazilian state" (Sorj, 1998: 38). President Cardoso described them as a fundamental restructuring of the legal framework governing land (*arcabouço jurídico da terra*) that signified the definitive political defeat of *latifundiários,* who were now "paper tigers" that no longer controlled Congress (Pompeu de Toledo, 1998: 321–322). Yet is such a conclusion warranted?

The Modest Impact of Other Reforms

Despite the relatively large scale of land redistribution under the Cardoso government, and the government's important legal changes, there is considerable evidence that other policy changes have had relatively little impact on the countryside.

Furthermore, important policy initiatives that could have been taken were not. This section will deal with some of these.

MST leader Stédile complained, for example, about the lack of enforcement of the law requiring the Public Ministry to be involved in land conflicts referred to in the previous section. He claimed that judges tied to large landowners did not respect the law, but instead continued to grant evictions ("*dar laminar para despejos*"), did not follow the procedures laid down for them, and did not listen to the Public Ministry (Stédile and Fernandes, 1999: 116). The noted autonomy of the Brazilian judiciary certainly lends plausibility to this account (Prillaman, 2000). The enforcement of other legal changes discussed in the previous section should also not be taken for granted. There is no evidence, for example, that the 1997 arms control law has been vigorously enforced. This is important, because despite an important decline in violence over land conflicts during the Cardoso government, rural violence is still a major impediment to the full enjoyment of civil and political rights by the poor in the countryside, especially in southern Pará and Maranhão.[22]

Another area in which policies have not had a major impact is the system of land titling. Formal, enforceable claims to property are unevenly distributed in the countryside. Small farmers and the rural poor in general face a double-edged sword with regard to the property rights regime: on one hand, they face barriers to obtaining formal legal title to the land they occupy, making them vulnerable to removal by large landowners and their gunmen. On the other hand, large landowners can sometimes obtain, through de facto possession, huge tracts of land to which they do not have legal title, thus "crowding out" the rural poor (Sorj, 1998: 38). In the words of one squatter in the county (*município*) of Conceição de Araguaina in Pará, "Here the best title is the biggest ax" (quoted in Alston, Libecap, and Mueller, 2000: 165).

A major reason for this state of affairs is a lack of efficiency in the demarcation of lands and their documentation and titling (*cadastramento*). Small farmers face barriers that prevent them from fully enjoying private property rights to the land they cultivate. Due to a costly, confusing, slow, and often politically manipulated and corrupt process of land registration, many farmers do not hold titles to their properties. Small farmers are much less likely to be able to obtain legal title than large farmers.[23] They are then usually unable to obtain credit with which to boost productivity through the purchase of new inputs or the adoption of more efficient techniques.[24] This has a big impact on rural poverty, because studies show that small and medium-sized farms in Brazil produce far more employment per acre, on average, than large ones.

Furthermore, many rural properties were simply taken from the public domain. This process is not limited to remote regions, but happens also in the more prosperous southeast. In the disputed area of São Paulo's Pontal do Paranapanema, for example, of the roughly one million hectares, only 20 percent were legally titled; the rest were "*terras devolutas do Estado*" or irregularly occupied by large landowners (Gonçalo, 2001: 22–23). There are also cases of large landowners receiving lands from the State without paying for them, then receiving fiscal incentives to produce, but not producing anything and simply holding on to the land (Gonçalo, 2001: 23). The illegal acquisition of lands, or claim-jumping (*grilagem*), is often associated with violence,

---

22. Government data show an average number of assassinations of rural workers of 91 in the period 1985–1994, dropping to 31 per year for the period 1995–2001. The CPT has slightly higher figures for the second period, but their data also confirm this trend. From Ouvidoria Agrária Nacional, as reported in "Crédito Ainda Desafia Reforma, Diz Governo" in *Folha de São Paulo*, January 6, 2002, p. A-8.

23. In a recent survey, of the total land area on farms of less than 10 hectares in size, only 65 percent of the land was registered. For land on farms between 1,000 and 10,000 hectares in size, the corresponding figure was 83 percent, and for land on farms larger than 10,000 acres, the number was 91 percent. From "Northeast Brazil: Market Assisted Land Reform: Private Property Rights for the Rural Poor" (1998): 39 (Table 8). This is a manuscript that was sent to me for review by *Public Administration and Development* in April 1998. I have been unable to identify its author. The data are from INCRA's 1992 *Estatísticas Cadastrais Anuais*. A hectare is roughly 2.5 acres.

24. From "Northeast Brazil: Market Assisted Land Reform . . ." (1998): 39 (Table 8). The lack of land titles is a larger problem in the northeast, where 64 percent of the farms smaller than 25 acres are located, than elsewhere. Only 41 percent of the land on farms smaller than 25 hectares is registered in that region.

because *grileiros* are often heavily armed hired hands committed to defending the land of their employers.

Improvements in the operations of the *cartórios*, the land registration agencies located in almost every município, have been reported—many have computers now, for example (personal communication from David Fleischer, May 18, 2001). In 2001, the government also passed a law to create a single land registry of all rural properties in the country under the control of the Ministry of Agrarian Development (Ministério de Desenvolvimento Agrário), a relatively new agency created by President Cardoso. It hopes that this will be complete by 2003 (from "Managing the Rainforests" in *The Economist*, May 12, 2001, p. 84). This could improve the situation described here. But it is a reform that came very late in the Cardoso presidency, and one whose effect—if there is one—will not occur until after President Cardoso has left office.

If smallholders are left vulnerable by a precarious, inefficient, and often politically manipulated system of land titling, they are also marginalized by the prevailing system of agricultural credit. The State still dominates the provision of credit for agriculture, and large landowners obtain a disproportionate share of these funds, which enable them to expand their properties, thus exacerbating inequalities in the distribution of land and perpetuating a cycle of immizeration for those on the bottom of the rural social hierarchy. Furthermore, large landowners have used their political power to default on loans at a high rate, resist foreclosure, and renegotiate loans to their advantage.[25]

A striking example of this came in 1995–1996, when large landowners used their political influence to persuade Congress to cancel indexation for inflation on outstanding agricultural loans—a move that cost the Bank of Brazil between R$1.8 and R$2.5 billion.[26] Large landowners also successfully lobbied Congress to give them another break on agricultural loans in 1999 (Martins, 1999: 117). These rural credit renegotiations epitomize the actions of a patronage-based State that uses its public power to facilitate the private appropriation of economic advantages, in effect punishing small and

---

25. In 1995, for example, over half the value of all outstanding agricultural loans made by the Bank of Brazil, a bank owned by the federal government, were for more than five hundred thousand *reais* (at that time, a Brazilian *real* was roughly equivalent to one U.S. dollar). Default rates on these large loans were high, and averaged 33 percent nationally. The debt was owed by 1,477 large landowners (less than one half of one percent of the total of 297,827 borrowers) whose default represented 73 percent of the value of all agricultural loans made by the Bank of Brazil that were not being repaid at that time. Owners of small and medium-sized farms, in contrast, generally repaid their debts. The default rates for loans up to R$30,000 was only 6 percent of the total loaned value, while the rate for loans up to R$150,000 was 8 percent. The state bank, in effect, subsidized the very largest landowners by refusing to subject them to a "hard budget constraint." From "Brazil: Market Assisted Land Reform . . ." (1998): 43 (Table 11). Data refer to outstanding loans as of May 31, 1995.
26. "Northeast Brazil: Market Assisted Land Reform . . ." (1998): 16.

TABLE 5-3. Collection of the Land Tax (ITR), 1998–2002,
in millions of *reais*

Year	Value	Weight in Federal Budget
1998	208	0.106%
1999	244	0.113%
2000	230	0.093%
2001	202	0.071%
2002 (proposed)	232	0.071%

Source: "Crédito Ainda Desafia Reforma, Diz Governo." *Folha de S. Paulo*, June 1, 2002, A-8.

medium producers who generally paid their loans back on time. (Some small producers have benefited, but large producers have been the major beneficiaries.) Rural debt renegotiation is also one of the causes of the fiscal deficits that have contributed to Brazil's economic instability during President Cardoso's second term (described in Eliana Cardoso's chapter in this volume).

If large landowners benefit from lax policies in land titling and politically motivated concessions and subsidies in the provision of credit, they are also notorious for evading taxes. The ITR has a high rate of avoidance (Leite, 1999: 158), and a study carried out as recently as 1999 showed that 98.7 percent of the 200 largest rural properties simply did not pay the ITR at all (Gonçalo, 2001: 22). The 1997 change in the ITR was potentially a significant step in the curbing of landowner's traditional free ride in the area of taxation. The new law also reduced the size of property on which the top rate can be imposed from over 15,000 hectares to over 5,000 hectares. Nevertheless, there are a number of potential loopholes in the law. For the government to charge a rate of 20 percent, it has to determine that 30 percent or less of the rural property is being productively used, but Brazilian landowners have shown great ingenuity in demonstrating land use, and in cultivating favorable rulings from local administrators. Furthermore, greater rates of utilization significantly diminish the tax rate for the largest-size farms (Cardoso, 1997: 83). Considering that Brazil's top corporate tax rate is 15 percent (World Bank, 2001: 306), and in some cases higher, these numbers suggest that rural properties are still relatively lightly taxed. Furthermore, despite the 1997 law, the real value obtained via the tax has declined from 1998–2001, and has also declined as a percentage of total federal revenue (see Table 5–3).

When one looks at the system by which land has been expropriated under the Cardoso agrarian reform, one also finds evidence that policies disproportionately benefit those already privileged by the agrarian political economy. Despite the fact that the success of the *Real Plan* brought about a marked reduction in the price of land, critics allege that the government continued to buy land at prices equal to or higher than those in effect before 1994 (Borin, 1997: 25). This appears to have been due both to judicial decisions and to collusion between INCRA officials and landowners (Sorj, 1998: 29). In a September 1999 study of over seventy cases in which owners of expropriated land had brought judicial actions against INCRA, the Extraordinary Ministry of Agrarian Policy (Ministério Extraordinário de Política Fundiária) estimated that the government had overpaid for land on the order of R$7 billion, or enough to place 300,000 families on the land (Martins, 2000: 125). The compensation paid to landowners is thus often far higher than the estimated value of land calculated by the Ministério da Reforma e do Desenvolvimento Agrário (Ministry of Agrarian Reform and Development, MIRAD) or INCRA (Martins, 1999: 124). This policy has amounted to a veritable give-away to large landowners, some of them the very idle and unproductive *latifundiários* whom modern agricultural markets were supposed to punish (Leite, 1999: 172). Because the cost of the land is part of the debt contracted by those resettled in the land reform program, the former landless "run the risk of paying for the poor management [and corruption] of INCRA for the rest of their lives" (Borin, 1997: 25). This is a striking example of the maxim offered by Sorj—the State takes the onus, the dominant class gets the bonus, and the subordinate groups are left with the crumbs—and indicates that some of the major beneficiaries of land reform have been landowners, rather than the landless.

Some observers disagree with the interpretation offered here. Alston, et al. (2000: 167), for example, write that "land owners historically have received less than the market value of their land in an expropriation," in part because INCRA pays for expropriated land in TDAs (*títulos de dívida agrária*), which are heavily discounted, and only pays cash for improvements to the property. In the same passage, they also write, "The land owner could also scheme with local INCRA officials or use the courts to set the compensation for expropriated land above its market value. Such actions, however, appear to be very isolated events." However, such an interpretation is belied by the Cardoso government's own rhetoric, actions, and data. The data about overpayment described above come from government sources. And in justifying the "market-assisted" land reform program, administered by the Ministry of Agrarian Policy, President Cardoso decried INCRA's "corruption." Government policy reforms, therefore, seem to be based on an assumption that overpayments for expropriated land were not "isolated events."

Finally, the Cardoso administration missed an opportunity for significant policy reform in the area of rural violence. Although rural violence appears to have diminished under Cardoso, the killings of rural workers and the landless by the military police and landlords' gunmen are still common in some regions, and usually go uninvestigated and unpunished. In the wake of the massacres of the landless in Corumbiara and Eldorado de Carajás, human rights activists called on President Cardoso to push for the passage of a constitutional amendment allowing the federal government to intervene in the investigation and prosecution of human rights violations when officials at the state level fail to carry out unbiased investigations. This "federalization" amendment, introduced in Congress in 1996, has not been passed. It could represent a major step forward in ending the impunity of perpetrators of violence against the rural poor, but the federal government did not prioritize it (Amnesty International, 1998: 32–33).

If one moves beyond land redistribution figures, therefore, and examines other, less-noted aspects of the Cardoso government's policies in land and agriculture, one can conclude that the government has largely maintained the general tilt of policy in favor of conservative modernization. This policy orientation gives little opportunity to the landless and the poor, punishes small and medium farmers, and generously rewards politically influential large landowners. Brazil may have a capitalist democracy, but its form of capitalism in the countryside is not very democratic. In agriculture, as elsewhere in the economy as described by Peter Kingstone in this volume, markets are still strongly shaped by political manipulation. For the poor, this results in a system in which access to land is limited, land distribution is highly unequal, property rights to land are precarious, land markets are underdeveloped, access to credit is dominated by large landowners who use their political influence to renege on their loan repayment and tax obligations, and they are subject to the possibility of violence at the hands of the military police or landlords' gunmen, with little protection from the state. Such a conclusion fits with the assessment of many observers that outside of macroeconomic reforms, the Cardoso government's accomplishments in the area of political and institutional reforms have been limited.

Conclusion

The extent of land redistribution under the Cardoso government was impressive and surprising, whether measured by the official government data or that of the opposition. The acquisition of land by previously landless rural people, as well as the securing of legal title to land by squatters previously without secure property rights, is an important achievement, because it means that marginalized Brazilians have, largely through their own tenacious efforts, obtained at least the possibility of inclusion in the economy and recognition as citizens in the political sphere. There was also an important decrease in rural violence during the Cardoso government. The land reform thus represents small victories for hundreds of thousands of people.

However, as the government redistributed some unproductive land to hundreds of thousands of people, a roughly equal number of small farmers, tenants, and squatters left the land as a result of prevailing policies of conservative modernization in agriculture. This economic model in itself would not necessarily be undesirable for Brazil as a whole, but in the absence of employment opportunities for the unschooled, the process represents the marginalization of a significant proportion of those Brazilians unlucky enough to be at or near the bottom of the rural social hierarchy.

In addition to redistributing land, the Cardoso administration has enacted a number of related reforms: to facilitate land expropriation, centralize the system of land titling, improve the collection of taxes on rural properties and progressively tax unproductive land, and control unregistered guns. This chapter suggests that these measures have not had a significant impact on the agrarian political economy in Brazil. Not all of the measures were actively enforced—a historic problem of the Brazilian state. Others were implemented late in Cardoso's term, or applied halfheartedly. Furthermore, an opportunity to federalize human rights abuses, thus diminishing impunity for rural violence, was missed. It is thus inaccurate to declare the Cardoso government's agrarian reform a "revolution" in the countryside.

I am not arguing that none of Cardoso's policies have resulted in major reforms. The achievement of price stability for eight years, for example, was a notable success of the Cardoso government. However, this chapter suggests that policies of conservative modernization—marked by the use of state personnel and resources primarily to serve a small but powerful set of large agricultural producers—continue in the Brazilian countryside. While these policies have gradually become more market and export oriented since the early 1980s, the Cardoso government does not represent a fundamental break with them. The resulting model is still a highly politicized one, in that access to and repayment of credit depend on political as much as market criteria. While the Cardoso government has bolstered the state's commitment to compensatory social programs for the rural poor, the productive structure is still dominated by the large producers most favored by government policies. In this sense the agrarian reform has been limited, and will probably eventually be seen as a modest but not fundamental modification of government policies in agriculture.

CHAPTER 6

Political Reform:
The "Missing Link"

David Fleischer

Background to Reform

Reform agendas are no novelty in Brazilian politics. Perhaps the first "reform agenda" was fostered in Brazil by the Marquis de Pombal during the colonial period (Maxwell, 1995). In the independence period, during the Second Empire (1840–1889), reforms were frequent, especially after the Triple Alliance War in the 1870s and 1880s, when successive cabinets labored under strong pressures for change.

With enhanced political autonomy granted to state governments by the first republican constitution and by the concentration of national power in the hands of the *mineiros* and *paulistas* in their *café com leite* power-sharing arrangement, "reform," especially of the economic system, became synonymous with enhancing profits for those elites. The First Republic elite was incapable of change in the 1920s, when minor (1922) and major (1924) military revolts highlighted rising demands for political, social, and economic reforms from mostly urban workers and an incipient middle class (M. C. C. Souza, 1974).

Modern Brazil's most thoroughgoing reforms were executed during the first presidency of Getúlio Vargas (1930–1945). The national armed forces finally consolidated their power over state military organizations. Import substitution began in earnest, and the state began a broad intervention in the nation's economy. The so-called "social question" was incorporated or co-opted into the reform agenda: modern social and labor legislation was adopted, complete with Labor Courts, retirement, health care systems, and workmen's compensation. In 1936 Vargas created the Departamento Administrativo do Serviço Público (Administrative Department of Public Services, or DASP), which was charged with reforming and modernizing public administration. In the same year the first comprehensive civil service laws were passed (Graham, 1968). Luciano Martins (1995) considers that this important attempt at modernization was tempered by a strong culture of patrimonialism and clientelism, which even the military regime of 1964–1985 was unable to alter substantially and resorted to parallel recruitment via the CLT and state enterprises.

Until 1945, most reforms were almost totally the initiative of the executive branch, with very little input from the Congress. However, after the 1946 constitution, many important questions concerning reform were successively locked into the Magna Carta, many times in quite detailed fashion, and thus necessitated high and difficult constitutional quorums of two-thirds and, later, three-fifths to effect change. This was the case in the early 1960s when progressive groups allied with President Goulart sought the approval of basic reforms, such as land reform, election reform, enfranchisement of illiterates, university reform, and others (Skidmore, 1967).

During the military period, when the opposition *Movimento Democrático Brasileiro* (Brazilian Democratic Movement, or MDB) increased the size of its delegations in Congress beyond 40 percent in both houses in the 1974 elections, the Geisel government and the pro-regime *Aliança de Renovação Nacional* (National Renewal Alliance, or ARENA) party found themselves unable to amend the constitution for lack of a two-thirds majority. Using the powers of the Fifth Institutional Act, Geisel resolved the impasse by temporarily closing Congress and amending the 1967 constitution by decree to reduce the requirement to an absolute majority. The Figueiredo government, fearful that it might even lose its absolute majority in the November 1982 elections, which would allow the opposition to amend at will, used the slim majority still held by the Partido Democrático Social (Democratic Social Party, or PSD) to amend the constitution in June and restored the two-thirds requirement (Fleischer, 1994).

Still, the twenty-one years of military rule produced frequent and profound reforms: on the political system at every turn; in the area of federalism and decentralization by empowering local government through federal revenue sharing (Sherwood, 1967; Mahar, 1971); on the tax system; on the expansion of public enterprises and "indirect" administration of new federal agencies (Deland, 1981); and on the participation of military officers as managers in command positions in the direct and indirect public administration (Barros, 1978). Again, all this happened with very little input from the Congress (Skidmore, 1988).

The 1988 Constitution

In the 1986 general elections, a new Congress was elected as a National Constituent Assembly (ANC). The ANC was convened in 1987 in a unicameral mode that included those senators elected in the 1982 elections. Adopting a "from scratch" modus operandi, the ANC was divided into eight committees and twenty-four subcommittees that drafted the future document's sections and chapters using a participatory methodology with strong input from public hearings and lobbying pressures (Fleischer, 1990; Eugster, 1995; Martinez-Lara, 1995; C. Souza, 1997).

The ANC shunned any major political reforms—such as those to the parliamentary system, open list proportional representation system, *desincompatibilização* (standing down from executive office), reelection of president and governors, obligatory voting, election finance, skewed regional representation in the Chamber, reforms in congressional organization and procedures, role of military, or the reorganization or reconfiguration of states. It limited changes to confirming the enfranchisement of illiterates, lowering the voting age from eighteen to sixteen, and creating three new states.

However, important changes were effected in other areas, especially the constitutionalization of many points that had traditionally been dealt with by normal legislation (Reich, 1998). In the economic order, harsh distinctions were made favoring domestic national firms in detriment of foreign enterprises installed in Brazil, and the national monopolies in the areas of petroleum, electricity, telecommunications, subsoil resources, coastal shipping, and gas distributions were reinforced.

In the public sector, employee associations achieved the incorporation of articles that granted automatic job stability to all civil servants with five years of service as of October 1988, linked salary adjustments of military and civil servants, and called for a unified civil service code (RJU) that was adopted in December 1990.

In the realm of social security, old and new guarantees were incorporated into the constitution, such as retirement based on time of service as opposed to contribution, proportional retirement, benefits equivalent to full last salary, no minimum age requirement, four months of paid maternity leave, seven days of paternity leave, no strengthening of collection procedures nor repression of fraud in benefit disbursements, and no rules against "double and triple dipping" or "cascades" of accumulations.

But, perhaps the most devastating impact on governability came from the reforms in the tax and fiscal areas by way of a reorganization of Brazil's federalism which left the national government in an very tenuous and delicate situation. Essentially, the ANC was driven by strong pressures from the grassroots and subnational governments, and reapportioned the national tax base by increasing the level of transfers to state and local governments, leaving less for the federal government, without a commensurate transfer of federal programs (Affonso and Silva, 1994).

Thus, as of 1989, the federal government was left "holding the bag": responsible for the same, and in some cases expanded, programs but with less resources for implementation. This created a chronic deficit, further aggravated by irresponsible state governments that, instead of using their new windfall resources wisely, squandered them on enlargement of payrolls and piled up new deficits via unredeemable loans and operations by state government banks and enterprises. These last ones were duly absorbed by Brazil's Central Bank, further worsening Brazil's current account deficit (C. Souza, 1997). In 1997 the federal government set out to rectify this situation by consolidating all state debts into a thirty-year repayment program and advancing the Fiscal Responsibility Law.

Political Reform

The rest of this essay will review the attempted reforms of Brazil's political system, focusing on electoral and party law, judicial reform, and corruption abatement. The discussion will also analyze the impact and consequences of the measures adopted.

Election and Party Systems

Many attempts were made to reform Brazil's election and party systems in the 1945–1964 period, and many analysts concluded that this was the "missing link" responsible for the failure of the structural and administrative reforms proposed by Presidents Jânio Quadros and João Goulart between 1961 and 1964 (Gordon, 2001; Skidmore, 1967; Soares, 2001; M. C. C. Souza, 1976).

The twenty-one-year military period of 1964–1985 saw many modifications of the election and party systems in a never-ending cycle of *casuísmos* (case-by-case changes), aimed at maintaining congressional majorities for its support party, ARENA/PDS, in the 1966, 1970, 1974, 1978, and 1982 elections. Many times the witchcraft returned to haunt the sorcerer, when the *casuísmos* failed to produce the desired results, and new measures had to be decreed by the executive (Fleischer, 1994).

Of the many political reforms considered since 1995, only the reelection amendment was approved by the first semester of 1997. Hotly debated since its introduction by Deputy Mendonça Filho (PFL-PE) in February 1995, this reform incited strong feelings, both pro and con, more in terms of the then incumbent mayors and governors than the president (Abrúcio, 1994 and 1998; Abrúcio and Samuels, 1997). Those mayors elected in 1992, whose terms would end in December 1996, pressured heavily to be included in the amendment, which, if passed in late 1995 or early 1996, would have allowed them to stand for reelection.

The Cardoso government procrastinated, fearing that approval might allow presidential hopeful Paulo Maluf, then incumbent mayor of São Paulo (with Brazil's third largest budget), to be reelected and thus enhance his chances for a 1998 run against Cardoso. It was also estimated that some thirty to forty senators planned to run for governor in 1998; they were not keen on running against incumbents, even those from their own party. Many thought that the latter could be appeased by applying the *desincompatibilização* concept that would require incumbents seeking reelection to temporarily stand down during the election campaign period (Fleischer, 1998a).

In a scene reminiscent of March 1988, when President Sarney defeated efforts aimed at both reducing his mandate to four years and installing a full parliamentary system by articulating a massive distribution of political goods to ANC members, the Cardoso government and some allied governors pushed the amendment through the Chamber of Deputies in early 1997, and the Senate finally approved it in May. The mayors elected in 1992 were not contemplated, but their successors elected in 1996 were included and were able to stand for reelection in 2000.

However, a rearguard action by the PMDB, PPB (Brazilian Progressive Party), and left parties in August/September 1997 included fetters on the reelection campaigns of incumbent governors and President Cardoso in the patched-up election law for 1998 (Law 9504, 30 September 1997). The restrictions included mandatory reimbursement by the president's campaign for use of federal human and material resources, such as the presidential jet, utilized during the campaign; all-out prohibition of the use of such resources by governors; the prohibition of both president and governors from participating in the inauguration of public works three months prior to the election; and the prohibition of using national/regional television and radio time for special announcements by the president and governors during the same period (Fleischer, 1997). The Senate deliberated an amendment that would eliminate the absolute majority criterion for the gubernatorial elections, but maintain it for the presidential election). On May 9, 2001, the Senate approved a bill (PEC) that, if approved by the Chamber, would oblige incumbent governors, mayors, and the president seeking reelection to step down on April 5, six months before the October 6 elections (A. Vasconcelos, 2001; Domingos, 2001). But the Chamber of Deputies stalled and killed this measure.

Two other changes were inserted into the 1998 election law: (1) the exclusion of blank votes from the calculation of the election quotient in each state, which hoped to lower the quotient and thus perhaps facilitate the election of more candidates from smaller parties; and (2) the 20 percent quota for women on the Proportional Representation (PR) party lists used in the 1996 municipal elections was expanded to 25 percent for the election of state and federal deputy. However, the benefits possibly accruing from the first change did not occur because the generalized use of electronic voting machines in 1998 greatly reduced the proportion of blank votes.

By 2000, Congress was in the final stages of another important political reform, regulation of the use of the *Medida Provisória* (MP) by the president. This artifice, which was conveniently overlooked in the hasty conversion of the draft constitution from a parliamentary to a presidential model after March 22, 1988, allowed the president to issue MPs that take effect immediately for a thirty-day period, but could be reissued indefinitely while awaiting congressional deliberation. This very powerful instrument was used to implement both the Collor stabilization plan in 1990 and the *Real Plan* in 1994, but it could not be used to alter the constitution (Figueiredo and Limongi, 1997). However, President Cardoso and his Congressional allies studiously avoided passage of this measure until early 2001, when it became evident that an amendment passed by the Senate would clear the lower house. Government leaders negotiated a solution with party leaders and brought the Workers' Party on board in support of restricting the use of MPs enacted in late 2001.

One of the restrictions on this powerful governability-favoring instrument is that if after the second ninety-day reissue period Congress has not acted on the MP, the agenda of Congress is blocked until the MP is deliberated. Paradoxically, this provision blocked the agenda in the Chamber of Deputies in favor of twenty-one MPs in late March 2002, and impeded passage of the PEC extending the tax on CPMF (tax on financial transactions). This was expected to create a shortfall of some R$6 billion in badly needed revenues after June 16 and to impact heavily on the 2002 campaign.

Other possible reform proposals in the political area, mentioned by Lima Jr. (1994), were deliberated by the Special Senate Committee for Political Reform (Machado, 1998) as of 1995, but none had passed by mid-2002. These are:

- Revising the skewed regional representation in the Chamber, regulating the "one-man, one-vote" concept. This had no chance of passage; to the contrary, Congress was considering further skewing regional representation by creating two new states and three federal territories in the Northern Region.

- Changing from an open to a closed list proportional representation system. This had a good chance of passage and would help: strengthen the quotas for women; elevate the media campaigns from ten seconds of "vote for me" to a real debate among parties regarding ideas and proposals; better regulate campaign finance (party only) with better monitoring; decrease the cost of PR campaigns; enhance party loyalty, because the party determines inclusion and rank order of candidates on the closed list; and eliminate some of the negative aspects of coalitions.

- Adopting a mixed election system, similar to the German model. This measure has considerable support.

- Imposing a threshold barrier of 3 or 5 percent for parties to be represented in the Chamber. Already passed in the Senate, this measure has a good possibility of approval in the Chamber (perhaps for 2006). It would help eliminate small and micro-parties, forcing their fusion with larger parties.

- Prohibiting coalitions in the PR elections and/or revising coalition criteria.

- Adopting party fidelity sanctions that would punish crossover voting and party switching. Already passed by the Senate and awaiting Chamber approval, this measure might be stricter than the current "one-year before election" prohibition on party switching, and oblige legislators to vote the party line at risk of losing their mandate.

- Moving to a six-year Senate mandate, with staggered elections every two years. This measure has little chance of being approved.

- Allowing Senate and Chamber presidents to also have the immediate reelection privilege, which had been eliminated by the military after 1964, and confirmed in 1988.

- Eliminating the one-year restriction on the tenure of chairs of standing committees in the Congress, thus restoring the continuity of the pre-1964 period.

- Tightening the criteria for the creation of new *municípios*. With a new unit being created every three days, it is estimated that of Brazil's 5,559 *municípios* nearly one-third are nonviable in fiscal terms.

- Strengthening restrictions on and reporting of campaign finance. The Senate has approved exclusive public campaign finance (R$7 per vote) that would prohibit any contributions from the private sector. However, it is doubtful that the TSE and TREs will be empowered to monitor abuses and punish offenders.

- Finally, reducing the current complete political immunity of legislators. A half-way measure was passed in late 2001 that allows the STF (Supreme Federal Court) to prosecute members of Congress directly without prior waiver, but maintains the special privilege of being tried only by the STF, which is almost equivalent to impunity.

Judicial Reform

The reform of Brazil's judiciary may be considered a subarea of political reform. Cited by many as one of the most important and urgent reforms, movement toward change has been very slow. The Chamber began deliberation on a judicial reform package in 2000, and was passed by the Senate in late 2001.

Of the main proposals, only two made substantial progress in 2002: first, the *efeito vinculante* (binding jurisprudence) would reduce federal court case loads by more than one-half because it would oblige strict adherence by lower courts to jurisprudence established by the STF and the STJ (Federal Appeals Court), and eliminate the *indústria de liminares* (industry of producing injunction requests) that clogs court calendars; and second, the elimination of *classista* judges chosen by labor unions or management associations on the labor courts has been approved and the *classista* judges are to be eliminated by natural attrition.

Other measures to eliminate nepotism in the judicial branch, especially the proposal for the creation of external control mechanisms, were vehemently rejected by judges and are currently not on the congressional agenda.

The Senate began deliberating a bill to revise the Civil Code in November 1997. A long-overdue revision of Brazil's Penal Code is another urgently needed reform. Moreover, a revision of the "Processes," separate legislation detailing procedures and rituals, of both Codes is even more important to avoid nearly indefinite postponement tactics by defense lawyers, a practice that is more or less equivalent to impunity.

A recent study conducted by IDESP (Institute of Economic, Social, and Political Research of São Paulo) interviewing 300 business leaders showed that 90.8 percent considered the agility of Brazil's judicial system bad or terrible. A majority responded that this situation inhibits new investments. Based on the quantification of the latter, BNDES calculated that Brazil's GDP could have been 13.7 percent higher than that registered in December 1997 (US$868 billion), or close to the one trillion mark (Thury Filho, 2001).

Corruption and Reform

Historians report that corruption, favoritism, bribes, tax evasion, and the like have been present in Brazil since the sixteenth-century colonial period. After independence in 1822, things changed little except for a more open press and more frequent accusations (Caldeira, 1999). When Brazil became a decentralized republic in 1889, corruption committed by members of the local political opposition was treated harshly by state governments. The 1930 Revolution was to have resolved these problems, but descended into the Estado Novo dictatorship in 1937 until Vargas was overthrown in 1945. The 1946 constitution restored democracy, strengthened the judiciary and prosecutors, and guaranteed freedom of the press. After Vargas returned via direct elections in 1950, the press and his political opponents began an intense campaign against the "sea of mud" in 1953 that eventually led to the president's suicide in August 1954 (Habib, 1994).

The massive economic and infrastructure development promoted during the presidency of Juscelino Kubitschek (with GDP growth rates over 10 percent) led to many accusations of corruption during the 1956–1961 period (Bilac Pinto, 1960). President Jânio Quadros, elected in October 1960, used a broom as his campaign symbol, but he resigned after seven months in office. During João Goulart's presidency (1961–1964) there were also many accusations of corruption and the April 1964 military coup was allegedly undertaken to stamp out communism and corruption. The military constituted numerous inquiries regarding alleged corruption by Kubitschek and other politicians, but they yielded no concrete results (Moura, 1967; Romero, 1967).

The ensuing military regime of 1964–1985 hobbled Congress, stifled the judiciary and prosecutors, and imposed rigid press censorship. These conditions were conducive to massive corruption in Brazil, as larger amounts of public funds were made available by rapid economic growth between 1967–1974 (Assis, 1983 and 1984a; Bueno, 1982; Grael, 1985; J. Leite, 2000; Schilling, 1999). When censorship was eased in the late 1970s, the press and federal prosecutors became bolder in their investigations (Cirano, 1982).

Brazil returned to civilian rule in 1985, after governor Tancredo Neves and Senator José Sarney were elected by an electoral college. A Senate investigation (CPI or Parliamentary Inquiry Commission) investigated accusations of corruption, such as kickbacks on construction contracts, over invoicing of emergency food imports (G. Carvalho, 1987) by the Sarney government in 1988. The investigation reported in favor of impeachment (Ferreira, 1989), but the acting president of the Chamber of Deputies decided not to transmit the report to the full Lower House for deliberation (Castello, 1989; Dimenstein, 1988 and 1989).

The Collor Impeachment. Former Alagoas governor Fernando Collor de Mello was elected in 1989 on a platform that promised to attack corruption and special privileges in the Sarney government (Gurgel and Fleischer, 1990). He adroitly selected the three key senators on the 1988 Senate CPI to be his vice president, education minister, and president of Telebrás, the state-owned telecommunications giant (G. Vasconcellos, 1989). By early 1992, Collor's ambitious programs of economic modernization and inflation control had stalled. Increasing reports of corrupt activities culminated in a devastating public account rendered by his younger brother Pedro Collor, in May of that year (P. Collor de Mello, 1993).

One of the first positive steps toward reducing corruption in Brazil was the installation of a joint CPI in June 1992 to examine the accusations against Collor and his associates. In less than three months of work, this CPI accumulated a vast amount of evidence, including personal testimonies, documents, and canceled checks, and submitted its report recommending impeachment in late August. On September 29, the Chamber of Deputies voted to install an impeachment proceedings by a much larger margin than the required two-thirds vote, and Collor was temporarily removed from the presidency. Finally, on December 29–30, the Senate approved impeachment and Collor was ultimately removed and lost his political rights for eight years. His vice president, Itamar Franco, served out the remainder of the five-year mandate until December 31, 1994 (Rosenn and Downes, 1999; Fleischer, 1999; Brooke, 1992; Weyland, 1993; Krieger, Novais, and Faria, 1992).

To date, over nine years later, indictments are still being brought before the STF, but only two lower-level operatives were convicted by a federal judge in Brasília: the mastermind ex-campaign treasurer Paulo Cesar Farias and Collor's private pilot Jorge Bandeira for income tax evasion, rather than corruption. Faria's wife died of a mysterious heart attack in a Brasília hotel room and Farias was killed in an even more mysterious murder-suicide alleg-edly perpetrated by his jealous girlfriend (Pinto, 1996). As a result, Collor can rightfully state that "the STF has given me a certificate of honesty."[1]

The "Budgetgate" CPI, 1993–1994. In August 1992, the Collor CPI began encountering cancelled checks in the paper trail that involved many politicians from diverse political parties. Before further research could drag down many members of Congress, the CPI abruptly closed its investigation against Collor and submitted its report to the Chamber of Deputies, calling for an impeachment vote (Fleischer, 1999). The Budgetgate CPI was consti-tuted some fourteen months later, in October 1993, and picked up exactly where the Collor CPI had left off to investigate a massive corruption conspir-acy involving the Joint Budget Committee in Congress.

This CPI's activities were intense and the evidence it gathered bombastic. The latter included some sixty kilograms of documents and eighty diskettes removed under federal court order from the home of the representative of a large construction company in Brasília. This documentation revealed a sophisticated cartel-type conspiracy to distribute federal government con-struction contracts by way of a circle involving executive branch employees (mostly in the Ministry of Transportation) and the Joint Budget Committee—hence the nickname, Budgetgate.

This CPI abruptly ceased its investigations and submitted its report in Jan-uary 1994, recommending the removal of some twenty members of Con-gress, further investigations of another fifteen, and declaring the innocence of twenty members. The final results were frustrating: four deputies resigned before the Chamber could vote on their expulsion and loss of political rights, eight were removed by their peers, including Deputy Ibsen Pinheiro, who had presided over impeachment proceedings in 1992, and twelve were absolved (C. Teixeira, 1996 and 1998; Nogueira, 1993). No further investigations have occurred and none of the accused were ever brought to trial. The Senate opted not to investigate or remove any of its members (Krieger, Rodrigues, and Bonassa, 1993; Wohlcke, 1994; Zancarano, 1994).

Budget Process Modifications. In 1993 and 1994, the congressional bud-get process continued with business as usual. However, the continuation of these questionable practices led to the resignation in July 1994 of Senator José Paulo Bisol (PSB–Partido Socialista Brasileiro, or Brazilian Socialist Party), the running mate of Luiz Inácio Lula da Silva (PT) for the October 1994 presidential elections. Bisol had an important role in the Budgetgate CPI. The following month, Senator Guilherme Palmeira (PFL), the running

---

1. The former president returned from self-imposed exile in Miami in 2001 to prepare his unsuccessful campaign for the Senate in the October 2002 elections. For his side of the story see F. Collor de Mello, 1996.

mate of Fernando H. Cardoso (PSDB) was also forced to resign for similar reasons. As a consolation prize, Palmeira was later named to the Federal Accounting Court (TCU).

Not until early 1995 did Congress significantly alter the budget process in line with the recommendations of the Budgetgate CPI. The submission of individual budget amendments, which had reached the unmanageable number of 150,000, was drastically reduced, as well as subsidy amendments benefiting designated NGOs (Nongovernmental Organizations) and nonprofit entities, many of the latter linked to the deputies and senators. Priority was given to collective amendments submitted by political parties or state delegations (for a description of the process in the 1946–1964 period see Ames, 1987).

Special Investigating Committee, 1994. Indignant at the evidence unearthed and CPI report suggesting corruption in the executive branch, president Itamar Franco constituted a blue ribbon Special Investigating Committee (CEI) in January 1994. The CEI investigated corrupt bidding practices, especially in the Ministry of Transportation, and submitted its report to President Franco in mid-December 1994, with an itinerary for further investigations that it proposed to undertake in 1995. Newly elected president Fernando H. Cardoso quietly extinguished the CEI in January 1995, stating that its investigations would be continued by the ministries of Justice and Finance (Carvalhosa, 1995). Nothing was done. During the next seven years the Cardoso government resisted several attempts to install CPIs to investigate corruption in his government (see also Suassuna and Novaes, 1994).

Both the Budgetgate CPI and the CEI prompted some modifications in the law for Public Procurement and Contract Procedures in 1994, or Law 8066. But in April 1996, within the context of considerable weakening of this law, the Ministry of Administration and Reform of the State (MARE) proposed the exclusion of state enterprises and a nearly total elimination of more rigorous procurement procedures for small projects and purchases (Maranhão, Pedone, and Fleischer, 1998).

Corruption since 1995. The difficulties of effectively evaluating levels of corruption in Brazil were vividly illustrated during the visit of U.S. President Bill Clinton to Venezuela, Brazil, and Argentina in October 1997. Journalists gained Internet access to a presidential briefing prepared by the U.S. Department of Commerce that described corruption as endemic in Brazil and specifically pointed out the problems of the judicial branch. Traditionally, visiting heads of state make courtesy calls to the Brazilian Congress and Supreme Court (STF) in addition to meetings with the president and officials of the executive branch, but in this case the STF snubbed Clinton and refused to receive him. Previously, this breach of protocol had only occurred with regards to Peru's president Alberto Fujimori, when the Brazilian high court snubbed him in solidarity with their Peruvian colleagues who had been summarily removed by Fujimori.

A study conducted by the Getúlio Vargas Foundation in São Paulo (FGV-SP) estimated that the direct and indirect economic impact of corruption on Brazil's economy cost some R$6,000 per capita per year (Silva, Garcia, and Bandeira, 2001; Silva, 2001). In 2000, Brazil counted a population of nearly 170 million inhabitants. A study funded by the Tinker Foundation indicated that if Brazil's judicial system were less dysfunctional, its GDP could be some 25 percent higher. The FGV study also concluded that if corruption were reduced, Brazil's per capita GDP would be US$13,700 rather than the current US$10,100. When per capita income is compared with the score on Transparency International's CPI for selected countries, Brazil appears in what is called the Risk Group together with Haiti, Zimbabwe, Mexico and low per capita income and relatively high perception of corruption.

Remembering the Clinton episode in 1997, in early February 2002 Brazil received another blast, this time from the Bush administration. Speaking at the World Economic Forum in New York City, Treasury Secretary Paul O'Neill bluntly stated that "Brazil's interest rates remain very high (19 percent per annum) because of corruption risk" (Purdum and Sanger, 2002; Rossi, 2002). The *O Estado de São Paulo* headline blazed "*Mercado teme corrupção no Brasil, diz O'Neill*"—O'Neill says, the market fears corruption in Brazil (Kuntz, 2002). Brazilian authorities retorted that "the Secretary should worry about U.S. corruption problems—notably the current Enron scandal," but the damage had already been done (Dantas, 2002).

Since 1995, Brazil has seen a series of corruption scandals exposed by the press. Some of these were investigated by the Congress and federal and state prosecutors. Few have been indicted and prosecuted, and hardly any have been convicted.

• *SIVAM.* Although the procurement contract for SIVAM (Amazon Region Electronic Surveillance System) was awarded to Raytheon during the Itamar Franco presidency in mid-1994, after Fernando H. Cardoso had left the Finance Ministry to launch his candidacy for president, a scandal irrupted in 1995 (Lewis, 1996).

• *Bank Scandals.* Early on in Cardoso's first year, a series of failed public and private banks suffered Central Bank intervention and were closed, liquidated, and had their ownership transferred and/or sent to public auction. Three episodes were especially complicated for Cardoso and the Central Bank. The Banco Nacional closed and was transferred overnight to Unibanco. The 1997 intervention of Bamerindus involved its CEO, Senator José Eduardo Andrade Vieira, and Cardoso's minister of agriculture and president of the Partido Trabalhista Brasileiro (Brazilian Labor Party, or PTB) (one of the parties in the governing coalition). The bank was quickly transferred to the bank, HSBC. During the subsequent Central Bank intervention, some R$5.7 billion appeared unaccounted for, and in 2002 the leader of the intervention team was indicted for fraud (Gramacho, 2002; Karam, 2002; J. Leite, 2000). In January 1999, the Marka/FonteCidam case involved accusations against a former Central Bank president and directors for insider trading and conducting false oversight/investigations.

• *"Precatórias" (Debt Bonds).* In 1997/1998, a Senate CPI investigated fraud and corruption in the issuance of debt bonds by state and municipal governments that were under court order to be used to pay their debts to creditors. Unable to pay, the courts authorized the issuance of debt bonds in the financial market. However, the funds were not used to pay the respective creditors but were instead siphoned off to other projects or ends. Recommendations for indictments in the CPI report were in vain as the accusations came to naught (Padrão and Caetano, 1997).

• *"Máfia dos Fiscais" (Mafia of City Inspectors).* In 1999/2000, a massive scandal in the city government of São Paulo, Brazil's largest city, literally exploded. An indignant young woman, whose attempt to establish a small physical fitness gym was blocked by a monthly kickback (*propina*) request by a city inspector in return for authorization license, helped prosecutors and police set up a televised sting. The resulting investigation revealed the involvement of scores of city officials and city council members. The scandal nearly caused the removal of the mayor and sent several people to jail. In the October 2002 elections, only two of the some fifteen accused city council members were reelected (Cardozo, 2000).

The investigations in São Paulo caused prosecutors to reopen previous corruption cases against former mayor Paulo Maluf (1993–1996). It was discovered that Maluf and family members had some US$200 million in bank accounts with Citibank in Geneva, Switzerland. However, the funds had hence been transferred to offshore accounts on the Isle of Jersey. The prosecutors visited Switzerland and hoped to have the incriminating documentation transferred to authorities in São Paulo. In the meantime, they discovered a very large loan by a German bank to Maluf's company in São Paulo (Macedo, 2002; Chade and Macedo, 2002).

• *Two Senate CPIs.* In 2000, the Senate installed two very explosive CPIs to investigate Brazil's judicial and financial systems. Both sectors had assumed they were off limits to any investigations by the legislature or executive branch, even during the military period.

First, Judiciary and Senate staff aided by prosecutors and retired police amassed some 1,000 dossiers of cases of corruption in Brazil's state and federal judiciary, ranging from nepotism, corruption of administrative funds, selling of sentences, sale of prison release orders, involvement with organized crime, and others. However, the fraudulent US$192 million cost overrun in the construction of the new labor court building in São Paulo (TRT-SP, Tribunal Regional do Trabalho, or Regional Labor Court) was found to involve a former TRT-SP president, Nicolau dos Santos Netto, who later fled the country, and then Senator Luiz Estevão (PMDB-DF). The judge was eventually returned to Brazil and was convicted, while Estevão became the first senator in history to be removed by his peers (Formiga, 2000). In addition, extensive corruption cases were discovered in state supreme courts. Examples of corruption in State Supreme Courts (TJs) and federal regional appeals courts (TRFs) exploded on a three-page exposé headed "the selling of judicial sentences" in a leading Rio de Janeiro newspaper in early March (Otavio and Brígido, 2002).[2]

Focused on the banking system, the second Senate CPI investigated the Marka/FonteCidam case and discovered other instances of bank fraud regarding the Central Bank's poor management of bank failures. A former Central Bank president and directors were accused and their indictment recommended. President Cardoso appointed one of the accused to be the first woman director at the Central Bank; in a close vote, the government prevailed and she was confirmed.

• *Organized Crime, Money Laundering, Drugs.* In 2000/2001, the Chamber of Deputies installed a CPI to investigate organized crime in Brazil. The results were devastating and demonstrated the level of sophistication and organization of these groups—plus the involvement of politicians, judges, police, prosecutors, lawyers, accountants, mayors, businessmen, and even the military. Several governors, members of the military, lawyers, state and local politicians are being prosecuted in 2002 (L. Teixeira, 2000).

• *Soccer.* Not even Brazil's beloved national sport was exempt, as in 2001 both the Chamber and the Senate installed separate CPIs to investigate the Brazilian Soccer Confederation and its international contracts, state federations, individual clubs, coaches, player agents, etc. The Chamber CPI final report was sent into limbo by the soccer deputies who were assigned to the CPI by their respective party leaders, but its evidence was transferred to the Senate CPI that issued a scathing report calling for the removal of two federal deputies, many indictments, and extensive modification in legislation for the sector (Bellos, 2002).

• *SUDAM* (Superintendência para o Desenvolvimento da Amazônia, or Superintendency for the Development of the Amazon Region) *and SUDENE*

---

2. For analysis of Brazil's dysfunctional judicial system, see Arantes (1997); Arantes and Kerche (1999); and Sadek (2000).

(Superintendência para o Desenvolvimento do Nordeste, or Superintendency for the Development of the Northeast). In 2001, a "battle of the titans" raged in the Senate between Senator Antônio Carlos Magalhães (PFL-Bahia) and Senator Jader Barbalho (PMDB-Pará) over the latter's election as president of the Upper House. The contention included accusations and dossiers over corruption of regional development funds administered by SUDAM (Amazon) and SUDENE (northeast). Investigations by the Federal Police, federal prosecutors, the TCU, and others, revealed that some R$2 billion had been embezzled from each agency. Among the accused were senators, deputies, governors, businessmen, and even cabinet ministers (Jungblut, 2002).

The evidence accumulating rapidly against Barbalho first forced his resignation from the Senate presidency and then, on the verge of being removed (and losing his political rights for eight years), he resigned his mandate. In January 2002, he began his campaign for governor of Pará, but the next month suffered a humiliating thirteen-hour imprisonment ordered by a federal judge in the state of Tocantins investigating the SUDAM corruption. He was eventually elected federal deputy

In March, 2002, another prominent politician fell victim to SUDAM corruption accusations, Governor Roseana Sarney (PFL-Maranhão). She and her husband were accused of embezzling SUDAM funds for unfinished development projects. The same federal judge who put Barbalho in jail ordered a search and seize operation by the Federal Police at the offices of Sarney and her husband in São Luís. The police confiscated incriminating documents indicating fraud, money laundering, and tax evasion—as well as R$1.34 million in cash (Policarpo Jr., 2002).

In the February 2002 presidential preference polls, Governor Sarney was technically tied with Lula (PT) for first place (23 vs. 26 percent), but polls conducted in the first week of March showed her losing ground. In a violent reaction, her political party (PFL) left the Cardoso coalition in Congress, thereby turning the presidential campaign upside down (Lima, 2002). After dropping in three successive polls, on April 13 Roseana Sarney resigned her presidential candidacy. In October 2002, she was elected senator.

• *Corruption CPI.* In April/May 2001, opposition parties, joined by a considerable number of deputies and senators from his alliance, signed petitions to install a joint CPI to investigate twenty-one key recent cases of corruption. The Cardoso government and allied congressional leaders finally beat back this effort, but only after considerable pressure to convince members to remove their names from the petitions.

• *Anticorruption Measures.* In evaluating the evolution of corruption in Brazil over past decades, many feel that the levels of corruption have not changed, but rather the intensity of revelations by a free press and increased levels of investigation and prosecution by police and prosecutors have given the impression that corruption has increased. More frequent and aggressive CPIs have been installed in Congress since the late 1980s to investigate corruption—especially the Chamber of Deputies CPI in 2000–2001 that investigated organized crime, money laundering, drug traffic, and arms traffic. Since the early 1990s, both houses of Congress have taken extreme measures, like the removal of peers, to deal with accusations of corruption within their own ranks (Fleischer, 2002a; Speck, 2000b). However, during a brief visit to Brazil in mid-1999, a Transparency International director concluded that congressional investigations are not important in combating corruption (Gaspar, 1999).

In late 2001 Congress reduced, though did not completely eliminate, the parliamentary immunity of its members from prosecution for "common crimes" like murder, corruption, theft, and white-collar crime. As a result, it is now easier for Congress to investigate, prosecute, expel, and strip its accused members of their mandates. Federal prosecutors can now open cases against members of Congress directly, without the prior wavier of immunity.

Table 6–1 demonstrates that there is a certain association between Transparency International's Corruption Perceptions Index for seventeen Latin American nations and their risk evaluations and spreads. Those with lower corruption perceptions in general have better risk and spread ratings by the international financial community, and vice versa to a certain extent. While Brazil has the fifth-best corruption rating among its Latin American neighbors, six nations have better risk and spread evaluations. Economic growth rates present a weaker correlation. When "Spearman's Rho" rank order correlation is applied to the four relationships, a fairly strong "positive" relationship exists between levels of corruption and risk (Moody's +0.72 and SandP +0.66)—that is, less corruption is associated with lower risk. The third indicator of risk (Spreads +0.46) presents the same relationship, although somewhat weaker. A relatively weak relationship exists between levels of corruption and GDP growth -0.39.

Congress attempted to install CPIs to investigate several alleged cases of government corruption in the second half of the 1990s, but the president and his allies in Congress were often able to beat back these attempts, claiming that they aimed at destabilizing the government. This led some observers to conclude that, although the president himself was probably not involved in corrupt activities, a thorough investigation would threaten the broader governing coalition. Responding to attempts to install an anticorruption CPI in early 2001, President Cardoso created a new agency, the Corregedoria Geral da União-CGU (Corrector General's Office), to combat corruption, but it had limited powers (Allen, 2002; Monteiro, 2001).

TABLE 6-1. Transparency International's Corruption Perceptions Index (CPI), 1999–2001 and Risk Ratings, GDP Growth, and Spreads for Selected Latin American Countries

| | Transparency International CPI[1] | | | | | | Risk,[2] GDP Growth, Spread | | | |
| | 1999 | | 2000 | | 2001 | | | | | |
Country	Rank	Score	Rank	Score	Rank	Score	Moody's	SandP	GDP%[3]	Spread[4]
Chile	19	6.9	18	7.4	18	7.5	Baa1	A-	+3.1	152
Uruguay	41	4.4			35	5.1	Baa3	BB+	-0.8	492
Costa Rica	32	5.1	30	5.4	40	4.5	Ba1	BB	+0.3	203
Peru	40	4.5	41	4.4	44	4.1	Ba3	BB-	+0.1	475
Brazil	45	4.1	49	3.9	46	4.0	B1	BB-	+1.8	843
Colombia	72	2.9	60	3.2	50	3.8	Ba2	BB	+1.5	598
Mexico	58	3.4	59	3.3	51	3.7	Baa2	BBB-	-0.3	286
Panama					51	3.7	Ba1	BB+	+0.9	375
El Salvador	49	3.9	43	4.1	54	3.6	Baa3	BB+	+1.4	234
Argentina	71	3.0	52	3.5	57	3.5	Caa3	SD	-3.8	3,943
Guatemala	59	3.1	62	3.2	61	3.2	Ba2	NA	+2.5	385
Dom. Republic					63	3.1	B1	B+	+1.5	371
Venezuela	75	2.6	71	2.7	69	2.8	B2	B	+2.3	1,078
Honduras	83	1.7	94	1.8	71	2.7	B2	NA	+2.0	NA
Nicaragua	70	3.1			77	2.4	B2	NA	+3.0	NA
Ecuador	82	2.4	74	2.6	79	2.3	Caa2	CCC+	+5.2	1,136
Bolivia	80	2.5	71	2.7	87	2.0	B1	B+	+0.5	NA
Spearman's Rho							+0.72	+0.66	-0.39	+0.46
Number of Cases							17	14	17	14

Note: Information supplied by Emy Shayo, Doug Smith, Paulo Vieira da Cunha, and Enrique Hidaldo-Noriega was used to complete the data on risk, GDP, and spreads.
1. A composite index using other "risk analysis indexes" with ranking done by domestic and international business leaders in each country on a scale of "zero" (high corruption perception) to 10 (low corruption perception). For the 2001 CPI, a minimum of 3 and a maximum of 12 of these indexes were used to compile the CPI for Transparency International. The 2002 CPI will be released in June 2002. For details see: http://www.transparency.org/cpi/index.html. Last date accessed: unknown.
2. Reported as of February 2002.
3. GDP growth reported for 2001 by *Latin American Consensus Forecasts*, February 18, 2000.
4. Spreads (EMBI') as of March 10, 2002 by IdeaGlobal.

Unfortunately, Brazil's very loose regulations for campaign finance are an open invitation for corruption-based funds to be channeled into multimillion dollar campaigns (Fleischer, 2000)—as the 1993/94 CPI (Fleischer, 1997), as the 2000 campaign for mayor of Curitiba clearly demonstrated. Prosecutors and police discovered that the reelection campaign of the PFL mayor of Curitiba actually spent R$33 million, instead of the R$3 million reported to the election court. Clearly, more rigorous campaign finance laws are necessary, with enhanced powers for the election courts to punish abuses, and without endless civil court injunctions to alleviate the accused and allow them to stand for election.

Currently, only three Brazilian institutions are actively involved in curbing corruption—the press, state/federal prosecutors, and congressional investigations. The CPIs usually have stronger and more intense investigative powers than the press and prosecutors, and the latter usually lend informal technical support to the CPIs and anxiously await their findings to enhance their cases.

Until the internal control agency is granted autonomous status, like the inspector generals in the United States, removed from within the Finance Ministry, and the external control body (TCU) is reorganized, depoliticized and fully empowered to investigate and prosecute the corruption activities uncovered by the internal control, like the General Accounting Office (GAO) in the United States, little progress will be made (Speck, 2000b). Also, Brazil's judicial system needs a thoroughgoing reform, with deep revisions in the penal code and the penal code process, and an external control body, to enable prosecutors to end the impunity caused by a dysfunctional judicial system (Arantes, 1997; Arantes and Kerche, 1999; Sadek, 2000).

In late March 2002, president Cardoso upgraded the Corregedoria Geral da União to become the Controladoria Geral da República-CGR (Controller General of the Republic). The internal control agency (SFCI) was incorporated into the CGR and the unit was attached directly to the president's office. This major reorganization must be approved by Congress; thus, the final role and powers of the CGR are as yet not defined.

Finally, Brazil's quite loose federal system affords considerable autonomy to state governors and local mayors, who many times use their powers and prerogatives to facilitate corrupt exchanges, build their campaign war chests, and favor family and political allies. Governors still maintain their special prosecution status (*foro especial*) to be exclusively tried by the Superior Court of Justice (STJ). Although the Cardoso government had succeeded in curtailing some of these prerogatives—sale or liquidation of all banks and public enterprises owned by state governments, the consolidation of the states' debts under federal refinancing, and implementation of the new Fiscal Responsibility Law that criminalizes overspending revenues—adequate internal control of expenditures by state governments is still elusive (Abrúcio and Samuels, 1997).

Conclusion

To a great extent, many of the structural and administrative reforms attempted by President Cardoso during his eight years in office were either not approved or partially enacted because major political reforms had not been completed. Had the "missing link," the political reforms, been enacted during Cardoso's first term—such as 1) political immunity (and impunity) eliminated completely; 2) the election laws modified to eliminate the open list proportional representation system; 3) reduction of regional inequalities in the Chamber of Deputies; and 4) stronger regulations for campaign finance, with heavy penalties for violations—the performance of Congress might have been quite different, especially in Cardoso's second term (Fleischer, 1998b). A thorough judicial reform would have given a new impetus to investments in Brazil, and reduced the drag on the nation's GDP growth caused by a dysfunctional judicial system.

In early 2001, Cardoso's leaders in Congress reached an agreement with the Workers' Party regarding a minimum political reform agenda, but even this was not enough to assure passage. Most of the political reform proposals still on the agenda in 2002 will again be deliberated by the new Congress in 2003 and beyond.

Part III
Institutions, Actors, and
Regional Context

CHAPTER 7

Competitive Federalism and Distributive Conflict

Alfred Montero

The evolution of Brazilian federalism continues to create both possibilities and obstacles for the deepening of state reform. If during the 1980s the governors and mayors were clearly positioning for their own political benefit and overspending in ways that threatened the national reform agenda, the 1990s saw a different dynamic. The loose and somewhat disjointed nature of the fiscal decentralization process shaped by the military regime, the subsequent transition to democracy, and the 1988 constitution, allowed reformist presidents during the 1990s to recentralize fiscal authority through the use of stop-gap measures.

In this chapter, I explain this ad hoc reassertion of executive authority by examining the decentralization process as a path-dependent, distributive game played in two arenas: the executive-legislative and intergovernmental (president-governors) spheres. I argue that bargaining leverage shifted to the presidency before and during the administration of Fernando Henrique Cardoso (1994–2002). This shift allowed Cardoso's administration to exert substantial control over subnational fiscal policy. The causes of this shift are path dependent and strategic.

Two major path-dependent factors aided the reequilibration of central authority: first, historical rivalries among Brazil's poor and industrial regions, and second, more recent fiscal rivalries involving competing investment incentive schemes. Both of these factors kept states from ganging up on the presidency in a sustained "all-on-one" fashion. Even when the states enjoyed common interests and favored coordination, these persisting divisions and rivalries weakened the credibility of their commitments to one another. Regional inequalities and persisting interjurisdictional competition have kept Brazil an asymmetrical, competitive federal state.

The president's strategic ability to shape a progressive reform agenda in the executive-legislative arena strengthened the presidency vis-à-vis the states and helped weaken interstate coordination. Intergovernmental distributive conflicts, involving and often overlapping the two arenas (executive-legislative and president-governors), have shaped the evolving federal pact (Afonso, 1996: 34). In the first arena, conflicts between the president and a bicameral assembly delineated the structural reform agenda in ways that affected the capacities and strategies of players in the second arena. In turn, the intergovernmental game involving presidents and governors helped configure the costs and possibilities for reform in the executive-legislative arena (Souza, 1998). On both levels, the presidency achieved strategic gains that gradually tipped the equilibrium of political leverage in its favor.

My argument assumes that the capacity of the state governments to engage in credible coordination is essential to determining the final outcome. While the states are seen by some scholars as "veto players" in the reform process, their capacity to reinforce the status quo is determined by the coordination of the governors, or what Tsebelis (1995) would term the "internal cohesion" of the veto players. This cohesion is, in turn, shaped by numerous and iterated strategic interactions with the president as he negotiates the terms of reform with federal legislators and the governors.

The analytical framework used here improves upon earlier studies of changes in the federal pact in Brazil. Several studies have focused on the way political institutions shape the Brazilian policymaking process by analyzing prohibitive factors such as balanced bicameralism and fragmented party systems (e.g., Willis, Garman, and Haggard, 1999; Garman, Haggard, and Willis, 2001; Mainwaring, 1999; Ames, 2001). Yet strictly institutional approaches alone cannot explain change in intergovernmental relations. Noninstitutional factors such as macroeconomic policy shifts and corruption scandals prompt changes in federal structures even when political institutions themselves do not change (Montero, 2002a). Furthermore, explanations that focus exclusively on the executive-legislative arena tend to ignore the capacities of the executive vis-à-vis the states in the intergovernmental arena. These approaches also tend to focus too much on the most proximate institutional factors and ignore historically specific and path-dependent conditions that explain the motivations, and hence the propensity to cooperate, of individual politicians and subnational governments (Montero and Samuels, 2003).

In the sections that follow I develop an understanding of the evolution of decentralization in Brazil as a path-dependent, two-arena game. In the first section I provide an outline of these levels of analysis and highlight the most relevant actors and processes in the Brazilian context. In the following section I examine the politics of the intergovernmental game in terms of these levels of analysis. This section lays out a periodization of the decentralization/recentralization process in Brazil during the bureaucratic authoritarian and most recent democratic periods. The final section offers my conclusions.

Distributive Conflicts in Brazilian Federalism as a Path-Dependent, Two-Arena Game

Distributive conflicts involving federal, state, and municipal governments have historically shaped the "pendulum swings" between centralization and decentralization that characterize the legacy of Brazilian federalism. Lacking either a coherent model of federalism or the sustained dominance of the states by the central government, the history of decentralization in Brazil is characterized by paradoxes and reversals. Periods of decentralization, such as the Old Republic (1889–1930), set the stage for recentralization by exacerbating the problems of national governance in a decentralized state. Episodes of centralized rule, such as Getúlio Vargas's *Estado Novo* (1937–1945), created precedents that enhanced decentralization subsequently. State governments, even in the *Estado Novo*, collected most taxes and implemented welfare policies. This experience would give the governors and mayors critical inroads into developing their capacities in the pluralist democratic period (1945–1964). The same was true during the bureaucratic authoritarian (1964–1985) and the democratic "New Republic" (1985–present) periods. Although the military centralized control over subnational governments, the generals also decentralized taxes that would become crucial to financing the governors' dispensation of patronage during the transition to democracy. Although the early history of the New Republic and the 1988 constitution was shaped by the interests of subnational elites, the president and central regulators of the economy, such as the Central Bank, gained an increasing capacity to restrain the unbridled tendencies of fiscal decentralization.

Examination of this latest transition reveals that the distributive conflicts that shape the federal pact in Brazil are themselves given form by certain path-dependent factors. These variables affected the distribution of intergovernmental leverage that mediated the politics of cooperation and conflict between the presidency and the governors during the 1990s. The arena of executive-legislative relations also regulated the relative bargaining power of the national executive and the governors. In the subsections below, I analyze each of these levels of analysis.

The Path Dependency of Intergovernmental Relations

Two persisting factors shaped the intergovernmental bargaining game in the 1990s in Brazil: one, continuing historical inequalities among the regions and two, the balkanization of political loyalties around competing subnational interests (*bancadas subnacionais*).

Regional inequalities in Brazil have historically shaped the interests of subnational governments, particularly among the poorest states. The rich southern and southeastern states of Brazil have three times the per capita GDP of the poorer northern and northeastern states. The southeast accounts for roughly 43 percent of the population, but 59 percent of the GDP and 66 percent of all industrial production. São Paulo alone is responsible for 38 percent of the GDP and 22.2 percent of the national population. By contrast the northeast has 29 percent of the population and only 14 percent of the GDP and 12 percent of industrial production. These socioeconomic inequalities have bred historical conflicts between states in each region (Souza, 1998; Selcher, 1998: 29–30). Northeastern resentment against the economic dominance of São Paulo and the southeast spurred efforts by the military to distribute fiscal resources to the poorer states, where its party, ARENA (the National Renovating Alliance), enjoyed conservative support. Congressional overrepresentation of the center-western, northeastern, and northern states prevented the political domination of the federal assembly by *paulista* interests. The same system carried over into the democratic period as the Congress, elected under the old rules, composed the Constituent Assembly in 1987 (Selcher, 1998: 34). The 1988 constitution set a limit of seventy federal deputies per state in the Chamber of Deputies, effectively sanctioning the mal-appointment of the lower house to São Paulo's detriment. The many small states of the northeast are also overrepresented in the Senate where each state retains three senators. Since the politics of the poor states tend to be more clientelistic than the Brazilian norm, overrepresentation has made of regional redistribution in policymaking more salient. In defense of their own interests, underrepresented states in the southeast and south have often responded with antagonism toward these mechanisms.

Another continuing aspect of the federal system is the persistence of subnational political loyalties, as opposed to partisan ones. Numerous studies have shown that the governors and local political machines, a few originating in the pluralist and bureaucratic authoritarian periods, continue to dominate Brazilian politics (Hagopian, 1992, 1996; Samuels, forthcoming). Local "notables" determine political career paths for federal politicians. Subnational office continues to be an important point in a politico's development, especially after serving in federal congressional office (Samuels, 1998, and forthcoming). These tendencies have weakened the party system and balkanized political loyalties around subnational interests.

An enduring aspect of this balkanized matrix of subnational interests (*bancadas subnacionais*) is that they have always had a history of competing over a common pool of fiscal resources. During the pluralist period, the *bancadas subnacionais* operated in support of governors contending for national development projects, public firms, and regional incentives (F. Oliveira, 1995: 82–84). State governments competed with each other for public sector investments during the bureaucratic authoritarian regime and especially as the generals expanded the Second National Development Plan (Montero, 2002b: chapter 3; Schwartzman, 1982). The *bancadas subnacionais* assumed center stage during the transition to democracy and the Constituent Assembly, where divisions between the northeast and south/southeast shaped the rules governing fiscal decentralization. The sequencing of subnational elections for governor prior to the direct election of the president and the fight over the rules of fiscal federalism to be codified in the constitution of 1988 enhanced the influence of these groups (Sallum, 1996; C. Souza, 1997, 1998). Yet the fiscal crisis of the state also made interstate competition over a more scarce pool of resources more intense, particularly with regard to infrastructure investments, (Rodriguez, 1995: 435–436).

Although joined around a generalized norm favoring decentralization, the *bancadas subnacionais* remained competitive due to regional inequalities. Escalating "fiscal wars" involving competing fiscal incentive schemes deepened interstate distrust in the post-1988 period. The commitment of the states to these fiscal wars reflects both a reaction to regional inequalities and the failure of the constitution to credibly prevent irrational competition (Affonso, 1995: 60). Interstate competition raised the costs of interjurisdictional coordination throughout the 1990s.

The Executive–Legislative Arena

In the executive–legislative arena the process of reforming fiscal federal institutions is fraught with obstacles. The requirement that significant reforms pass through two separate three-fifths votes in both chambers of Congress keep presidents from submitting major legislation until they have bargained to generate sufficient votes. The fragmentation of party loyalties in a multiparty, open-list proportional representation system adds significantly to the president's bargaining costs. Each piece of legislation is contingent on the outcomes of numerous deals involving ministerial and subministerial appointments, the outcome of "decree games" in which presidential initiatives lie in limbo before being voted on, and pork-barrel discretionary spending projects negotiated between the president and party leaders, interest groups, and individual politicians (Ames, 2001; Power, 2000).

Despite these hindrances, the overall pathway of reform has been progressive. During Cardoso's two terms, the five center-right parties "allied" to his government—PSDB, PMDB, PFL, PTB, and PPB—provided somewhat consistent support to the president's reform agenda, but the executive had to dispense ministries, pork, and other favors to sustain these loose coalitions (Mainwaring, 1999: 313–317). Presidential decree power (*Medidas Provisó-rias*) reinforced the reform agenda, but congressional approval required that Cardoso distribute patronage. These concessions allowed Cardoso to sustain a macroeconomic and structural adjustment agenda that moved forward, albeit slowly (Almeida, 1996b and in this volume). More importantly, each reform was reinforced by the bargains that preceded it (Couto, 1998: 72–73; Montero, 2000). Macroeconomic stabilization policies such as the Fiscal Sta-bilization Fund (FEF), passed in February 1994, allowed the federal govern-ment to retain 20 percent of constitutionally mandated federal transfers from tax revenues to the states and municipalities, making these resources avail-able for stopgap fiscal adjustments. By enhancing fiscal pressures on subna-tional governments into expanding, the FEF made subsequent presidential side payments that much more valuable. Cardoso also used his enhanced pre-rogatives over revenue sharing to coerce Congress to extend the FEF, making it more of an ongoing de facto fiscal reform. Cardoso was able to use these threats strategically to create support for other pieces of stopgap fiscal adjust-ment legislation—the Camata Law, the Kandir Law, and the Law of Fiscal Responsibility (LRF). The progressive and cumulative nature of the reform agenda was shaped by several factors.

To begin with, the president was able to take advantage of weak party dis-cipline and coherence to forge policy-specific coalitions. This was particu-larly evident in macroeconomic reform where the multidimensional nature of the policy and the broad range of provisions upon which the executive could cajole individual deputies to support him made passage more probable (Ames, 2001: 264–265). In this context, presidential patronage traded off leg-islators' short-term interests in acquiring pork with the long-term interests of their office. Given high turnover, especially in the Chamber, legislators were willing to take short-term compensation in return for their votes on behalf of structural reforms that would limit access to patronage later (Weyland, 2000a: 50; Power, 1998a: 61–62). This served to divide and limit subnational opposition to the FEF and subsequent legislation.

Then, the progressive sequencing of reform helped move the agenda for-ward. The success of the first phase of reforms, which involved macroeco-nomic stabilization (*Real Plan*), the National Destatization Program (PND) (privatization), and the emerging autonomy of the Central Bank, strength-ened the president vis-à-vis legislators. The success of the *Real Plan* created support both in the legislature and among business constituencies for fiscal reform. Passage and periodic renewal of the FEF was costly in terms of pork, but it gave Cardoso more bargaining chips for later reform negotiations by enabling the president to exert influence on the fiscal accounts of the states and their *bancadas subnacionais*. The *Real Plan*'s success in reducing inflation and the economic team's tactic of maintaining high interest rates raised the costs on the erstwhile state practice of rolling over debt. This made the states more receptive to Central Bank intervention in state banks and to the privatization of enterprises owned by the state governments.

Finally, corruption scandals prompted Congress to move reform forward at different points. The FEF's passage was enhanced by the "budget mafia" scandal on the Joint Budget Committee in October 1993, which discredited Congress and forced the retirement of several ranking deputies. Fearing a popular antipolitical backlash that would surely have strengthened Lula's persisting lead in the presidential polls, conservative politicians supported Cardoso and his *Real Plan*. While passage ultimately relied on promising compensation to municipalities and distributing government appointments and benefits to individual politicians, support for the FEF was a residual of this momentary political shift (Melo, 1997: 69–70; Couto, 1998: 66–67). The *precatórios* scandal of the late 1990s raised serious concerns about debt bond issuance and this led to new limits on the practice. Ongoing corruption scandals, and particularly the 1999–2000 "Lalau" case, once again focused public attention on official malfeasance in the months prior to the passage of the LRF.

By winning large and small battles in the assembly, Cardoso became increasingly equipped to win in a second arena: that of intergovernmental distributive conflict, which involved the presidency and state governors. The Kandir Law, the Camata Law, the FEF, and the LRF greatly expanded Cardoso's bargaining position in comparison to his predecessors, yet this shift in presidential leverage was far from automatic. The president's strategy was instrumental in dividing subnational opposition.

The Intergovernmental Game

As in all coordination games, intergovernmental coordination has multiple equilibria. Different configurations of intergovernmental bargaining will lead to distinct reform outcomes. Two variables are important: (a) the ability of states to credibly commit to reinforce each other in the face of federal attempts to limit subnational autonomy (Solnick, 1998); and (b) the capacity of the center to use selective benefits and costs to divide the states. The first variable is essential for coordinating interjurisdictional resources in opposition to federal efforts to restrain subnational autonomy. The credibility of commitments by the states to such coordination is crucial. Historic rivalries and other forms of competition will undercut the credibility of horizontal coordination. Steven Solnick (1995: 57), referring to the Russian case, puts it simply: "Ultimately, the viability of any bargaining coalition will depend on whether subnational actors distrust each other less than they each distrust the

TABLE 7-1. Intergovernmental Bargaining

		Credibility of Governors' Commitments	
		High	**Low**
President Capacity to Sanction	**High**	Some-on-one	One-on-one (Advantage to the Federal Government)
	Low	All-on-one	One-on-one (Advantage to the States)

center." For the federal government, the capacity to foment interjurisdictional rivalries and selectively reward and punish states will mitigate subnational coordination.

Table 7–1 models intergovernmental coordination. Where interjurisdictional commitments are credible and the executive's capacity to dispense sanctions is low (lower left cell), the configuration of intergovernmental bargaining will take the form of "all-on-one." Credible interstate coordination acts to veto federal reform and maximize subnational autonomy. If the center's capacity for distributing selective costs and benefits is high, then efforts by the center to divide states will prevent the "all-on-one" scenario but allow for some subnational coordination ("some-on-one"). Federal reforms will be limited due to the capacity of the coordinated group to hinder the universal application of a change in rules. Even partial reforms will require significant concessions to states in the coordinated group. Where interstate commitments are not credible, states will oppose reform individually. "One-on-one" configurations that give an advantage to the central government (upper right cell) provide federal reformers with the capacity to impose universally applicable reforms. However, application requires the selective distribution of side payments of both positive and negative sanctions to keep states from coordinating their opposition. If the center's sanctioning capacity is weak, the configuration of intergovernmental bargaining remains "one-on-one" but states will have the advantage in individual bargains by being able to hold out for improved terms (lower right cell). Under these conditions the federal government cannot impose uniform restrictions on all states.

Only by converting some-on-one or one-on-one (advantage to the states) configurations to the one-on-one (advantage to the federal government) matrix will the center be able to implement universal restrictions. If the center is initially successful in changing the matrix, the iteration of the game will further undercut the ability of the states to make their interjurisdictional commitments credible. The costs of distributing selective costs and benefits will decline as initial reform successes reduce subnational autonomy and hence the capacity to forge interstate collective action. As the credibility of federal will and capacity to limit subnational autonomy increases, the costs of interstate coordination also increase. This "policy feedback" effect helps explain the progressive path of reform despite Cardoso's weakened congressional position following the 1998 elections.

Path-dependent factors shaped the initial game in both the legislative and intergovernmental arenas in ways that gave Cardoso the opportunity to gain leverage over the states. The weakness of parties, which otherwise would have allowed state delegations a means for coordinating cross-jurisdictionally, helped fragment the *bancadas subnacionais*. Historic rivalries between northeastern and southern states that continued into the democratic period kept the states divided, although negotiations over the constitution produced moments of universal collaboration ("all-on-one") regarding the rules of fiscal federalism. Yet as powerful as the states were in universalizing a set of fiscal rules in the new constitution that protected their interests, the persistence of rivalries and partisan weakness undercut prolonged coordination. This was more than apparent in the emerging "fiscal war" among state tax incentive schemes to attract investors during the late 1980s and throughout the 1990s. Cardoso's ability to periodically take advantage of these rivalries prevented the intergovernmental game from becoming "all-on-one." The dominant configuration was "one-on-one" in favor of the states. The governors retained a capacity to resist constitutional fiscal adjustment and to individually negotiate debt workouts with the federal government. Broader coordination (a "some-on-one" matrix) was limited due to the historic rivalries deepened by the "fiscal war."

With the *Real Plan*, the costs of financing state debt and the "fiscal war" soared. This shift in the political economic context of federalism aided Cardoso's efforts to strengthen regulations of subnational spending and finance. As central monetary authorities—the Central Bank, the CMN (National Monetary Council), and the Finance Ministry—gained leverage over state banks and fiscal accounts, the center's capacity to sanction expanded, undercutting interjurisdictional commitments to coordinate subnational opposition. The slow but progressive passage of enabling legislation that gave the federal government increased control over fiscal transfers, and set limits on subnational spending, gradually shifted the intergovernmental bargaining matrix from a "one-on-one" configuration that advantaged the states, to one that tipped in favor of the executive.

Tipping the Intergovernmental Equilibrium to the Executive

The three levels of analysis outlined above interacted in the Brazilian context in complex ways. During the bureaucratic authoritarian and early democratic transition periods, the states gained important fiscal and policymaking authority. But subnational rivalries and constitutional and extraconstitutional precedents would later facilitate ad hoc recentralization. In the meantime, the expanded fiscal powers of the states deepened perverse macroeconomic and financial crises that would bedevil national reform. State profligacy, particularly in the form of competing tax abatements to attract foreign investors ("the fiscal war"), would help divide the states and later increase the fiscal pressure on the governors to commit to structural reform. The *Real Plan* would end the years of megainflation and finally set the stage for a series of stopgap fiscal reforms that would take place in the dual arena of executive-legislative and intergovernmental relations.

The Bureaucratic Authoritarian and Democratic Transition Periods

Although it is tempting to generalize the bureaucratic authoritarian period as one of centralization and the democratic period (the New Republic) was one of decentralization, the periodization analyzed here shows little evidence of a distinctly sequenced centralization-decentralization process. Rather, each period created precedents that shaped and even enhanced the opposite process. The military centralized control over fiscal federalism but it also devolved important taxation powers to the states that would prove crucial to the autonomy of state governments during the democratic period. The states expanded these powers during the New Republic, and particularly during the Constituent Assembly, when they moved to an "all-on-one" position. But they also accepted precedents that would enhance federal regulation of fiscal federalism during the 1990s. Moreover, the path dependencies of subnational rivalries remained apparent in both periods. During the authoritarian regime, the military solicited subnational support among the conservative center-western, northeastern, and northern states. During the New Republic, the rich states opposed efforts by poor states for redistributive fiscal rules and all engaged in an escalating "fiscal war."

The bureaucratic authoritarian period initiated with the coup of 1964 strengthened federal authority over the states and municipalities in unprecedented ways. In late 1965 the military government centralized control over state governments as a means of undercutting subnational politicians who were poised to resist the deepening of authoritarianism (Sallum, 1996: 30–32). Institutional Act number 3 suspended the direct election of governors in February 1966 and gave the military regime the power to veto candidates put forth by state legislators. In addition to the military's centralization of security forces (e.g., police, state militias, etc.), the regime also took greater control over subnational taxation and spending. Through a constitutional amendment in 1967, the federal government gained control of ten out of the country's fourteen taxes. States administered the tax on the exchange of real estate (*Imposto sobre a Transmissão de Bens Imóveis*, ITBI), the new value-added tax, and the tax on the circulation of goods (*Imposto sobre Circulação de Mercadorias*, ICM). Yet the military government controlled ITBI and ICM rates and determined how revenues would be spent.

The military also used its discretion over resources to reward supporters and punish opponents to the regime. The armed forces used decentralization to build support for the regime among the conservative states of the north and northeast by creating new fiscal transfers (Selcher, 1990). These states had small tax bases and therefore depended upon transfers from a revenue-sharing fund (*Fundo de Participação dos Estados e Municípios*, FPEM) that was split 50–50 between states (FPE) and municipalities (FPM). More than 51 percent of total revenues for the northern states and more than 26 percent of total revenues for the northeast came from fiscal transfers (Sallum, 1996: 37). At the same time, the generals undercut the southeastern states, where most of the civilian opposition was based, by moving or granting new public firm investments in alternative areas. During the liberalization period (1974–1985) developmentalist projects were allocated to states under the control of regional elites that had shown their dedication to the regime.

The dynamic changed with the direct election of the governors in 1982. These contests, which occurred seven years before the president was directly elected, made the governors leaders of the popular movement against authoritarianism and the chief civilian negotiators of the terms of transition (Almeida, 1996b: 225). Empowered by a reservoir of democratic legitimacy, the governors mobilized support through distributional and clientelistic networks in favor of increased federal transfers and enhanced subnational control over ICMS (Abrúcio, 1998). In 1983, the Congress passed the Passos Porto Amendment, which expanded the FPEM funds and enhanced subnational discretion over these resources. Another fiscal reform in 1984 (the Airton Sandoval Amendment) increased subnational tax collection authority. Thus imbued with political and resource autonomy, the *bancadas subnacionais* emerged in their strongest position yet during the New Republic. They exerted their influence most clearly in the Constituent Assembly of 1987–1988, where they played a leading role in shaping the rules governing fiscal federalism in favor of subnational autonomy (C. Souza, 1997; Martínez-Lara, 1996).

The *bancadas subnacionais* succeeded in locking in constitutional rules that decentralized fiscal resources. The 1988 constitution eliminated federal taxes on transportation, electricity, fuel, and mining and combined these into the ICMS. It also expanded the Passos Porto Amendment by increasing state and municipal transfers. The growth of federal transfers and the expansion of the ICMS led to a drop in the federal share of tax revenues and an increase in state shares. Municipalities had their share of ICMS raised from 20 to 25 percent. State constitutions bestowed other powers onto the states, including the autonomy of state banks from central monetary authorities. The governors then used these banks to finance expenditures and dispense patronage (Sola, 1994: 165; 1995).

The 1988 constitution, however, was not a complete subnational coup against the federal government. First, the politics of the assembly deepened historical rivalries among the *bancadas subnacionais*. While the poor northern and northeastern states pushed for redistributive tax rules, the southern and southeastern states fervently opposed such efforts. Second, the new constitution did not prevent the federal government from imposing borrowing constraints on subnational governments—just the contrary. The constitution authorized the federal government to limit the growth of subnational debt, a precedent that would prove useful during the 1990s as presidents, their finance ministers, the Central Bank, and the National Monetary Council (CMN) maneuvered to do just that. Finally, the constitution proscribed the financing of state expenditures through state banks.

The Vicious Financial and Monetary Circle
The states had achieved a brief coordination of their common interests in the Constituent Assembly. This allowed them to garner resources and use them with little regard for macroeconomic stability or fiscal responsibility. The right to be irresponsible might have been a universal norm, but regional rivalries and the "fiscal war" would keep the governors from forming a more coordinated strategy in response to more concerted efforts by presidents in the 1990s to recentralize. However, presidential capacity to recentralize was limited initially due to President José Sarney's dwindling popularity and the fragmented congressional support of his successors. As a result, the configuration of intergovernmental relations throughout this period remained one-on-one (advantage to the states).

The dangers of fiscal decentralization in the context of macroeconomic instability were more than apparent. The governors' potential for excessive profligacy was great as many had already proven adept at maneuvering fiscal resources to their clientelistic bases during the transition (Hagopian, 1996). Not surprisingly, state spending expanded during the 1980s as the governors consolidated their political machines through appointments, expansion of government payrolls, and project spending. By 1995, the states had 3.6 million civil servants; double the number in the federal government (Afonso, 1996: 50). State payrolls averaged over 65 percent of current receipts.

The military had allowed the states' banks to finance government expenditures by carrying state bonds, issuing finance, and emitting money. Such practices continued during the New Republic as spending escalated according to electoral cycles. By 1992, the debt of the state banks was twice their total liquidity. Seignorage increased inflation and when state banks encountered liquidity problems in the early 1990s, the Central Bank was compelled to bail them out, generating a "moral hazard" problem (Hillbrecht, 1997: 60; Silva and Costa, 1995). By this time the states owed their banks US$22.8 billion and subnational governments composed roughly half of Brazil's operational deficit (Afonso, 1996: 37). What Lourdes Sola (1995: 48) calls the vicious financial and monetary merry-go-round ("*ciranda financeira e monetária*") undermined federal efforts to create and maintain price stability. The profligacy of the states added to the dismal failure of seven consecutive anti-inflation plans from 1985 to 1993.

Paradoxically, other aspects of what seemed to be unbridled and dangerous fiscal decentralization would set the stage for ad hoc recentralization later. True to their history of regional rivalries, the states used their newfound policy authorities and resources to compete against each other. As industry tended to concentrate in São Paulo and development policies designed for poor states, such as the Superintendency for the Development of the northeast (SUDENE), failed to reverse regional inequalities, the governors of poor and developing states created competing tax abatement schemes to lure foreign direct investors (Oliveira, 1995: 84–87; Rossi and Neri, 1995). In addition to competitive incentives, the governors spent on behalf of economic constituencies. In pursuing their own political interests, the governors were also protecting various interest groups linked to their states. The governors spent on behalf of indebted agrarian and industrial interests and failing banks (Almeida, 1996b: 225). These positions were competitive in that they not only opposed national reform efforts, but also sought to protect economic interests in their states by passing the costs of adjustment off to rival states.

Although the *bancadas subnacionais* were able to coordinate in "all-on-one" fashion during the Constituent Assembly, the years that followed saw escalating interstate competition that reduced the credibility of commitments to coordinate subnational interests. The 1988 constitution granted the states the authority to offer tax incentives on ICMS and many states did so in an attempt to attract automotive firms during the 1990s. The "fiscal war" escalated during the 1990s as states such as Rio de Janeiro, São Paulo, Minas Gerais, Rio Grande do Sul, Ceará, and Bahia, in particular, competed very publicly for automotive investments. Despite attempts by reformist governors, such as Eduardo Azeredo (Minas Gerais), to coordinate a common strategy to limit the costs of fiscal competition, the states retained their competitive posturing (Cavalcanti and Prado, 1998; Arbix, 2000).

Persistent efforts by state governments to weaken interstate coordination of fiscal policy followed the perverse norm that competition was preferable to cooperation (Rodriguez, 1995: 438–440). This could not have been more apparent than on the National Council of Fiscal Policy (CONFAZ), a constitutionally mandated entity under the command of the Ministry of Finance and composed of all the state finance secretaries. CONFAZ's purpose was to regulate state fiscal incentive schemes, but the *bancadas subnacionais* crippled CONFAZ by requiring that all decisions be made unanimously. Since all state governments preferred to have the authority to employ tax abatements competitively, no new scheme was proscribed by CONFAZ. States tended to barter their votes on the council in exchange for approval of their own programs (Affonso, 1995: 60).

As interstate coordination weakened, the federal government developed capacities for dealing with the problems generated by the ciranda, although they would not be fully utilized until much later. First, the Central Bank gained the ability to intervene state banks temporarily under Decree Law 2321. This experience for the Central Bank would prove important during subsequent governments as the failure of state banks would require more permanent solutions resulting from Central Bank intervention. Second, while the Sarney administration appeared impotent in the face of the *ciranda*, it took important steps to reinforce the powers of the executive in ways that would prove crucial to later macroeconomic stabilization efforts. Most notably, Sarney's interpretation of the constitutional power of decree as allowing him to reissue provisional measures (*Medidas Provisórias*) expanded the presidency's legislative authority (Power, 1998b: 204–205). It is doubtful that, absent this precedent, the *Real Plan* and ancillary fiscal reforms would have occurred during the 1990s (Couto, 1998: 77).

Partial Reequilibration: Collor and Itamar
Neither the Fernando Collor de Mello (1990–1992) nor the Itamar Franco (1992–1994) governments produced durable corrections to the problems posed by the *ciranda monetária e financeira*. However, these two presidencies initiated important neoliberal structural reforms that would play a role in building support for fiscal restructuring during the Cardoso administration. More important, these administrations practiced techniques that enhanced the powers of the presidency in the economic reform process. Collor and Itamar used their line-item veto authority, the power to issue and reissue provisional measures, and the presidential prerogative to shape annual budgets as the primary mechanisms to implement reforms. These experiences would prove

valuable to Cardoso in his relationship with Congress and the governors, for he would soon far exceed his predecessors in the exercise of executive authority.

Collor's initiatives in structural reform, and particularly the PND, created an early record of successful reform upon which Franco and Cardoso could rely. Most important, these subsequent administrations were not saddled with the responsibility of overseeing the restructuring of firms to be privatized nor did they have to fight the first and most difficult judicial contests against the opponents of structural reform. The modalities of privatization, which paid generous side payments to workers, divided working-class opposition to structural adjustment well before Cardoso's presidency (Montero, 1998). Opposition in the legislature to the structural adjustment agenda also changed in the 1991–1995 period, as support by a broad array of parties of the center and center-right in favor of the PND ran in excess of 60 percent (Almeida and Moya, 1997).

Several moves during the Collor and Itamar administrations helped stave off the deepening of the *ciranda monetária e financeira*. First, Collor threatened state banks with Central Bank intervention unless they initiated procedures to stop the taking on of nonperforming debt. While these threats were not backed up as strongly as they would be later, they were accompanied by more credible actions by central monetary authorities. Second, the federal government curtailed the states' access to credit. In May 1990, the National Monetary Council enforced stricter limits on state banks seeking to issue loans to the public sector. These signals repelled private investors away from state debt. Then, in 1993, the Senate passed constitutional restrictions on the emission of new state bonds used to roll over debt. Third, both Collor and Itamar raised federal tax revenues through crackdowns on tax evasion and administrative improvements to the main tax-collecting agency, the Secretaria da Receita Federal. Much of the increase in tax revenues was accorded to funds not subject to revenue-sharing with the states. The COFINS (Contribution for the Financing of the Social Security System) and the CSLL (Employers's Social Contribution for Social Security) increased between 1992 and 1995 by 173 and 66 percent, respectively (C. Souza, 1998). These funds amounted to 40 percent of federal revenues in 1994 and they continued to claim a larger share in subsequent years during the Cardoso administration (Montero, 2000: 68; Samuels, 2001: 10–11). Finally, both administrations decentralized service responsibilities, particularly in health care.

Perhaps the most important precedent for the exercise of presidential authority was Collor's penchant for implementing macroeconomic reform, including his ill-fated stabilization plans (*Collor I* and *II*), through the use of *Medidas Provisórias*. Although Cardoso faced the need to enact sweeping constitutional reforms that fell outside the purview of these decree powers, the use of *Medidas Provisórias* would prove crucial in implementing the *Real Plan* in 1994.

Shifting the Context of the Intergovernmental Game: Cardoso and the *Real Plan*

The inauguration of the *Real Plan* and the subsequent election of Fernando Henrique Cardoso in 1994 marked a turning point in the executive-legislative and intergovernmental arenas. Although the three previous administrations were unable to consolidate a constitutional reform agenda, they left valuable precedents for Cardoso to employ in both arenas. Unlike his predecessors, Cardoso could count on growing support for fiscal reform in Congress and the business sector, and an enhanced capacity by central monetary and financial regulators to implement restrictions on subnational debt and spending. The states, which had briefly coordinated their interests for the Constituent Assembly and then reverted to a one-on-one (advantage to the states) during the *ciranda financeira*, showed no signs of being able to unleash an unbridled fiscal decentralization of the state. A combination of the end of inflation, the increased regulatory power of central agencies, and stopgap fiscal reform legislation such as the FEF set the stage for recentralization.

Macroeconomic stabilization continued to dominate the economic reform agenda throughout the Collor and Franco governments, but the acute sense of crisis that permeated this issue by 1994 was unprecedented. Thus by the time Fernando Henrique Cardoso, Franco's finance minister, was prepared to launch what would become Brazil's most successful stabilization measure to date, the *Real Plan*, in 1994, significant support existed for a stepped-up program of economic restructuring (Mainwaring 1999: 314–315). Most major businesses, including those that had been privatized under Collor and Franco, had already initiated productive restructuring and were eager to see an end to megainflation (Kingstone, 1999). In contrast to the political fragmentation evident in Congress, a "pragmatic consensus" existed among Cardoso's economic team, business, and some liberal wings of major parties such as the PSDB, PMDB, and the PFL in support of inflation-control and some structural adjustment (Melo, 1997: 70–71; Almeida, 1996b). One recent study by Power (1998a) found that an absolute majority of representatives in the 50th Congress (1995–1999) described themselves as economic liberals.

Having succeeded in controlling inflation and surviving the Mexican peso crisis, Cardoso's government could count on a reserve of political support among centrist and conservative parties in Congress and major segments of business for fiscal reforms (Couto, 1998: 68; Power, 1998a: 60–62). Given an earlier shift in Congress in favor of the PND and structural adjustment, Cardoso faced not an ardently divided legislature set against macroeconomic and structural reform, but one willing to move the agenda forward, and to do so with legislation proposed by the president rather than the Congress (Figueiredo and Limongi, 2000a). The passage of the FEF in February 1994 was an early indicator of this shift.

The price stability created by the *Real Plan* laid bare the need to adjust fiscal accounts. In a reversal of the classic logic that posits central bank autonomy as a precondition for monetary stability, the price stability created by the *Real Plan* greatly strengthened the central monetary regulatory bodies—the Central Bank, the CMN, and the Finance Ministry. These entities gained leverage over the states and the state banks, who opposed centralization of monetary authority (Sola, Garman, and Marques, 1998). The *Real Plan* undercut the ability of the governors to use their state banks to finance expenditures. By cutting off the cash-strapped state banks from interbank credit, they were forced to turn to Central Bank bailouts. Central Bank intervention in the state banks removed these as financiers of state spending, further pressuring state fiscal accounts. Meanwhile, the end of megainflation increased these pressures by raising the real costs of servicing debt and eliminating the tactic of using inflation to reduce public payroll and supplier costs. The need to raise interest rates to stave off inflation effectively increased state and municipal debt and discouraged further borrowing (Dain, 1995: 359).

The *Real Plan* reduced information asymmetries that had previously bedeviled federal attempts to control subnational spending. First, the *Real Plan* enhanced the Central Bank's ability to measure subnational debt by eliminating "floating" debt with state banks (Afonso, 1996: 40–41). Second, by forcing Central Bank intervention in state banks and negotiating debt workouts, federal agencies gained insights into the composition and amount of subnational debt. Finally, the credit crunch in the private sector and federal restrictions preventing states from contracting foreign debt greatly restrained the degree to which state governments could significantly expand their primary deficits.

The *Real Plan* became a turning point in the intergovernmental game as Cardoso was able to employ the stick of Central Bank intervention in state banks and the carrot of debt workouts to compel and cajole the governors, one after another, to implement fiscal reforms and privatization of state utility and financial going concerns (Affonso, 1997; Montero, 2000). Under the Program to Support Restructuring and Fiscal Adjustment in the States, the federal government began negotiating the terms of debt workouts. These required the governors to privatize state firms, transfer holdings to the federal government, and initiate downsizing of the civil service. The workouts involved exchanges of state bonds for treasury bonds and Central Bank bonds. Given high interest rates on federal bonds (e.g., 22–25 percent in 1995), the stock of bond debt grew during the mid- to late 1990s. States contracted federal loans to pay off payroll and contractors' obligations. The National Treasury thus garnered more than 87 percent of all subnational debt. By mid-1999, the central government had rescheduled the debt of 24 of 27 state governments and bailed out the states involved in a US$22 billion public bond scandal (the *precatórios*). These conditions are indicative of a shift from a "one-on-one" (advantage to the states) configuration to a "one-on-one" (advantage to the federal government) configuration.

Three pieces of legislation heightened the fiscal pressures on the states to comply with the terms of federal intervention. The FEF continued to constrain state government accounts, forcing most to consider privatizing their major public enterprises (Tavares, 1997). The Camata Law, passed in March 1995, threatened states with the suspension of constitutionally mandated federal transfers if they failed to reduce their public payrolls to under 60 percent of net annual revenues. The federal government then reduced state revenues by exempting all primary and semi-manufactured exports from ICMS in September 1996. The Kandir Law, named after Cardoso's planning minister, Antônio Kandir, added a vague promise that state governments would be compensated for their revenue losses. Yet delays and false promises hindered compensation. Reimbursement for their losses became a generalized demand of the governors. However, Cardoso held out the possibility more as a carrot to cajole subnational support for structural adjustment than as a serious commitment.

As the FEF and the Kandir Law became special targets of subnational protests, the presidency took additional steps to keep the states' opposition uncoordinated. Cardoso exacerbated the fiscal war by continually avoiding opportunities to legislate impediments to competitive fiscal incentives. He even added to the competition by offering selective federal incentives to prospective investors. In March 1997, Provisional Measure 1532 escalated interstate tensions by offering federal tax incentives for automotive investments locating in the northeastern, northern, and center-western areas. In a highly public example of the extent to which Cardoso would go to keep the states divided, he promised federal incentives for a new Ford plant in Bahia that was originally promised to the opposition governor of Rio Grande do Sul. The deal sparked competition between the northeastern states that rallied behind Bahia and the industrial southern states, but it had a more generalized effect of reminding the governors that they were competitors. ·

As the presidency assumed the new leverage accorded it by the Camata and Kandir laws, federal monetary authorities closed off some of the financial channels that would otherwise have allowed the governors to continue the *ciranda financeira*. In August 1996 the CMN was able to halt states' issuance of new bonds until their annual revenue exceeded their debt. This restriction effectively eliminated new bond finance for a period in most cases exceeding ten years.

Cardoso used his prerogative to shape the annual budget (*Lei de Diretrizes Orçamentárias*—LDO) to distribute discretionary carrots to state *bancadas* in return for political support for reform. After the 1993 budget scandal, key congressional leaders avoided taking on greater protagonism over the budget (Werneck, 2000: B2). The breakup of the "budget mafia," in which a few deputies controlled amendments to the budget, distributed the share of budget "pork" more evenly. But Cardoso used his discretion over the programmed transfer of funds to reward supporters and punish opposition deputies (Ames, 2001: 230). This helps to explain why the PFL, an archetypal clientelist party, provided some of the most consistent support to Cardoso's reform agenda during the 50th Legislature (Power, 1998a).

Whatever the combination of carrots and sticks in the president's employ, the strategy worked to push the fiscal reform process forward. The pace of subnational structural adjustment picked up markedly during the 1997–2000 period as the governors sold off their state banks and utility companies as part of their debt rescheduling agreements with the federal government. During this time, seven state-owned or recently federalized state banks sold (BANERJ, Credireal, Bemge, Bandepe, Beneb, Banestado, and BANESPA) for US$5 billion. Seven more, with assets totaling US$8 billion, awaited sale at the end of 2000. The list includes financial institutions from the four largest debtor states—São Paulo, Rio de Janeiro, Minas Gerais, and Rio Grande do Sul, which together account for 90 percent of all subnational debt. Additionally, numerous utility, public works, and transport companies have already been sold off, generating over US$23.5 billion as of 1999. The federal government gained shares in privatized firms and bargained for other concessions as part of specialized packages negotiated with each state government.

The permanent quality of subnational adjustments such as privatization suggests that, unlike previous attempts to limit the governors' profligacy, Cardoso has been able to engineer several endgame conditions. First, federal restrictions on the growth of subnational debt are much tighter and permanent. In June 1998, the CMN halted the states' abilities to contract new foreign debt. In September 1998, the Senate passed Resolution 78 empowering the Central Bank to impose debt ceilings and other limits on subnational borrowing, including proscriptions against the emission of bonds until 2010. Second, debt workouts elicited commitments to restrain the growth of new debt. States agreeing to reschedule their debt were prohibited from emitting new debt notes (although agreements have not stopped capitalization of interest on continuing bond debt). Finally, the "one-on-one" dynamics of the intergovernmental game have produced selective benefits for the federal government as particular states have used their resources in creative ways to restructure their debts. For example, the state of Rio de Janeiro granted the federal government the state's royalties from petroleum exploration (10 percent of annual receipts in the sector) for thirty years in order to halve Rio's debt with Brasília.

To be sure, federal solutions to the problem of state debt incurred massive fiscal costs. The restructuring of state banks cost an estimated US$43.9 billion in federal loans to the states at below-market real interest rates not over 6 percent. These costs might be greater still in the absence of hard budget constraints on subnational government. However, with the passage of the Law of Fiscal Responsibility (LRF) in June 2000, the presidency may finally be in a position to fundamentally alter the intergovernmental game.

Endgame(?): The Law of Fiscal Responsibility

A condition Barbara Geddes (1994) identifies as one requisite for congressional support for reform is the rough parity of advantages/costs among politicians. In the wake of the extension of the FEF and implementation of the Kandir law, many governors and federal legislators complained that the costs of fiscal austerity were being shifted unfairly to the subnational level, while the president and his ministers had unrestricted access to patronage. The LRF, however, offered a credible set of commitments that the federal government would also "tie its hands" by adopting the same stringent spending limits. This prompted more congressional support for the LRF than would otherwise have been possible (Greggianin, 2000). Although some judicial challenges lingered into the end of 2000, the measure passed in June and survived with few modifications into 2001.

The LRF mandates that states and the federal government follow a stringent set of spending ceilings. Articles 19 and 20 establish a spending limit on payroll of 60 percent of revenues, which is divided among the various powers (executive, legislative, judicial, and public ministries). As of the end of 1998, expenditures on the civil service were 65.7 percent of current revenues. The LRF commands that 50 percent of the excess be cut within the first year of the law (2001), with the remainder to be eliminated within the following year. Article 17 determines that no new spending can occur without a corresponding increase in revenues. Article 35 sets limits on contracting of new debt until all old debt is paid. Most important, the LRF ended the moral hazard of having the Central Bank roll over state bank debt by prohibiting further rescheduling of subnational debt after May 2000. Taken together, the LRF's proscriptions are substantial, as are the penalties for noncompliance:

the freezing of federal transfers, restrictions on external finance, and criminal penalties for officials found guilty of violating the law.

By forcing states to finance current expenditures with revenues, states and municipalities have had to enforce drastic cuts and bureaucratic restructuring but also initiate structural reforms. For example, after November 2000, Mato Grosso do Sul's governor, José Orcírio Miranda dos Santos ("*Zeca*") of the Workers' Party, cut the number of political appointees in state government by half, initiated voluntary retirement programs for the civil service, increased workers' pension contributions, and increased tax revenues (*The Economist*, 2001, 35). Other states, such as Bahia, used proceeds from state privatization to finance public pensions and reduce civil service costs (Lavoratti, 2000). Similar reforms have emerged in several states. In the municipalities, the use of new management systems and technologies has improved service delivery and revenue performance (Afonso and Mello, 2000). Overall, the fiscal health of subnational governments is steadily improving. Since the time that the LRF was first discussed in Congress in 1999, the overall fiscal standing of the Brazilian states has moved from one of primary deficits to surpluses. To be sure, the sustainability of these efforts remains the main question. The advent of the LRF will help. Through the beginning of 2001, the LRF remained (despite several court challenges and intense lobbying by newly elected mayors) the source of a new level of hard budget constraints imposed on states and municipalities by the center (Mignone, 2001: 6).

In the wake of the LRF many states have also taken a second look at their fiscal incentives schemes (Cavalcanti, 2000: A3). Complementary Law 101/ 2000 requires that states increase taxes to compensate for the concession of tax revenues to firms. Independently, the governors have also started to use the courts to impose restrictions on the use of fiscal incentives by their rivals. These restrictions will not eliminate the "fiscal war" but they will compel governors to be more fiscally strategic and politically judicious in the way they engage in interjurisdictional competition (Herrisson and Frazão, 2000).

Overall, the LRF broadens the president's capacities to limit subnational profligacy. However, a couple of caveats are worth noting. First, the implementation of many of the LRF's key provisions will depend upon the maintenance of good relations between the executive and the legislature. For example, changes in subnational debt levels must still be approved by the Senate in response to a formal request by the president. This provision opens the door to the possibility that a president will compromise the fiscal probity of a sound request in order to get the Senate's approval for another piece of reform legislation. Second, actual implementation will depend on the capacity of state and municipal governments, and not just their interests. The LRF employs a number of "sticks" to extract compliance, but it is short on "carrots" to enable subnational governments to provide public services while they attempt to meet fiscal targets. The National Bank of Economic and Social Development (BNDES) and some international financial institutions such as the World Bank and the Inter-American Development Bank are actively promoting efforts to improve subnational government capacity. Yet it is not clear that time is on their side. Growing regionwide and global financial crises may deepen the parlous situation of many subnational governments and take them beyond these kinds of help.

Conclusion

The LRF was only the latest in a series of stopgap fiscal reforms that tended to slow and in some aspects stop the *ciranda monetária e financeira*. Such legislation enabled the president in the second arena of intergovernmental distributive conflict, even as several years of "fiscal war" fed by historical regional inequalities and rivalries kept the governors from coordinating in a sustained manner. Path-dependent factors and strategic choices in both the legislative and intergovernmental arenas tipped bargaining leverage in favor of the executive, producing an ad hoc reequilibration of fiscal authorities.

A more exclusively institutional approach to explaining change in Brazilian federalism would emphasize the heavy costs and inefficiencies of the process due to the weakness of political parties and the pervasive obstacles created by numerous "veto players" in the country's politics. Given the slow, stopgap nature of the reforms and the lateness of seemingly "endgame" conditions created by the LRF, the evidence in this chapter would support such evaluations. However, the capacity of institutional theories to explain the dynamics of decentralization in Brazil is limited since political institutions and the number of veto players did not change significantly during the process. Noninstitutional or "historical institutional" factors involving presidential strategy and path dependency explain how the changing distributive context of the intergovernmental game altered the politics of decentralization in ways that favored recentralization.

The Brazilian experience demonstrates the importance of studying the politics of decentralization with a broad temporal and multidimensional lens. Analyses that focus exclusively on executive-legislative dynamics, the party system, the interests and powers of the governors, or the legislative policy-making process miss the way that the intergovernmental distributive game overlaps these areas and subsumes them into two linked arenas. Both are shaped by historical legacies involving interjurisdictional rivalries and presidential powers.

For Brazil, the story revealed in this chapter suggests that although policymaking regarding fiscal federalism remains disjointed and costly, presidents may still engineer progressive reforms of the system. Unable to produce the sweeping constitutional reform he wanted in 1995, Cardoso settled for a prolonged, two-term strategy that will no doubt make him the most successful Brazilian president in the country's short democratic reform period. Yet enduring success may depend on a more assertive reform of the very fiscal and political institutional constraints that have made the recentralization process so stopgap and tortured.

CHAPTER 8

Industrialists and Liberalization

Peter Kingstone

The Roman Emperor Domitian once claimed that emperors are "necessarily wretched since only their assassination can convince the public that the conspiracies against their lives are real" (Suetonius, 1957: 308). To some extent, this statement is an apt analogy for Brazilian industrialists who endured a variety of unflattering portrayals as a consequence of their almost incessant complaining about the neoliberal reform program. Industrialists complained about a lack of strategic vision, a lack of program coherence, a lack of policy stability and predictability (and under Collor, credibility), and a lack of interest in policy beyond monetarist approaches to price stability. In exchange, many academics (for example, Lal and Maxfield, 1993 or Nylen, 1992) and members of the Collor and Cardoso administrations (the two key neoliberal reform presidents) cast industrialists as "obstacles to modernization," "cartorialists," "oligopolists," and "protectionists." This negative image has persisted, even though the evidence from at least 1996 on has tended toward confirming industrialists' complaints. This image downplays the coherence of industrialists' critique of government policy and misses the extent to which they support the general policy direction.

This chapter argues two points. First, time has proven many of the industrial community's complaints to be well justified. Most importantly, the industrial community argued that an array of issues—especially the tax system—created a "Brazil Cost" that undermined competitiveness and weakened Brazil as an exporter of manufactured goods. Second, despite the Brazil Cost and complaints about the economic reform process, industrialists have actively engaged in competitive restructuring. The result has been real and significant change at the microlevel with domestic producers remaining crucial players in the economy. Yet, important issues remain unresolved with uncertain consequences for the future. Industrialists have been calling since the late 1970s for a national discussion of development. This paper suggests such a call is warranted.

Criticism of the Brazilian Industrialist Community

Criticism of the Brazilian industrialist community, especially from São Paulo, typically has had two elements. In one argument, industrialists are portrayed as hypocrites because they say that they support reform publicly, but oppose it privately (Nylen, 1992; Diniz and Boschi 1993a). In another view, industrialists are presented as vocal and visible obstacles to "modernization" (Cardoso and Figueiredo, 1992).[1] Both views point to the same sets of behaviors: industrialists have actively lobbied government agencies and ministers for individual benefits and have been a virtually constant source of criticism of government policy since the beginning of the reform process generally and the commercial liberalization process specifically. Thus, these characterizations appear to have been warranted. Yet, the superficial reaction bears further examination.

The first view recognizes that, in public at least, industrialists have often taken positions in support of the reform process generally and commercial liberalization specifically. Yet, the contention is that the public position is only for show and conceals a commitment to the old status quo of state protection and subsidization. One troubling aspect of this view, however, is that there is no clear argument as to why industrialists would take this public position and especially why they would adhere to it relatively consistently from the late 1980s on. If businesspeople are hypocrites then there should be some plausible basis that explains why.

The second view, articulated by officials in both the Collor and Cardoso governments, takes the burden of responsibility off the government. In that view, bad or incoherent policy, or administrative inability to deal with macroeconomic shocks is dismissed as a principal cause of obstacles to reform. But this view—besides being potentially viewed as highly self-serving for government officials—ignores the considerable evidence of business support for reforms as well as the considerable evidence of competitive restructuring at the microlevel.

There are several potential sources of evidence for industrialists' support of commercial liberalization in particular and neoliberal reform in general. Certainly, industrial leaders in a variety of organizations articulated pro-reform positions throughout the late 1980s. The strongest source of evidence,

---

1.   In addition, this position has been a view articulated by both the Cardoso government and the Collor government. Both governments have faced extensive criticism from the business community and Collor faced in addition a political mobilization designed to weaken or control him. Both governments have had good, self-serving interests to dismiss industrialists' criticism as the complaints of "cartorialists."

however, may come from the National Confederation of Industry's (CNI) annual surveys on commercial liberalization from 1991 to 1995 (Confederação Nacional da Indústria, various years).[2] For example, the 1995 survey showed strong support in every sector of industry. At least a large majority favored commercial liberalization, even in those with the highest levels of opposition, such as textiles or rubber.

Thus, both industrialists' behavior and attitudes present something of a puzzle. On the one hand, evidence from a variety of sources suggests meaningful support for the reform process and for commercial liberalization specifically. On the other hand, the evidence also points to virtually incessant criticism of the government with respect to the reform process and considerable anecdotal evidence of active business lobbying for narrow, particularist benefits. Rather than dismiss evidence of one set of behaviors or another, it is worthwhile further considering the sources of industrialists' attitudes and behavior. Most importantly, the "hypocrite" and the "protectionist opposition" views underestimate three factors: the way the organization of business and government affect the pattern of lobbying; the evolution and content of industrialists's complaints since at least 1978; and the relation between macroeconomic instability and microlevel adjustment efforts.

Evolution of Industrialists' Concerns

The São Paulo-based industrial community was an important partner in Brazil's developmental project, especially starting in the 1950s as both Getúlio Vargas and Juscelino Kubitschek aggressively promoted import-substitution industrialization (Addis, 1999; Leopoldi, 1984). São Paulo became one of the crucial centers of support for nationalist, development policy, and not surprisingly prospered considerably under the program. Thus, perceiving Paulista industrialists as nationalist opponents of neoliberal reform is certainly consistent with their past behavior and beliefs.

The Paulista industrialist leadership, however, began to articulate an alternative set of views, dating at least back to the "Democratic Manifesto of the Bourgeoisie" of 1978. The Manifesto was an open letter in the *Gazeta Mercantil* to the military government signed by eight of the most influential industrialists in the country. The letter captured considerable attention for its call for an end to military rule. It also articulated a set of concerns about the economy and the need to rethink the country's national development strategy. By 1978, it was becoming clear that ISI was reaching its conclusion and the Democratic Manifesto signatories argued that a new government-busi-

---

2.   Research conducted by Gesner Oliveira at CEBRAP found high levels of support in 1990–1991 (Oliveira, 1993). Similarly, my own interviews in the early 1990s (Kingstone, 1999) also found high levels of support for the shift in policy.

ness partnership was needed to identify and overcome the challenges of continued development. The call was reiterated in the less noted "Document of the 12" of 1983.[3] By that time, the Brazilian economy was in serious disarray and its structural problems apparent to industrialists.[4]

The set of concerns about the gap between the developed world and Brazil increasingly expressed themselves under a label invented in the National Development Bank: competitive integration. This view, held within the industrial community and among some members of the bank, argued that Brazil had to move away from ISI toward an active and full integration with the world economy. This view was not a strict neoliberal view.[5] Instead, the competitive integration view point argued for a role for government as a partner in the integration process. The idea was to manage the character and pace of integration so as to ensure that the Brazilian economy opened on its own terms with a commitment to maintaining competitive domestic producers.

The competitive integration view identified two critical problems in the Brazilian economy. First, the economy was bifurcated, with a relatively competitive, modern segment and a relatively uncompetitive, backward segment. While the former was conscious of the problems that existed and was concerned about maintaining competitiveness, the second was not. This backward segment was a drag on economic development and highly vulnerable in the event of an economic opening. Thus, competitive integration needed to focus on policy mechanisms that could help close the gap between the two segments. The second problem was that the economic crisis of the 1980s and the failure of the government to respond was hindering the efforts of the modern segment to stay competitive and therefore widening the gap between Brazil's best sectors and the developed world.

The competitive integration called for two government responses to this issue. First, industrial leaders wanted policymakers to define a strategic vision for economic development and for competitive integration. In practice, that meant having government and industry work out an understanding of which sectors were crucial to maintain and promote, and therefore where government priorities would lie. Industrialists sought some guidance in a

---

3. Both the original "Document of the 8" (or the Democratic Manifesto) and the later "Document of the 12" are reprinted in the *Gazeta Mercantil*'s Balanço Anual of 1996–1997 (p. 17–22).
4. Industrialists' perception that something had to change was reinforced further by the experience of exporting—a strategy many firms followed to escape the domestic recession. Attempting to export their way out of recession demonstrated to many industrialists that the technological gap between the developed world and Brazilian producers was growing.
5. A more liberal view was emerging out of other organizations, such as the Liberal Institute, founded in Rio and then established in São Paulo (Gros, 1993). Yet, the Liberal Institute, like the "Campaign against 'Statization'" of the 1970s, had a prominent nonbusiness and intellectual component. Moreover, at its founding in 1983, the Liberal Institute certainly lacked allies in a government that remained committed to ISI.

context of tremendous macroeconomic and economic policy uncertainty. Rather than have individual and potentially suboptimal investment strategies, industrial leaders preferred to follow an investment strategy linked to an overall vision of Brazilian development. Once such a strategic vision existed, the competitive integration view called for government policymakers to identify the most efficient and effective policy tools for promoting their strategic ends.

Of course, such a plan never really materialized. The military rulers spent the remainder of their years focusing on strict monetarist solutions to debt, deficits, and inflation. Sarney's economic policymaking was characterized by instability and ineffectiveness. Although the Sarney administration did produce an industrial policy in conjunction with business representatives, the plan was almost entirely ignored. Instead, the Sarney administration brought two new problems to the industrial community. On the one hand, bad economic policy brought levels of economic disarray the likes of which industrialists had never encountered. Brazilians were battered by extremely volatile growth rates coupled with a steady upward spiral of inflation. At the micro-level, the effect was utterly chaotic. Industrialists coped by speculating financially and by continuously raising margins on continuously shrinking volumes. Firms survived and many even continued to earn profits, but among industrial leaders there was no question that the strategy was unsustainable.

The second problem that emerged with the Sarney administration was the 1988 constitution, which was widely condemned by the business community. Business leaders were furious about several crucial elements, including the extensive detailed labor legislation, ceilings on interest rates, the system of federal transfer payments, and restrictions on foreign investments. This last issue was salient particularly in sectors such as energy and telecommunications where industrialists felt it was clear that the State could no longer invest and domestic producers lacked the resources to take its place. Some analysts regard the 1988 constitution as a victory for business groups because they were able to mount a substantial campaign to forge a "center" bloc that successfully tempered or repealed many articles opposed by business (e.g., Payne, 1994). Within the industrial community, however, the perception is that business groups lost as the constitution retained many of its worst problems—evidence of business organizations's failure to get involved in the writing of the first draft (Kingstone, 1999).

In any event, the two issues played an instrumental role in encouraging the formation of new business organizations, such as the Pensamento Nacional das Bases Empresariais (PNBE) or the Instituto dos Estudos de Desenvolvimento Industrial (IEDI), and reforms in existing organizations, such as within the Machine Tools and Equipment Syndicate (ABIMAQ/SINDI-

MAQ) and within the Auto Parts Syndicate (ABIPEÇAS/SINDIPEÇAS). Both new and reformed organizations played an important role in generating criticism of the existing pattern of business-state relations, of government policy, and of the country's development strategy generally. Increasingly, the set of demands emerging from different sources echoed a similar set of themes—many of them consistent with the view of competitive integration. Among the most important themes, industrial leaders called for a withdrawal of the state—again not on strict neoliberal lines. But, industrialists recognized that state regulation of a wide array of areas, such as prices for example, had become politicized and erratic. As a consequence, state regulation was producing more harm than good. Furthermore, the bankrupt state was incapable of investing in key areas and incapable of paying its bills and was thus crowding out private investment through its extensive borrowing requirements. In short, industrialists called for a removal of the elements that produced market distortions and discouraged investment. As part of that, a number of business organizations explicitly called for commercial liberalization, privatization, and liberalization of foreign investment rules (IEDI, 1990, 1992a; Kingstone, 1998).

It is important to reiterate that these calls did not emerge from an ideological commitment to neoliberalism. Nor were the specific business proposals strictly neoliberal in their design. Instead, industrialists articulated a pragmatic approach that was designed to address the clear failures of government policy at the microlevel. Industrialists' policy recommendations contained nationalist elements in the sense that they were oriented toward maintaining and promoting domestic producers. They also contained neoliberal elements because it was abundantly clear by 1990 that the State had lost the capacity to drive development, and foreign capital and technology was needed in order to resume sustained growth. At the core of the various proposals coming out of the industrialist community lay a concern with competitiveness: both a diagnosis of the factors dampening competitiveness and a set of policy recommendations for improving it.

Ultimately, the onset of serious neoliberal reforms with President Fernando Collor in 1990 did not proceed in the ideal way envisioned by diverse groups including PNBE and IEDI. Despite meaningful business participation in some aspects of the design of reforms (such as the trade liberalization or the Brazilian Program for Quality and Productivity), the Collor government did not consult much with the industrial community. In fact, Collor's government added the insult of demonizing industrialists to the injury of excluding them from policy deliberations (Kingstone, 2000). The onset of neoliberal reforms without active coordination between business and government made a number of industrialists' preferences moot. For example, in interviews, some industrialists expressed the hope that the government would work with industry to develop leading conglomerates, along the lines of Korean "chaebol." By the early 1990s, it was clear that this was not going to happen. IEDI, in particular, developed a vision of industry-government partnership to foster a new development strategy. Yet, by the mid-1990s, that idea had also become moot. Instead, industrialists were forced to adapt to the realities of adjustment to freer trade even though the macroeconomic environment remained highly unstable (Kingstone, 1998).

Nevertheless, the focus of industrialist leaders remained on competitiveness. By the mid-1990s, industrialists had abandoned the language of competitive integration and instead focused more explicitly on the factors that continued to limit the success of domestic producers and the development of the economy. These factors were linked together under the label of the "Brazil Cost"—a term that referred to a specific set of problems external to firms that hindered competitive adjustments. The thinking behind it was again pragmatic (Federação da Indústria e Comércio, 1997). For industrialists, it was fair to demand competitive adjustments in the firm. Every individual firm and sectoral association was responsible for doing what it could to increase competitiveness. Firms and sectoral associations, however, could not solve systemic problems that depended on government policy. Thus, industrialists pointed to the inefficiencies of the tax system. They pointed to rigid and excessively detailed labor laws that restricted managerial autonomy, increased the cost of labor, and ultimately resulted in lower levels of employment. They observed that the failure to reform the social security system (Previdência) and the civil service system had direct and perverse consequences for the country's macroeconomic performance. Finally, they also expressed concern with the level of real interest rates and the overvaluation of the exchange rate, although many industrialists in surveys and in interviews understood the link between interest rates, exchanges rates, and the maintenance of the *Real Plan*.

Industrialists' proposals came out in a variety of forms and from a variety of organizations, although increasingly with the leadership of the CNI. Many of the proposals were developed in conjunction with professional economists, through think tanks such as the Liberal Institute or the Roberto Simonsen Institute of the Federation of Industry of the State of São Paulo.

The Cardoso government paid closer attention to industrialists' concerns than the Collor government. The Cardoso administration was much more careful to choose ministers of industry and of planning who are sensitive to industry's needs. Members of the government made visible efforts to meet with industry leaders in crucial organizations such as the Federation of Industries of the State of São Paulo (FIESP). Industrialists' proposals have been incorporated, to some extent, into government policy, probably most notably in the Kandir Law of 1996 and its set of export and competitiveness-oriented measures. Overall though, the Cardoso government has subordinated economic policy to the demands of financial stability. As a consequence, industrialists' concerns have not been effectively addressed and the São Paulo-based industrial community continues to appear as a vocal, critical community that is frequently and easily dismissed as a defender of narrow self-interests.

That dismissal is unfortunate. There is no question that São Paulo-based industrialists defend their self-interests—much like any other group. Nevertheless, many of their criticisms over the past twenty years have been accurate and fair. From roughly 1978 on, leaders in the industrial community have articulated a set of recommendations that have flowed from a coherent view of the problems of competitiveness in Brazil. Despite considerable changes at the microlevel, the Brazilian economy continues to perform below potential, for many of the reasons indicated throughout the 1990s by the industrial community. Yet, if business organizations and leaders have articulated a coherent message about development policy, it is still true that much of their lobbying behavior has been oriented to narrow, particularist benefits. That contradiction seems to give greater weight to the claim of hypocrisy. Understanding the split between the two sets of behaviors requires further discussion of the organizational bases of business behavior.

Organized Business and the Problems of Collective Action

Why do business leaders articulate a coherent development vision while at the same time actively pursuing private benefits for themselves—even when those contradict their public positions or challenge the integrity of development policy? The answer lies in three different aspects of business-state relations and business and state organization. First, business interests organized themselves in narrow, sectoral, and particularist organizations as opposed to broad and encompassing organizations. Second, the Brazilian government remains highly fragmented in terms of its control over the allocation of benefits to business. Finally, the persistence of a "politicized marketplace" and politicized access to government resources forces firms to continue to lobby for their own individual interests or risk losing out to competitors that continue to operate politically.

Mancur Olson's work on collective action led to crucial observations about the relationship between the composition of groups and the kinds of collective goods they seek. Groups with very broad membership ("encompassing organizations") have an interest in promoting policies that enlarge the overall pie so that each of their very many individual shares is larger.

Narrow, particularist groups, however, have no incentive to concern themselves with the size of the overall pie. Rather, the incentive for particularist groups is to obtain targeted benefits that provide a sizable payoff to their few members regardless of the size of the pie or for the consequences of their behavior for the growth rate of the pie.

The organization of business interests in Brazil is highly fragmented, by design, into multiple particularist organizations (Diniz and Boschi, 1979). The corporatist system of organization that dates back to the Consolidação das Leis do Trabalho (CLT) of 1937 divides business interests into sectoral and often regional specific associations. The logic of this organization prevents cross-sectoral associations from forming. In fact, the character of the associations also has the tendency to discourage large, powerful firms from relying on their associations, thereby fragmenting business interests even further. Industrialists have been able to create reasonable facsimiles of encompassing "peak" associations in several instances and in several ways. For example, the effort to amend the writing of the 1988 constitution was led by a short-lived organization called the Union of Brazilian Businesspeople (UBE) (Schneider, 1997b). Similarly, FIESP and the CNI—the most important corporatist federations—have at times functioned like a peak association in the sense that they have been able to coordinate lobbying efforts on an ad hoc, short-lived basis. But the general condition is of highly fragmented, uncoordinated lobbying by different associations and firms—often in competition with each other for the same targeted benefits. The tendency since the 1970s has been toward even further fragmentation (Weyland, 2000b; Diniz and Boschi, 1993b).

Theorists have observed that business organizes itself into peak associations primarily in the context of significant threats of expropriation or a highly mobilized, radical labor movement (Durand and Silva, 2000). Those threats have been almost completely absent in Brazil. With the exception of the Goulart (1961–1964) regime, industrialists have been a highly favored political constituency. Even in the case of Goulart, it is not clear how much of a threat of expropriation existed and the 1964 military intervention rapidly made the question moot. Industrialists in the period of neoliberalism have not enjoyed the same central position as they did in the past, but they remain an important political constituency. Thus, there is no particular indication that the logic of business organization, with its resulting behavioral consequences, is likely to change.

The likelihood of continuity is greater given the organization of the Brazilian government. Control over resources remains highly decentralized, so that different ministries and agencies have considerable discretion over how to allocate their resources. The fragmentation of the party system exacerbates this tendency. Thus, the government and/or the finance minister may have a particular set of preferences about how resources are used, but they cannot effectively control how ministers, agency heads, and members of Congress actually behave.

This lack of centralized control further weakens whatever incentive business may have to organize collectively. In such a context, the costs of organizing and lobbying multiple agencies, ministries, and party caucuses or congressional blocs are prohibitive in relation to the likely benefit. By contrast, this context means that firms and sectoral associations can target specific pools of resources and lobby for them at relatively low organizational cost—especially in relation to potentially considerable benefits. Thus, benefits such as modifications to tariffs or import tax exemptions, access to government credit lines, lowered interest rates, or tax exemptions are all narrow, particularist benefits that can be obtained at little organizational cost, with potentially great individual benefit regardless of the consequences for policy or government finances, etc. Making the tax system more efficient, or reforming the pension system to ease the state's fiscal problems, is vital to the success of all Brazilian producers. Lobbying the government to make it happen is expensive, complicated, and ultimately unlikely to yield much reward.

Finally, the situation described above means that firms and sectoral associations must seek rents even if their policy preferences lean toward strict neoliberal policy. A firm that allows its competitors to obtain special benefits without trying to obtain equal or better treatment is inviting poor performance or even bankruptcy. Firms compete with each other in areas like obtaining BNDES credit, or defining which products may receive import tax exemptions. As in the past, this struggle often turns on political influence and access rather than on technical merits. The old situation of *cartórios* described by Fernando Henrique Cardoso some thirty years ago probably no longer holds. Thus, the combination of organizational fragmentation and politicized access to benefits preserves the old *cartório*-style behavior even though important segments of industrialists and industry leaders have embraced the need for change.

Evidence of Reinvention

The industrial economy has undergone some significant changes over the decade of neoliberal reform. Two crucial policy changes have made changes inevitable: tariff reductions and deregulation. Tariffs began a steady course of reduction beginning in 1990 and reached their planned conclusion in 1994. At the same time, President Collor significantly deregulated the process of foreign commerce to remove the significant host of bureaucratic obstacles that had existed previously to impede imports (Kingstone, 1999). Change has come from several sources. First, domestic producers have undertaken significant adjustment efforts, following different patterns depending on the sector. Second, the later 1990s saw very considerable increases in foreign direct investment, with important consequences for character and quality of production in the domestic economy. Third, newly privatized firms have emerged as critical players within the private economy. Finally, sectors recently opened to private and foreign investors have emerged as more important and prominent players within the domestic economy. All together, the results show considerable changes in aggregate measures of economic performance.

In the late 1980s, it was possible for firms to operate with little attention to productivity, quality or efficiency. Trade and financial liberalization changed that rapidly. Industrial leaders concerned with these issues found it difficult in the late 1980s to convince their peers of their importance. Even after the start of Collor's tariff reduction program, sectoral participation in the Brazilian Quality and Productivity Program (PBQP) varied widely, with some sectors aggressively promoting learning and adaptation and others barely considering it. Yet, the drop in tariffs and the increased possibility of import competition drove firms to rapidly respond. The pattern of response varied by sector. For example, auto-parts experienced an extraordinary wave of mergers and acquisitions as firms were forced to adapt to the new global paradigm of systems production. Machine tools and equipment producers increasingly dealt with the mix of import competition and poor conditions supporting adjustment by becoming licensed importers themselves and offering a mix of locally produced and imported goods (Santana, 1997). Pulp and paper producers sought greater scale and took advantage of their considerable access to the BNDES and the presence of high-quality sector-specific machinery and equipment producers (Santos, et al., 1996). In all sectors, firms sought to increase productivity and efficiency, increase the level of exports, and downsize their workforce.

Foreign direct investment played a crucial role as well. The total amount of foreign direct investment entering Brazil between 1987 and 1994 was slightly more than US$9 billion. Brazil took more than US$9 billion in 1996 alone in the beginning of a trend in which FDI (Foreign Direct Investment) has increased almost every year since then. By 1999, over US$30 billion entered Brazil in direct foreign investment, of which only US$8 billion came from privatization (MDIC, *Boletim Estatístico* 2001). Multinational investment has included expansion of existing operations, notably in the auto sector in response to the government's auto industry policy. It has also come in the form of new players in the industrial economy, frequently through joint ventures or acquisitions, such as through the highly visible purchase of Metal

Leve and then Cofap by the German auto-parts giant, Mahle. Finally, multinationals also entered into the economy through privatization and the opening of sectors previously closed to foreign capital, such as Enron in natural gas.

Multinational corporations have played important roles as carriers of technology and know-how. They have been less vulnerable to the "Brazil Cost" through their greater access to capital on global finance markets. They have helped domestic producers survive and adjust through joint ventures and other strategic alliances. And, of course, they have helped stimulate adjustment through greater competitive pressure within the domestic economy.

Newly privatized firms have also emerged as crucial players. Firms like Usiminas and Embraer have become models of efficiency and competitiveness. Usiminas was so successful in turning itself into a highly competitive producer that it was identified by industrialists as one of the leading firms in Brazil, and its CEO, Rinaldo Soares, was voted the industrial of the year in the *Gazeta Mercantil*. Embraer has become one of Brazil's leading exporters and a key firm for Brazil as evidenced by recent struggles with Canada over the trade conflict between Embraer and Bombardier. In fact, exports of planes reached US$5.5 billion in 2000 and represented 5.5 percent of all Brazilian exports (MDIC, *Boletim Estatístico* 2001).

Finally, newly opened sectors have allowed a host of new players to enter into the economy with significant long-term consequences. The most obvious example is in telecommunications. Prior to the privatization of Telebrás in 1998, the telecommunications system in Brazil was decaying due to years of inadequate investment, was costly, and, in many areas delivered poor service. Four years later, numerous private telecommunications firms rank among the biggest firms by sales. Costs have come down dramatically with potentially crucial long-term consequences for productivity in the Brazilian economy.

The data on performance in the industrial economy point clearly to some meaningful changes. Most notably, productivity from 1994 to 2000 increased on average 9 percent per year in the manufacturing sector with increases reaching as high as 20 percent per year in some sectors. To some extent, it's probable that some of those gains came simply from cutting the workforce (Rossi and Ferreira, 1999). Employment in industry (minus mining, energy, public utilities, and construction) fell from over eight million to just over seven million between 1994 and 2000 while production in many sectors remained constant or even increased. Nevertheless, firms also invested at a much more rapid pace in the 1990s than they had in the 1970s, with more attention to modern equipment and research and design. For example, investments in the capital goods sector averaged over US$2 billion per year from

1996 to 1999.[6] Surveys by the CNI in 2000 and 2001 suggest that industrialists were concentrating their investment plans primarily in R&D and production improvements as opposed to the priorities of the early trade reform period, which placed emphasis on rationalizing production and increasing quality control (Confederação Nacional da Indústria, 1991). In another indicator of change, the number of firms with the ISO 9000 quality certification rose from thirteen in 1990 to well over 6,000 by 1999. The annual rate of certification rose from an average of roughly 200 between 1990 and 1995 to an average of roughly 1,000 per year between 1996 and 1999 (MDIC, *Boletim Estatístico* 2001).

Exports increased by as much as 20 percent over the period 1994 to 1999. Increases, however, varied by sector and not all sectors performed as well. Over the same period, import competition increased markedly as the level of imports rose substantially. Between 1994 and 1999, imports more or less doubled, with the largest percent increases occurring in basic materials and intermediary goods and with the smallest increases in consumer durables (MDIC, *Boletim Estatístico* 2001). Machine tools and equipment have felt the increase in imports particularly sharply, as investment in capital goods has increased considerably over the period 1992 to 1999, with the share of imports rising sharply over the same period. Mergers and acquisitions occurred at a brisk pace. In fact, over 1,500 occurred through the mid-1990s, concentrated in areas like finance, food processing, and auto-parts (Bonelli, 2000). In short, the industrial economy experienced considerable, meaningful change. Brazil's industrial economy in many important respects is not the same as it was in 1990 and is certainly much better placed today for global competition than it was then.

Sources of Continuity

The Brazilian industrial economy has changed considerably since 1990. There are, however, several important sources of continuity. To some extent those sources of continuity point to lingering difficulties in Brazil's development of a competitive domestic economy. The Cardoso government brought both price stability and a clearer commitment to the overall policy direction. Thus, longer time horizons permitted firms to plan investments and the results showed both in domestic investment levels and in foreign direct investment.[7] Nevertheless, significant obstacles to adjustment continued. First and foremost, Cardoso's primary policy priority was price stability through the *Real Plan*. In the absence of effective reform of several key

---

6.   Data noted above are drawn from the Ministry of Development, Industry, and Commerce, *Boletim Estatístico*, 2001.
7.   Data on investment are also available in the Statistical Appendix of the Interamerican Development Bank, Annual Report. Observations above are drawn from the 1997 report.

sources of government deficits, the plan depended on substantial foreign capital inflows, high real interest rates, and an overvalued exchange rate. Some economists and business leaders questioned the necessity and viability of keeping high real interest rates and an overvalued exchange rate. Even within the government, some felt that at the very least interest rates could not be sustained at high levels over a long time. Yet, each sign of instability—such as from the Asian Flu or the Russian Ruble Crisis—forced the government to fall back on these policies.

Two perverse effects flowed from this policy orientation. First, the frequent changes in interest rate policy and uncertainty about the exchange rate complicated planning adjustments, even though the broad outlines of the program remained stable. Second, maintaining a high real interest rate and an overvalued exchange rate undermined other policy goals, such as export promotion or promotion of quality and productivity improvements. The exchange rate, generally thought to be overvalued at between 10 and 20 percent, hurt the competitiveness of Brazilian exports and, along with real interest rates, created strong incentives to import goods, even when low-cost domestic inputs existed. High real interest rates hurt investments in technological improvements as well as the capacity of domestic firms to offer financing through programs like the BNDES's finance program. Thus, even after stabilization, obstacles to adjustment persisted.

The obstacles to adjustment and to increasing competitiveness reveal themselves in the fact that Brazil remains a relatively "closed" economy. Even in 1997—its peak year for imports—imports represented only about 7.5 percent of GDP: relatively unchanged from before commercial liberalization. Export performance has also failed to develop the way government policy had hoped, despite a series of export promotion plans and incentives. Exports also remain at roughly 7 percent of GDP and the structure of exports suggests that the exporting sectors in 2000 are the same ones for the most part that were successful exporters in 1990. Furthermore, there has been considerable debate about whether increased Brazilian trade reflects real improvements in competitiveness or simple diversion of trade to less competitive markets, principally those of the Mercosur region (Markwald and Machado, 1999). Evidence from the CNI and Agosin suggests that multinational investors continue to see investment in Brazil as oriented toward capturing shares of the domestic market—not toward exports. Thus, to the extent that exports are a critical component of increasing domestic competitiveness, the evidence suggests that Brazil's success has been quite limited.

Finally, the contradictions/weaknesses in government policy identified by industrialists over ten years ago continue to be central issues for the business community and continue to act as limits on the competitiveness of the domestic economy. Remarks from an interview with Rinaldo Campos Soares, CEO of Usiminas, reveal the extraordinary continuity of the problems facing Brazilian firms. Elected as *Gazeta Mercantil*'s "National Leader" of 1996, Soares observed that commercial liberalization brought into sharp relief the set of problems that Brazilian firms needed to overcome to increase their competitiveness. One set of obstacles was internal and under the control of the firms. The other set of obstacles was external and depended on government policy. Chief among those obstacles were the inefficiencies of the tax system and the burdens of social obligations (as well as the serious deterioration of Brazil's economic infrastructure and the woeful inadequacy of health and education). These issues figured prominently in the concerns of the Democratic Manifesto letter of 1978 as well as the "Document of the 12" of 1983. By 1999, a CNI/FIESP/Vox Populi survey of industrialists on the principal obstacles to strengthening national producers showed that deterioration of the infrastructure had disappeared as an issue.[8] Leading the list, however, was the tax system, social contributions, and inadequate or overly bureaucratic access to credit (one other crucial issue was excessive interest rates). In short, the set of concerns had changed only a little between 1978 and 1999.

Conclusion

Since at least 1978, domestic industrialists' leaders and government representatives have been engaged in an awkward dialogue. Industrialists have been engaged in a twenty-year-long defense of "national" industry through promotion of competitiveness and a managed integration with the global economy. Over the course of that time, government representatives have varied in their response: distracted under Sarney; hostile under Collor. Under Cardoso, industrialists have received a varied response, depending on the timing and the specific minister or agency. Ministers in the Planning Ministry or the Ministry of Industry (under its various names), such as Serra, Dornelles, or Kandir, have tended to be more responsive to industrialists' concerns. Pedro Malan, by contrast, has tended toward being dismissive. The effect has been very patchwork. Industrialists have had some of their concerns reflected in a set of policies aimed at promoting competitiveness and exports. Many industrialists have had their concerns met through informal access to government agencies. Yet, overall, Brazilian economic policy continues to be oriented to maintaining stability and addressing emergencies as opposed to defining a long-term strategic vision of development.

---

8.   This CNI/FIESP/Vox Populi survey is available at http://www.cni.org.br. Last date accessed: unknown.

In 1978, industrial leaders believed that the country would benefit from an ample discussion of such a vision. It has never happened. In its place, industrialists have adjusted to the changing context on their own. The pattern of adjustment leaves some questions that merit further consideration. Does it matter that Brazil no longer really has a guiding development strategy? Brazil is neither a genuinely open economy nor a developmental or guided economy. Instead, it is occupying an ill-defined space in which the market is still politicized to a significant degree. Does it matter that the country is not able to improve its export profile? Does it matter that ten years of neoliberal reform have not solved the problem of a bifurcated market? Is the failure to solve that problem due to the lack of a guiding philosophy? What is the role of "national industry" and should there be a distinction between "national industry" and domestic production that includes both Brazilian and multinational capital? All of these are questions that industrialists have been raising for nearly twenty-five years. There are no definitive answers. The evidence to date, however, does suggest that Brazilian industrialists are a robust and adaptive lot. It is not clear whether leaving them to adjust on their own, without reference to a guiding, developmental strategy comes without costs.

CHAPTER 9

Entrepreneurs:
The PNBE

Eduardo Rodrigues Gomes and *Fabrícia C. Guimarães*

Surprisingly or not, entrepreneurs have had a number of difficulties in playing an important role in the shaping of Brazil's new democracy and in the construction of an open, deregulated economy in Brazil. Despite the fact that they have ended up supporting and benefiting from the market-oriented reforms, they have not managed to reach an influential political position in Brazil's new politico-economic model, either through their old corporatist organizations, or through fresh collective actions they developed in the last decade and a half (Weyland, 1998a; Schneider, 1998; Kingstone, 1999).

The corporatist institutions have undergone a troublesome process of modernization in their organizational structures and of the services they render to members. In addition, they have also taken some time to restructure their lobbying activities in order to deal with the complexity of the new democracies, which lack an interventionist executive power (Canosa, 1999; Kirschner and Gomes, 1999; Weyland, 1998a; Schneider, 1998; Kingstone, 1999; Addis and Gomes, 2001; McQuerry, 1996).

Entrepreneurs' new extracorporatist movements, on the other hand, have not been able to open any new valuable channel for the exercise of political power, to say nothing of the fact that many of these collective actions have not lasted very long (Diniz and Boschi, 1993a; Kingstone, 1999; Weyland, 1998a; Nylen, 1992, 1993; Schneider, 1998).

Within these businesses' new collective actions, however, one autonomous association of small and medium entrepreneurs based in São Paulo has actively articulated interests, voiced concerns, and staged demonstrations in the political arena with a significant impact in the last fifteen years, despite having also gone through some downturns. The National Thought of Entrepreneurial Base (Pensamento Nacional das Bases Empresariais, or PNBE), was born from within the corporatist system but it became an autonomous business movement, and gained paramount political importance during the Sarney and Collor administrations.

The PNBE ended up losing its importance at the national level as time went by, although it still tries to have a say in national issues and remains quite active in São Paulo. The PNBE appeared on the front page of one of Brazil's main newspapers and in television headlines, by staging demonstrations against Congress' apparent lack of clear and firm intent to suspend the mandates of two of its members who were charged with accusations of breaking the secrecy on an important House vote. On that occasion, approximately forty PNBE members went to the street to publicly send pizza-shaped cards to Senate members to remind them of the importance of the issue, and that it could not end in a "pizza feast."[1]

PNBE activities, and its lasting trajectory, contrast sharply with other entrepreneurs' collective actions, making it an exceptional case of an autonomous business movement that deserves more attention, especially because it has not been the object of specific analysis.[2]

This chapter explores the reasons behind the PNBE "success story" by discussing to what extent it has been in tune with Brazil's transformations, namely the transition to democracy and the market-oriented reforms. It also analyzes the extent to which the PNBE may have been a suitable answer to the crisis of the corporatist institutions, by accounting for its interactions with the Federation of Manufacturing Industries of the State of São Paulo (Federação das Indústrias do Estado de São Paulo or FIESP).

This study on the PNBE may shed light on the dilemmas faced by business entrepreneurs in inserting themselves in the favorable political environment of new democracies with open economies, such as Brazil. Despite the gains that may come from liberalization in the medium or long term, business has also had to face the fact that it lost its privileged access to the state, and that the transition to this new model has depended on an autocratic executive branch exercising significant autonomy from organized interests, including those of entrepreneurs.

This ends up being an almost unsolvable dilemma, either during the process of transition itself or in the moment of institutionalization, and this study of the PNBE "success story" may contribute to the advancement of the understanding of the political incorporation of business in new democracies (O'Donnell, 1994).

---

1.   This results from the fact that in Collor's impeachment process, the expression "finishing with a pizza" became synonymous to not wanting to do anything about an important subject.
2.   As this chapter was being finished, a book on PNBE was published (Bianchi, 2001). Although dealing with some of the issues focused on here, Bianchi is mainly interested in showing PNBE's lack of real potential to solve the "crisis of hegemony" the author sees in Brazil's bourgeoisie.

This chapter is composed of five sections in which we cover the origins of the PNBE (section two), the institutional and ideological format it assumed and its relations with FIESP (section three), and its main actions in the national scene and social projects since 1987 (section four). In the fifth and last part, we present our conclusions about the PNBE's unique characteristics and trajectory in Brazil's transition.

Origins and First Steps

What came to be called the National Thought of Entrepreneurial Base appeared in the mid-1980s, as a movement of new and young leaders of several sectors of São Paulo's manufacturing industry, who were unsatisfied with the oligarchization of the principal corporatist-class association in the state, the Federation of the Manufacturing Industries of the State of São Paulo, FIESP (Kapaz, 1998; Grajew, 1998).

At that point, a couple of young industrial entrepreneurs had reached the presidency of some unions of FIESP and began to try to imbue the entities in their hands a broader representativeness and a more active political role, in tune with the "rebirth of civil society" seen during the first moments of Brazil's transition to democracy (Stepan, 1989; O'Donnell and Schmitter, 1988).

Later on, these same entrepreneurs tried to make similar changes in FIESP, but they had little or no success. Emerson Kapaz, one of PNBE's leaders, remarks that some members of the group were called "shiites" at FIESP meetings, an expression borrowed from the fundamentalist religious movement in Iran which is used to convey a sense of radicalism, commonly used in Brazil to refer pejoratively to the most radical left (Kapaz, 1998).

After many collisions within FIESP, this group came to the difficult decision of building its own organization, though initially they only wanted to reform FIESP.

As a result of an initiative of one of its members, Paulo Butori, they began to meet in the Auto Parts Industry Syndicate (Sindicato da Indústria de Autopeças, or SINDIPEÇAS). Butori, in fact, brought up the idea of using the new movement's name as a way to convey the somewhat loose intentions of the group: a reflective and representative group of entrepreneurs committed to democracy as a means and goal for political action, something that was not an easy agenda to undertake during the transitional period in Brazil.

Butori and Kapaz, along with Luiz Carlos Delben Leite, president of the Capital Goods Industry Syndicate (Sindicato da Indústria de Bens de Capital, or SINDIMAQ), Salo Seibel, from SINDIPEÇAS, Oded Grajew, from the Brazilian Toy Industry Association (Associação Brasileira da Indústria de Brinquedos, or ABRINQ), Luís Peres Michelin, and Adauto Pousa Ponte, were not only prominent figures of their sectors, but also medium entrepreneurs, naturally sensitive to the claims of their group. Usually overlooked by FIESP, these claims were becoming increasingly important (Nylen, 1992).

However, the official public launching of the movement occurred only on June 9, 1987, in a large meeting in the Anhembi Convention Palace, in the city of São Paulo. Organizers relied on the euphoria remaining from the stabilization brought by the *Cruzado Plan* as a means of attracting attendants, particularly the importance the Plan had given to productive activities as opposed to the financial sector. These entrepreneurs, and business people in general, considered that the financial sector had been the most privileged sector in all stabilization plans during previous inflationary periods (Kapaz, 1998; Carneiro and Modiano, 1990).[3]

The event was also arranged with the purpose of verifying the reach and repercussion of the proposals that guided the organizers, besides protesting against the "growing statization of the Brazilian economy" seen in the ongoing Constituent Assembly.

Members of PNBE were uncertain about the results of the call for the meeting, and Grajew said the date was chosen with a "bit of intuition" (Grajew, 1998). As it turns out, the choice could not have been better because the meeting was crowned a true success: approximately two thousand five hundred small and medium entrepreneurs participated, representing ninety-eight unions, associations, and entrepreneurial federations from São Paulo and from other states.[4]

Paulo Butori, one of the newborn movement's leaders, became so optimistic with the outcome of the meeting that, backstage at the Anhembi Conventions Palace, he announced his intention of "organizing one in each state and to end in Brasília, with a national encounter, if possible, with the workers's participation."[5]

One immediate result of the meeting was the creation of a "mobilization group" within the PNBE to plan actions for a national agenda and to handle the day-to-day functioning of the PNBE, as well as its institutional formalization. At that point, the leaders of the PNBE had also made clear their intention of looking for an "understanding with the workers."[6]

PNBE was born with so many and such grand expectations that some entrepreneurial leaders of other traditional class organizations invited to the launching of the movement simply did not show up. The president of FIESP, Mário Amato, justified his absence because it would "expose the entity to a risk." But he apparently followed the unfolding of the PNBE's first public

---

3.   *Folha de S. Paulo*, June 10, 1987.
4.   *Gazeta Mercantil*, June 9, 1987, and *Folha de S. Paulo*, June 9, 1987.
5.   *Gazeta Mercantil*, June 10, 1987.
6.   *Folha de S. Paulo*, June 10, 1987.

meeting, which undoubtedly turned out to be an important political demonstration.[7]

In fact, Amato explicitly tried to protect FIESP from the challenges of the
PNBE, not only at that time but consistently, assuming fairly enough that the
new movement had "good intentions." He basically portrayed the PNBE as a
collective of nice and perhaps idealistic people, sometimes pushy, and with
some good ideas, although unsuitable for the time the country and FIESP
were going through (Amato, 1997).

After this initial step, the movement did not stop and a second meeting
was held in the same place four months later. As in the previous meeting, the
invitation for the new encounter was conveyed through 117 business associations, and there were about 1,000 entrepreneurs in attendance, representing
approximately 184 class entities.[8]

The prominent part of the second encounter was the presence of the Minister of Finance, Bresser-Pereira, who accepted to openly discuss national
economic problems with an audience of small and medium entrepreneurs.
His comments, however, were considered too generic, having apparently
avoided subjects as the high financial costs of the banking sector, the control
of government expenses, and the lack of credibility of the current economic
policies.[9]

This was how the PNBE was actually born. The movement, therefore,
appeared in the middle of the 1980s as a reaction against the FIESP's limitations in adapting itself to the new economic and social times of Brazil: a temporarily stabilized economy, within a democratic regime in the making, and
with a Constituent Assembly in session. This reaction came from small and
medium entrepreneurs who had long been left out of politics, had reached
leadership positions within FIESP, and had decided to try to change the organization to face those central and unavoidable issues of Brazil's liberalization
and democratization.

Moreover, in trying to be consistent with its motivations, the group that
formed PNBE began to organize along the principles of "grassroots democracy" and to act along the same democratic rules, that is, choosing to deal
with the most important issues at stake in Brazil, necessarily based on an
internal democratic decision-making process and externally through open
dialogue with other relevant social actors, such as workers and government.

This was a difficult and demanding collective project for business, but it
was undoubtedly tuned to the PNBE's origins and motivations and ended up
fitting the unfolding of Brazil's transition, at least for a significant period of

---

7.   *Gazeta Mercantil*, June 9 and 10, 1987.
8.   *Folha de S. Paulo*, October 10, 1987.
9.   *Folha de S. Paulo*, October 6, 1987.

time. This project was carried out for at least a decade and a half, and the PNBE's uniqueness would become clearer with the passing of time, but not immediately with the institutionalization of the movement.

Institutionalization and Second Challenges to FIESP

In the beginning of 1988, the leaders of the PNBE began to discuss the transformation of the PNBE-movement into the PNBE-entity, having explicitly assumed the need for a slower structuring process to avoid the risk of failure they had already seen happen in other initiatives (Grajew, 1998).[10] As a consequence, it was only in 1990 that the PNBE made the transition from a movement to an entity, gaining a formal structure, with clearly defined objectives, strictly consistent with its original democratic motivations.

According to its statute, then formulated, the principal objective of the PNBE was "to contribute for the improvement of the democracy and for the political formation of entrepreneurs—be they from small, medium or large business, any sector or region—through their participation in the discussion and decision processes of relevant national and social questions of general interest" (PNBE, 1990).

Additionally, according to this founding document, the PNBE intended to work as a "catalyst of ideas, organizer of debates and driver of projects and political actions to contribute to the development and accentuation of the role as citizen of each entrepreneur," a statement that indeed opened up a varied group of roles that PNBE intended to assume at other moments (PNBE, 1990).

In its self definition, the PNBE was characterized as a movement devoted to the fight for democracy and for its constant improvement, assuming democratic rules as the only means to reach this goal. In other words, the PNBE had a platform of a concomitant valorization of democracy in a substantive and procedural way, something thought achievable only through the types of democratic actions mentioned above.

Framed along this orientation, the PNBE was organized based on an inclusive and dynamic representative structure, emphasizing the active participation of its members in general assemblies, ordinarily held at least three times a year and allowing absentee voting, and in other loci.

These same assemblies were in charge of choosing the PNBE's board of directors, named the Group of National Coordination (Grupo de Coordenação Nacional, or GCN), possibly for taming its position of power in the top of the institutional hierarchy of the movement. It is not for any other reason that people say that the entity is an "upside down pyramid."

---

10. *Gazeta Mercantil*, January 8, 1988.

For the same reasons, the Group of National Coordination is constituted by a relatively large number of members, under constant turnover: it is formed by twenty effective coordinators, with a two-year mandate and ten substitute coordinators, with a mandate of one year each. In each annual election, ten effective coordinators and all the substitutes are replaced.

The highest representatives of the PNBE are chosen by this group, constituting the Executive Coordination (Coordenação Executiva), formed by the first and second general coordinators, in addition to three executive coordinators and three substitute coordinators. The general and executive coordinators are always chosen for a six-month mandate, and are allowed reelection for two consecutive additional periods of six months.

Besides typical organs of representative entities such as the Fiscal Council, Working Groups, and Task Forces, the PNBE looked to build a national structure organized around "regional nuclei" that, in spite of the name, could have merely a municipality as its covered area. The PNBE, however, never succeeded in covering the whole country, and it remained essentially rooted in São Paulo.

The PNBE's institutionalization did not ease relations with the FIESP, which were tense even before this formal step had taken place. In 1988, for instance, the PNBE group opposed a proposal from Mário Amato to create an Advisory Council that would choose just one president for FIESP and CIESP, Center of the Manufacturing Industries of the State of São Paulo (Centro das Indústrias do Estado de São Paulo—CIESP). CIESP is an autonomous noncorporatist business organization associated with FIESP, which has firms as its members. Amato's proposal would basically reinforce the importance of the affiliated unions as voters in the choice of the board of directors of CIESP, originally chosen by affiliated firms.

Although Amato's initiative caused a number of disputes between him and the PNBE, which saw this latest move as an antidemocratic one, the election criteria was kept the same.[11]

On the other hand, some time later, Oded Grajew presented a plan geared toward the opposing goal of increasing the number of members of CIESP, which was around nine thousand in a universe of a hundred and twenty thousand companies in the state. But FIESP did not go along with Grajew's proposal.[12]

Two years later, however, the PNBE had what could be considered a victory outside of the corporatist realm, something that generated a number of positive repercussions for the movement: Emerson Kapaz, one of the most important names in the PNBE, reached fifth place in an informal national

---

11. *Folha de S. Paulo,* June 10, 1998.
12. *Folha de S. Paulo,* June 11, 1988.

election of the most influential political leaders, called by Brazil's most important business newspaper, *Gazeta Mercantil*. The poll, which consulted a large number of business people all over the country, also recognized him as a regional class leader of Brazil's southeast.[13]

Taking advantage of the recently conquered prestige and, at the same time, relying on the PNBE's motivations (but without receiving its endorsement), Kapaz announced his interest in succeeding Mario Amato as president of FIESP, in an explicit opposition to that organization's status quo.

Although Emerson Kapaz was not officially a candidate from the PNBE, the unfolding of the dispute was felt directly within the movement. With the entrance of Kapaz in the dispute for the leadership of FIESP, the entity underwent a crisis, with some of its members disagreeing with the way the candidacy of Kapaz appeared, not to mention opposition to the candidacy itself.[14]

As the campaign went on, support for either of the two candidates fluctuated and, most of the time, names that were behind Emerson Kapaz shifted to Carlos Eduardo Moreira Ferreira, a situational candidate. Moreira Ferreira tried to exploit the division in the PNBE concerning candidates to the leadership of FIESP, when he collected a group of depositions of several associated founders of PNBE, manifesting support to his own candidacy in a campaign video.[15]

However, the sorcery turned against the sorcerer, because a direct effect of the video was the breaking of the apparent neutrality that the PNBE was adopting. The PNBE presented a manifesto supporting Kapaz, with the signatures of 169 of the entity's 188 members.[16]

Regardless, Moreira Ferreira won the FIESP presidency with 95 votes against 24 for Kapaz. In CIESP he also obtained more votes, but with a very small difference, 1,731 against 1,591 votes.[17] According to the statute of CIESP, there should be a second run in case any candidate had not reached the absolute majority, as was the case. Kapaz, however, gave up the second run, stating that "the lack of legitimacy of the electoral process of FIESP was fully demonstrated."[18]

In sum, after publicly gaining force through Kapaz's candidacy to FIESP/CIESP, the PNBE tested its importance without losing the contest in a broader sense. The electoral competition seems to have shown that the business representative framework was at least biased, as indicated by the con-

13. *Gazeta Mercantil*, October 30, 1991.
14. *Jornal da Tarde*, March 30, 1992.
15. *O Estado de São Paulo*, July 15, 1992.
16. *Folha de S. Paulo*, July 15 and 16, 1992.
17. *Folha de S. Paulo*, September 30, 1992.
18. *Folha de S. Paulo*, August 1, 1988.

trast between FIESP and CIESP voting, and this message had resonance within the business class, as was later to be seen.

The restrictive representative rules and institutional practices of the corporatist organization appeared to be among the main issues of contention separating the PNBE from FIESP during its first year of existence. In any case, the PNBE moves affected FIESP even further because Moreira Ferreira incorporated some names from the PNBE into his staff after the election, and also began to enact some organizational reforms within FIESP.

This is not the whole story about relations between PNBE and FIESP, but let us now turn to the PNBE's political and social actions in the extracorporatist scenarios, where conflicts with FIESP also took place, amidst important political initiatives taken by the PNBE.

PNBE in the Extracorporatist Scenario

Since its appearance, the PNBE engaged in a series of initiatives related to the most pressing political, economic, and social issues at stake in Brazil in the mid-1980s, as evidenced in the official public launching of the movement in June 1987.

At that point in the Sarney administration, the PNBE mobilized against the apparent statist tendency of the Constituent Assembly, but also supported the different attempts for the building of anti-inflationary social pacts, especially after the failure of the *Cruzado Plan*. For the PNBE, controlling inflation was indeed a priority for Brazil, and it both supported proposals for a social pact with that goal and mobilized its bases in the same direction.[19]

In late 1988, after the failure of the *Cruzado Plan*, the discussions about inflation had gone to a search of controlling both prices and wages, but it was quite difficult to get a substantive policy outcome.[20] In spite of the workers' and entrepreneurs' active involvement, government representatives remained passive, not presenting relevant proposals.

Later on, recognizing a paralysis in the negotiations, seven entrepreneurs from the PNBE simply—and quite unusually—decided to visit Israel, accompanied by two union leaders, Luiz Antonio de Medeiros and Gilmar Carneiro, in order to get a close understanding of Israel's successful experience in controlling inflation, which had been made possible by a social pact in 1985.

The Brazilian delegation, having discussed with economists and employees of the Israeli government the principal points of the anti-inflationary pact, became convinced of the importance of simultaneously attacking the problems of inflation and of the balance of payments.[21]

---

19. *Gazeta Mercantil*, June 16, 1988, *Folha de S. Paulo*, July 22, 1988.
20. *Folha de S. Paulo*, October 27, 1988.
21. *Folha de S. Paulo*, November 22, 1988.

Upon return, the seven PNBE entrepreneurs met for three hours with the Minister of Finance, Maílson da Nóbrega, to describe the Israeli experience and its possible application in Brazil, but no changes were made.[22] In fact, Maílson da Nóbrega later revealed that the economic situation Brazil was going through at that point was simply unmanageable and that nothing could realistically be done, except to roll the problems from one day to the following.

Besides these problems, 1989 was also an electoral year and the PNBE began to call for a series of public debates with the candidates for the presidency of the Republic. The movement succeeded in having candidates Guilherme Afif Domingos, Fernando Collor de Mello, Luiz Inácio Lula da Silva, Leonel Brizola, and Mário Covas debate at their organization. According to Salo Seibel, this was an initiative opposed "to the private audiences, where only the entrepreneurial elite and the elites, in general, have access to the rulers," in clear contrast with the corporatist establishment.

This was the first direct presidential election after the end of the dictatorship and, after a heated dispute in the two-round electoral process, Fernando Collor defeated Lula from the Workers' Party with a conservative moralizing platform. Despite having no major affinity with the PNBE orientation, the Collor administration ended up being 'the [PNBE's] golden opportunity', according to Kapaz (1998).

In the face of difficulties in suspending a price and wage freeze that had brought inflation to zero in the first days of the Collor government, the Minister of Finance, Zélia Cardoso, called the PNBE to open negotiations with the private section in order to define which steps should be taken. This was a demanding call because the government had gone through a series of conflicts with the entrepreneurs as a result of the freezing of liquid assets involved in the plan, and of the autocratic orientation followed by Collor.

In any case, the PNBE accepted the challenge and unceasingly tried to build that agreement along the lines of sectoral chambers involving workers, again without success. However, the PNBE faced both difficulties in dealing with other sectors of the government and opposition from FIESP.[23]

FIESP was deeply dissatisfied with and critical of the PNBE initiative of accepting open dialogue with the government and its top bureaucrats. In fact, several more orthodox entrepreneurial leaders even pressed some union leaders to end the meetings between Zélia Cardoso and the entrepreneurs of the PNBE. Paradoxically enough, the silence of FIESP seemed to convey the idea that the corporatist entity was supporting everything that the government did.[24]

---

22. *Folha de S. Paulo*, January 6, 1989.
23. *Folha de S. Paulo*, March 25, 1990.

Later on in October 1990, in a new attempt toward a social pact, the negotiations between workers and entrepreneurs were resumed, seeking the formation of a "national understanding." In these new efforts, Oded Grajew and Emerson Kapaz met regularly with Jair Meneguelli and Gilmar Carneiro, Meneguelli having identified the PNBE as a "representative of the future."[25]

Once again, after having established agreement on some points, the government did not agree with decisions about prefixing price and wage increases, or the compensation of residual wage loss with previous inflation. The economic situation was tough and the government stepped in with new executive decrees aimed at achieving stabilization, without giving information to the groups involved in the negotiations prior to the decrees.

As a result, the PNBE and two workers' unions, the General Confederation of Workers (Confederação Geral dos Trabalhadores, or CGT) and the Unified Center of Workers (Central Única dos Trabalhadores, or CUT) went to Congress as a way of opening new means of maintaining a negotiated format of policymaking. However, this meant a significant expansion of the number of actors involved, and the difficulties increased to the point of making it an unworkable solution.[26]

The attempts toward collaboration with the Collor government did not prevent the movement from criticizing that administration. In December 1991, for example, the PNBE coordinated a meeting in the Anhembi Palace of Conventions with entrepreneurs, syndicalists, and other representatives of civil society to evaluate the administration. Approximately three hundred people attended and the result was a manifesto proposing longer periods of financing of the public deficit, an encompassing tax reform, and efforts toward distribution of income based on an expansion of production, larger employment, and higher wages.[27]

Concerned with a possible recession, members of the PNBE decided to meet regularly with other entrepreneurs and syndicalists in another initiative denominated as the Labor-Capital Forum (Fórum Capital Trabalho), at the University of São Paulo.[28] The objective of the forum was to conceive of short-term actions aimed directly at combatting the effects of the crisis, and, in the long term, to elaborate projects for the already scheduled constitutional reforms.[29]

Assembling conflicting views, the issues discussed went from state reform to changes in the Brazilian land structure. No government entity par-

---

24. *Folha de S. Paulo*, April 6, 10, and 18, 1990.
25. *Folha de S. Paulo*, October 16, 1990.
26. *Gazeta Mercantil*, December 12, 1990.
27. *Gazeta Mercantil*, December 10, 1991.
28. *Gazeta Mercantil*, December 7, 8, and 9, 1991.
29. *Folha de S. Paulo*, December 17, 1991.

ticipated in the forum because "the words and the actions of the federal government's act are incoherent," according to Oded Grajew, the PNBE's coordinator at the time.

The discussions lasted six months and the final report presented suggestions concerning several themes, especially issues of labor-capital relations: participants defended the rupture of the corporatist model, restriction of state intervention in labor issues, and also the reliance on direct negotiation as the best and permanent way for solving conflicts of the actors' antagonistic interests.[30]

In mid-1992, the PNBE joined other social and political entities in protesting against recently disclosed corrupt practices in the House of Representatives in the creation of the federal budget. This social effort became the Movement for Ethics in Politics that was conducted through several public manifestations against those corrupt practices in major Brazilian cities.[31]

The accusations of corruption led all the way to the president of the republic, Fernando Collor, against whom a process of impeachment was opened with support of the PNBE.[32] In any case, after Collor's impeachment in October 1992, the PNBE continued to work for the formation of social pacts in Itamar Franco's government, the former vice president who was then placed in power.

For instance, as early as the end of 1992, the movement presented to President Itamar Franco, through his Minister of Foreign Affairs, Fernando Henrique Cardoso, a document containing a proposal for a social pact in order to combat inflation, in this case through the creation of a Permanent Forum of National Union (Fórum Permanente de União Nacional), where an empty chair would symbolize those excluded from the economic process.[33]

Franco, however, stuck to the same technocratic pattern of policymaking as his predecessors, and had a stabilization plan formulated behind closed doors centered on the full indexation of the economy to the dollar. Different from previous efforts, this plan did not involve any kind of political control of price and wages, and no change in the basic economic rules. In fact, it was a gradual process of full indexation of the economy, aimed at introducing a new stable currency named the *real*, and initially based on the introduction of a new monetary device, named URV (*Unidade Real de Valor*, or Real Value Unit), with a daily quotation, to which all prices and wages should be converted.

The implementation of the *Real Plan* was an economic and, later on, political success. In its early stages, however, leaders of the PNBE called

---

30. *Gazeta Mercantil*, June 19, and December 7, 8, and 9, 1992.
31. *Folha de S. Paulo*, August 9, 1992.
32. *Folha de S. Paulo*, September 4, 1992.
33. *Folha de S. Paulo*, October 7, 1992.

attention to entrepreneurs' newfound possibility of converting prices into the new monetary unit above the inflation adjusted level, something that could threaten the new policies and should therefore be seriously combatted by the government.[34]

The PNBE also dealt with the conversion of wages to URV, Kapaz having declared that, in this transition, it would be important for wages to increase, in order to give credibility to the plan.[35]

The achievement of stabilization through the *Real Plan* brought other subjects to the fore. In July, the first coordinator of PNBE complained against the protection of elite interests by saying: "The *Real Plan* should proceed if it was aimed at saving the production sector, and not the banks, of bankruptcy. Otherwise, it is a play that doesn't put an end to the inflation."[36]

Despite criticism from the left, the *Real Plan*'s economic success opened the possibility for a presidential candidate to challenge the rising support Lula was receiving for his 1994 presidential bid. The choice fell on the minister who had been at the forefront of the *Real Plan*, Fernando Henrique Cardoso. But his candidacy was not easily formed, at least for PNBE members, who advanced serious concerns about his alliance with the Party of the Liberal Front (Partido da Frente Liberal, or PFL), given the party ties with the authoritarian regime and its clientelistic roots. In any case, Cardoso ended up beating Lula with 52 percent of the vote.[37]

PNBE however retained its unique method of political engagement: for example, PNBE looked to open a channel of direct negotiation with the president, to allow a direct consultation of the presidency with entrepreneurs and workers: "We proposed to the President the creation of a permanent forum with him or with the Vice President aimed at having a permanent discussion of major national problems, and involving entrepreneurs and workers, but we felt that there was no political will among the governing circles."[38]

According to Kapaz, the election of Fernando Henrique represented a lot of what PNBE had dreamed of and fought for, and the entity increasingly went back to institutional projects of social intervention, although it maintained its political concerns in São Paulo, and to a couple of economic and political issues such as public morality, fair competition, among others.

Since the mid-1990s, for example, the PNBE tried hard to make Brazil's Anti-Trust Commission, named Council for Economic Defense (Conselho de Defesa Econômica, or CADE) work efficiently, but had no success in this effort. In more concrete terms, the PNBE also engaged itself in a long battle

34. *Folha de S. Paulo*, January 18, 1994.
35. *Folha de S. Paulo*, February 22, 1994.
36. *Folha de S. Paulo*, September 27, 1994.
37. *Folha de S. Paulo*, August 3, 1994.
38. Interview with Jack Strauss, São Paulo, 1998.

against what the members considered a collusive arrangement for taking care of vehicles' registration and licensing in the city of São Paulo.

Despite being mildly supportive of Cardoso's government, the PNBE became critical of some of its actions, for example, his efforts to pass the bill that made his reelection possible, given that his initiative involved the support of the members of the legislature under charges of corruption. This and other localized critiques of the Cardoso administration and its process of privatization did not have much effect.

As the movement of critical concerns and propositive actions toward national issues faded out, PNBE became increasingly devoted to projects of intervention in "emblematic social problems," something that it indeed had always been involved with, although not as much as it had been since the mid-1990s.

This other side of the PNBE derives from its goal of working for the construction and improvement of democracy. The substantive dimension of the political regime was also incorporated as a locus for action of this entrepreneurial group, reinforcing its uniqueness among new collective actions from business sectors in Brazil.

Already in the beginning of the 1990s, for instance, ecology became an important subject for the entity, and the PNBE created, in December of 1991, the Working Group on Environment with the objective of promoting ecological projects with the unique mark of the movement. According to the coordinator of this group "the difference between our group and other similar entities lies in the fact that we consider the conquest of citizenship and best distribution of income as indispensable points in the combat to the environmental destruction."[39]

In April 1992, in the midst of a growing concern with ethics in the country, the entity created an award that became very important, the PNBE Award of Citizenship (Prêmio PNBE de Cidadania), that would annually honor prominent figures in defense of citizenship. The award has been given to people like the socially oriented Minister of Health Adib Jatene, a street vendor who denounced extortion from city officers in São Paulo, among others, not to mention the one who could be considered the "founding father" of nongovernmental organizations devoted to social causes in Brazil, Herbert de Souza (Betinho).

Later on, in 1994, the PNBE joined the Institute for the Development of Health (Instituto para o Desenvolvimento da Saúde), a nongovernmental organization aimed at elaborating and promoting effective health policies. Kapaz, who was then coordinator of PNBE, pictured IDS "as part of the revolution of citizenship in the health area."[40] The following year, the movement

---

39. *Gazeta Mercantil*, December 3, 1991.

developed a project with the International Labor Organization (ILO) with the goal of eliminating child labor, an initiative which received great repercussions inside and outside PNBE.[41]

Among all of PNBE's concerns with social issues, perhaps the ones in the educational arena have been the most widely considered. The movement recognized a high repetition index, resources badly used and distributed, ineffective teaching methods, and the absence of a process of evaluation of the teaching, as some of the main problems of Brazil's educational system.

The PNBE decided to face them initially through the project Enterprise-School Cooperation, that proposed the "adoption" of public schools by private companies, which would support the latter financially, in exchange for allowing business to participate in the school administration to collaborate to solve the above problems.[42]

Interestingly enough, as the 1990s were coming to an end, PNBE joined a couple of other class associations and private foundations to create the São Paulo Institute Against Violence (Instituto São Paulo contra a Violência) essentially aimed at enhancing the city resources to control urban violence, a problem on the rise in major Brazilian cities.[43]

Last but not least, the PNBE also carried out another social project destined to support homeless adults in São Paulo without taking them from the streets. Created by the coordinator Jack Strauss, it was named "My Street, My House," and centered on the creation of living centers in the empty spaces under the city viaducts to provide minimum identity resources for this population, assumed as unrecoverable for "normal" social life, starting from a personal toilet and sleeping spaces.

Without producing more than one center in downtown São Paulo, the project was transformed into an autonomous association with the same name as the project, and it has remained operational through voluntary personnel and business support (Strauss, 1998).

Without reaching its goal of supporting the entire homeless population of São Paulo, this project gained a life of its own and illustrates the potential and limitations of social intervention by PNBE.

This is what PNBE became in the second half of the 1990s: a mixture of social and political actions located increasingly in São Paulo, carried out along with internal activities such as congresses, seminars, debates, although, as time went by, the latter projects of social intervention in emblematic social problems became the cornerstone of the entity.

---

40. *Folha de S. Paulo*, October 7, 1994.
41. *Pensamento Empresarial*, 9, 1995.
42. *Pensamento Empresarial*, 2, 1993 and 8, 1994.
43. *Folha de S. Paulo*, November 25 ,1997.

However, these other dimensions of PNBE activities helped to keep this institution alive, without diminishing its concern for broader political issues. The sending of pizzalike cards to the Congress in early 2001 is an example of the latter attitude, among others.

Conclusion

The PNBE appears to have been an alternative to the traditional corporatist politics, embodied by FIESP: it was born from a critical position with relation to the latter's lack of action in the face of the country's democratization and liberalization, as well as its lack of representativeness of the concerns of the whole business community.

From this standpoint, the PNBE built a platform of action on the national political scene, trying to influence the country's transformations loosely along social-democratic ideas: it fought for a more substantive, redistributive democracy, based on tripartite policymaking, at the same time assuming an important, indispensable role for the market.

By and large, they succeeded in presenting their claims on the national political arena, largely in tune with the unfolding of Brazil's transition, that went from a project centered on the search for resuming growth through concerted policies to an orientation based on market-oriented reforms. It saw this as the only way out of the country's problems, largely implemented through an autocratic executive power (Diniz, 1997). Although practically none of these PNBE ideas were realized, in the long run, they may have had an impact in terms of building and giving public legitimacy to social democrat perspectives.

But that is not the whole story. In order to do that, and considering its critical view of FIESP's becoming an oligarchy, PNBE also tried to establish a new organizational format and practices based on an inclusive, participatory democracy. PNBE aimed at contributing to the building of Brazil's democracy, based on a equally democratic format. In the long run, the critical view of FIESP's lack of representativeness echoed in the institution: the election and platform of the last president of FIESP, Horácio Piva, was clearly regarded as an outcome of PNBE concerns (Kapaz, 1998).

Being deeply concerned with democracy in substantive terms, the PNBE also engaged in a variety of initiatives of social intervention. To this extent, the PNBE carried out different interventions on projects in education, the environment, and for children, among others. Additionally, the PNBE has been awarding a prestigious PNBE Award of Citizenship to outstanding contributors to citizenship-building in the country.

The PNBE success story therefore may be rooted in this double personality of an organized interest group turned social movement or nongovernmental organization, which, in turn, mirror the dilemmas of business politics in new democracies: although being a very favorable scenario for capitalists, the autocratic role played by the executive branch gives little room for organized interests, including business's interests. It should, then, not come as a surprise to find business in a peripheral position, such as PNBE's.

Working-Class Contention

Salvador Sandoval

As the decade of the 1980s drew to a close, the Brazilian labor movement was at its height in mobilization capacity. By 1989, strike strength was ten times that of the beginning of the decade when the "new unionism movement" first dawned. Without a doubt by the end of the 1980s, one can confirm that the Brazilian labor movement, especially as represented by the Central Única dos Trabalhadores (CUT), had reached a historic level of development able to lead strike actions in separate occupational sectors as well as command national general strikes, as in the General Strike of 1989 in which over twenty million workers participated. On the institutional side the CUT represented the consolidation into a national organization of a previously fragmented progressive labor leadership (Sandoval, 1993).

Thus by the beginning of the 1990s labor's force in the political arena was formidable as was its corresponding political party, the Workers' Party (Partido dos Trabalhadores). As Figure 10–1 illustrates, strike activity level in 1990 reflected the tendencies of the previous decade, when the labor movement had reached a certain level of organizational maturity. In this first year, organized labor led 1,952 separate strikes with an average of 4,654 strikers per event.[1] Over the entire decade though, one finds that labor's trajectory was in fact inverse to that of the 1980s. In focusing on strike performance as a quantitative measure of labor's capacity to mobilize workers in contentious actions, as depicted in Figure 10–1, the decade of the 1990s can be divided into three distinct periods or phases representing different political and economic conjunctures and patterns of labor mobilization.

Phase I encompasses the years of 1990 to 1993 when labor was struggling against the effects of hyperinflation. Considering that these years were

---

1. Departamento Inter-Sindical de Estudos Sócio-Econômicos, strike data 1990–1999, calculations by author.

FIGURE 10-1. Labor Strikes and Average Number of Strikers, 1989–1999

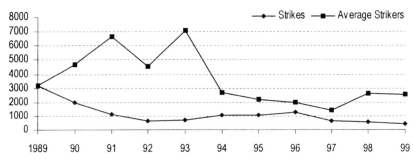

Source: Strike data 1990–1999: DIEESE until October 1999; strike data 1989, Sandoval (1993), p. 170.

marked by severe economic instability as the country rapidly slipped into a hyperinflation spiral, labor's response was direct. Union mobilization against the corrosion of wages due to the 25–30 percent monthly inflation produced strike actions with characteristic dimensions. There was a significant decrease in the number of strike actions from 1,952 in 1990 to 732 in 1993 and rising slightly between 1993 and 1994. Though strike actions significantly decreased, the average number of strikers increased to record heights. By 1993, the average number of strikers was 7,095 workers per strike. As hyperinflation drained the lifeblood of the people, workers joined strike actions in increasing numbers to protest and defend their interests.

Even though one can see in this phase a fluctuation in average number of strikers it is important to note that in spite of the fluctuation, strikes represented a growing number of participants in these collective actions. The only exception was in 1992 when both strikes and average number of strikers took a downward curve most likely as striking was substituted by the political turmoil over the crisis in the presidency of Fernando Collor and his eventual impeachment that year. As unions, labor centrals, student and neighborhood organizations, politicians, church clergy, and economic leaders mobilized in favor of impeaching the president, working-class strike activity slumped both in terms of strike events as well as in average number of strikers. This was not unexpected, as strike behavior has generally receded whenever national political issues reach critical points and mass mobilizations are directed against targets other than labor-related ones.

Phase II begins in 1994 and comprises 1994, 1995, and 1996, the years immediately following the monetary stabilization program. The *Real Plan* was enacted in July 1994 as an unorthodox economic program to halt the spiraling inflation. Economic stabilization under the plan would prove to be a fundamental factor in undermining labor's mobilization capacity from this phase on. As the curves in Figure 10–1 indicate, strike activity, in terms of number of strikes, increased slightly over the previous period (Phase I) but average number of strikers declines at a rapid rate reaching the lowest level since the late 1970s. Strike actions were focused mainly in specific firms with the participation of employees while the large occupational category mobilizations ceased. In this respect, the relevance of Phase II can only be understood in relation to Phase II and Phase III. In the overview, we find that Phase II reflects the difficulties that the labor movement had, and in particular the CUT, in dealing with the new socioeconomic conditions created as a consequence of economic stabilization.

The data for Phase III clearly depict strike activity in a period of growing economic recession. In the recessive economy strike actions continued to decline and average number of strikers also had an insignificant increase over the 1994 and 1996 period. Needless to say, the causes for this decline are, in part, explained by the effects of economic recession on workers' disposition to challenge employers in a period of growing unemployment and economic uncertainty, but as we argue in the remainder of the chapter, the decline in labor union mobilization also resulted from the undermining of the CUT rank-and-file base and the inability of the CUT to respond to the consequences of stabilization and subsequent neoliberalization of the Brazilian economy.

The Changing Profile of Strike Demands

Looking more closely at the years between 1994 and 1999, the period of the stabilized economy, we find that the decline in strike activity was due to changing economic conditions, as evident in the change in the profile of strike demands over the three phases into which the decade is subdivided. Strike actions in the first phase (1990–1993) advocated demands predominantly proactive in nature, focusing overwhelmingly on issues of wage increases as a result of the galloping inflation that marked those years. After economic stabilization in 1994, strike demands underwent important changes clearly differentiating the subsequent Phases II and III. Between 1994 and 1997 (Phase II) proactive strike demands began a gradual decline as defensive demands increased significantly at the same time. This is best exemplified in the specific demands made by strike actions at this time (DIESSE, Boletim, 1999: 11). In Phase II, wage demands decrease almost 40 percent between 1994 and 1996 while demands over employers' compliance to contract agreements rose from 18 to 44 percent. During this time, demands over job security remained at 10 percent for the three years in question.

In Phase III the most change in the profile of strike demands are present. Beginning with 1997, as strike actions and worker participation plummet, strike demands reflect the new social-economic conditions of recessive

FIGURE 10-2. Strike Demands, by type, 1994–1999, percent

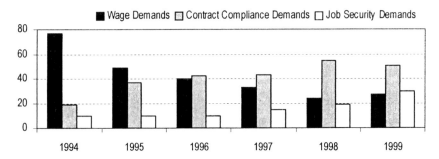

Source: Data adapted from "5 Anos do Plano Real," *Boletim DIESSE*, Separata, July 1999, p.11.

neoliberal government policies. From 1997 on, defensive demands over-whelmingly dominate workers' demands while proactive demands become progressively less prominent.

A closer look at the specific strike demands in this phase, depicted in Figure 10–2, shows that higher wage demands play a less important role, falling to 25 percent in 1998 and 28 percent in 1999. On the other hand reactive demands like contract compliance and job security issues become predominant among the issues raised in strike actions. Contract compliance demands account, on the average, for 50 percent of the demands in all strikes at this time. More interesting is the fact that job security demands have an important increase from 15 percent in 1997 to almost 30 percent in 1999. In this sense, of all the strikes conducted in the period, 30 percent of them made demands about job security and 50 percent also made demands related to compliance to contracts or legal provisions. The shift from proactive to defensive demands in worker mobilizations further points to the effects that the new economic situation had on working-class mobilization. Not only did stabilization decrease inflation, it also created the conditions for fundamental changes in basic structures of the economy.

While strike scholarship has clearly established the now commonplace fact that recession tends to reduce the predisposition of workers to strike, this is not entirely clear that it explains the pronounced decline of labor militancy in the Brazil case. Over the decade of the 1980s, under conditions of spiraling inflation and periodic recession, workers' unions were far less restrained and workers were more predisposed to mobilize their resources in collective actions against employers and government authorities and often against threats and actions of state repression. Why then in the 1990s, with a highly organized union movement under the CUT, has labor been less efficacious in its capacity to mobilize workers against the effects of neoliberal policies and globalization? Certainly one partial explanation is the recession, but to fully understand labor's demobilization it is necessary to focus on how economic stability and restructuring have undermined the CUT social bases, and CUT's capacity to provide responses to new economic demands.

While the 1994 *Real Plan* brought hyperinflation under control, the Brazilian economy was already showing signs of structural change from the beginning of the decade, changes that would come to undermine the social basis of the "new unionism" more than a decade after its founding. The impact of an economy in recession as in the years 1997–1999 would partially account for the sharp drop in strike activity, if it were not for the fact that this decline began at the beginning of the decade after a very successful decade (1980s) of labor militancy and organizing. My argument is that the changes in the economy and in the social structure that began in 1990 contributed significantly to a weakening of the CUT rank-and-file base and created serious dilemmas for union leaders in formulating systematic and cogent union responses to the negative effects of stabilization and neoliberalization.

Over the 1980s, strike rate data show that only a few occupational categories stand out as the pillars of labor militancy: metalworkers, especially automotive and steelworkers, bank workers, and government employees, teachers, and health workers (Sandoval, 1993: 163).

Examining the evolution of employment between 1989 and 1999 for these economic sectors where the CUT found its greatest support and militancy, one finds that of the occupational categories that had been the mainstay of CUT militancy (metal/automobile workers, bank workers, and civil servants), only government workers did not experience significant changes in employment over the decade.

Crisis in the Social Bases of the CUT: The Case of the Metalworkers

Automotive workers in the metropolitan region of São Paulo were the cradle of the "new unionism" movement in the late 1970s and one of the cornerstones of the CUT, demonstrating their determination and combativeness by participating in the major mobilizations throughout the 1980s and providing the CUT with the core leadership necessary to consolidate a national labor movement. Yet by 1990, in Phase I, employment declined less severely from 95 to 78 percent. After 1994, though, work in the sector continued to decline throughout Phase II. In the last period, between 1997 and 1999, employment for automotive workers had reached a historic low of about 58 percent, having lost just less than half of the jobs in the sector since 1990.

Job loss in the sector can be attributed to factors related to changes in the technological bases of production and the effects of the growing recession seemingly linked to government's economic policies aimed at supporting

Cardoso's reelection. With stabilization under the *Real Plan* and increased foreign investment many automotive and metalwork companies sought sites outside the traditional industrial belts of the cities of São Paulo, Belo Horizonte, and Rio de Janeiro to build new industrial plants and assembly units.

Cities that had been traditional strongholds of the "new unionism" faced growing unemployment due to technological changes, to recession, and, just as important, to the flight of industrial investment to other regions of the country. As authorities from less industrialized cities and states used direct fiscal incentives to attract new industrial investments, the older industrial centers began to suffer the gradual processes of deindustrialization, as was the case of the automotive and metalworks industries of the metropolitan areas of São Paulo and Belo Horizonte.

A study of the evolution of industrial employment between large and small cities (Silva, 1999: B1) points out the shift in both the number of jobs leaving from the larger cities to smaller ones as well as the shift in the bulk of wages that accompany these changes. Figure 10–3 shows that in 1970 large cities accounted for 70 percent of the jobs. By 1998, small cities had succeeded in attracting 52.6 percent of the jobs and large cities were left with only 47.4 percent.

Between 1991 and 1998, the São Paulo industrial belt lost 474 metalwork factories that relocated to the interior of the state or some other states. This represented a loss of over 25,000 jobs in this sector alone. While in 1993 the metallurgical industries employed 32.6 percent of the labor force in the city, by 1996 this had been reduced to only 21 percent. This decline of industrial employment in the large cities is also reflected in the shift in wages from the capitals to the interior. In 1970 large cities accounted for 82.9 percent of the wages paid in the industrial sector and the small cities for only 17.1 percent. By 1998 there had been a noticeable change. Large cities now account for 64.3 percent and small cities have increased their share to 35.7 percent: small cities have doubled their share of wages in the last thirty years. Average wages in São Paulo were around R$1,200; in the interior average wages in the metal industries were approximately R$840.

The migration of both preexisting industries and new ones to other regions away from the traditional industrial areas not only created immediate problems of unemployment and reskilling of workers for local unions, but on the national level the CUT was confronted with competing union interests. Mainstay unions in the traditional industrial regions faced fleeing investment, while unions and the working-class populations of the less industrialized regions were strong lobbies against continued industrial concentration in the São Paulo–Belo Horizonte–Rio de Janeiro triangle.

FIGURE 10-3. Industrial Employment, by city size, 1970–1998

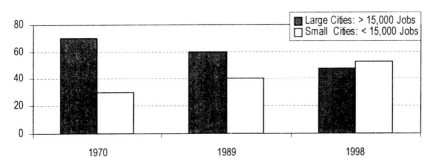

Source: Adapted from M. Pochmann/UNICAMP, reproduced by *O Estado de S. Paulo*, 11/08/99, p. B1.
Municipalities with 15,000 or more employees represent 85 percent of the industrial product.

The fact that local populations and local state governments mobilized their resources—tax incentives, tax exemptions, low interest public loans—to attract industry away from the traditional regions placed the CUT in a delicate position between its traditional union base and the emerging industrial unions in the industrializing cities of the interior. This dilemma has meant that the CUT has been unable to come up with any coherent and cogent stance with regards to industrial expansion.

The flight of industrial capital from the large metropolitan areas to secondary cities in the interior has been a serious blow to the capacity of core metalworkers' unions to respond to the multiple forces that stabilization and neoliberalization have brought upon the working class. Facing a shrinking job market and the deindustrialization of the traditional areas of unions' strength, the metalworkers' unions were confronted with yet another challenge: the privatization of the Brazilian steel industry. The steelworkers' unions made up another arm of the metalworkers' militancy along with the automotive workers. Over the decade of the 1980s the steelworkers represented a key base for the CUT and their presence in the union movement was noteworthy.

Beginning with the ill-fated Fernando Collor presidency and continued with more determination in Fernando Henrique Cardoso's presidency, dominant political elites assumed the commitment of privatizing the extensive industrial and banking holdings under government ownership. In terms of labor militancy, key in this broad public sector were the employees in Brazilian steel industry and the state-owned banks.

The debates within the CUT over the privatization issue brought to a head the political dilemma faced by the progressive unionists with regard to the situation of the state-owned enterprises: on the one hand these enterprises were economically deficient due to excessive political patronage that resulted in mismanagement, featherbedding practices, and lack of market competitiveness, and, on the other hand, they represented a strategic sector for the national economy. As the debates developed within the CUT against privatization, it became clear that CUT leadership and political supporters, though positioned against privatization, were unprepared to offer viable alternatives to the distortions in the steel complexes, while local union leaders and steelworker rank-and-file favored privatization, seeing it as the only form of correcting these distortions and ultimately curtailing political patronage. As each steel complex was auctioned, local union leaders and their workers confronted CUT and student activists on the streets protesting in favor or against privatization. In the aftermath of the confrontations in each privatized company, the union locals voted to leave the CUT, remaining independent unions, instead of joining the more conservative labor confederation, *Força Sindical*. Between 1991 and 1997 ten Brazilian steel complexes were privatized bringing nearly US$6 billion to the national treasury (Biondi, 1999: 39).

The loss of the steel rank-and-file to the CUT was yet another blow that contributed to the weakening of the metallurgical union base of the "new unionism." This, coupled with the growing problems facing the metalworkers' unions and rank-and-file in the older industrial areas, has meant that one traditional stronghold of labor militancy has been seriously curtailed.

Crises in the Social Bases of the CUT: The Case of the Bank Workers

Like the metalworkers, bank workers also faced changes that sapped the capacity of the union leadership to mobilize their following. In the first place, bank workers faced massive unemployment as a result of economic stabilization. The logic of hyperinflation made it necessary for banks to provide customer services on an extensive scale as well as to guarantee that money transactions be conducted as swiftly as possible given the high daily devaluation rates due to inflation. Because of this, all banks, up until the 1994 *Real Plan*, maintained a large contingency of workers as tellers and in the processing functions to guarantee speedy transactions under the pressure of daily inflation. In order to further respond to the challenges of high daily inflation rates, banks quickly adapted themselves to computerized procedures that made transactions more rapid, while costumer services remained highly labor intensive prior to 1994. Nevertheless, over the period between 1990 and 1994 (Phase I) employment in the banking sector already was indicating a strong decline from almost 100 in 1990 to 77 percent in 1994.

Certainly the bulk of the jobs lost in this period were due to the growing computerization of the banking system. As depicted in Figure 10–4, until

FIGURE 10-4. Bank Employment and Automatic Banking Trends, 1990–1999

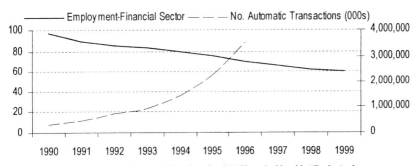

Source: Employment data: Ministério de Trabalho, Caged and RAIS as cited in table "Evolução do emprego foram . . ." in *O Brasil Desempregado*, São Paulo: Fundação Perseu Abramo, 1999, p. 18. Automation data: *Suma Econômica*, October 1996; Federação Brasileira de Bancos, 1996.

1994 banks had already established their bases for computerized banking. One finds a steady tendency to grow both in terms of the doubling in the number of ATM units installed in Phase I and in terms of the increase in automatic transactions that grew dramatically in the period. Thus, as banks automated their systems, employment in the sector took a corresponding decline. After the 1994 *Real Plan*, the tendency toward bank automation climbed as indicated in the increased number of transactions and financial institutions added yet another facility to an already expanding ATM system: the home office banking services. This, as Figure 10–4 illustrates, occurred in the years between 1994 and 1996 that marked a threshold in the restructuring of the banking labor market with the further elimination of jobs.

These changes in Phase II and Phase III point to a direct decline in the evolution of bank employment (see Figure 10–4) which by 1999 reach almost 50 percent of the 1990 level. The massive dismissals of bank workers over the decade severely weakened the unions' capacity to mobilize the rank-and-file as workers became less predisposed to risk their jobs in work stoppages.

Furthermore, unions were slow to recognize that computerization of the banking system during the hyperinflation years was a prelude to further automation once economic stability occurred. By the time the effects of stabilization were acknowledged by the union leadership as a clear danger, banks had already laid the groundwork for very sophisticated banking systems.

In addition to the shocks coming from technological changes in the banking system, unions were also confronted with the dilemmas of privatization of the state-owned banks that like their counterparts in the steel mills were plagued with political patronage, corruption, featherbedding, and deficit lending. Since state-bank employees have been the backbone of labor militancy among the rank-and-file, bank workers' unions were hard-pressed to maintain their influence on employees as public banks were turned over to private owners and labor relations in these banks changed drastically.

Through the decade over 90 percent of the state-owned banks were privatized, leaving only the bank of the State of São Paulo, which was auctioned off in 2000. The loss of the state-owned banks as the backbone of the bank workers' unionism was a hard blow to the union movement, even though state-owned bank employees, in conjunction with their union leaders, strongly resisted privatization.

A fourth factor that impacted the mobilization capacity of the bank workers' unions was the series of financial crises that involved a number of large national private banks after the end of hyperinflation. The closing of these important private financial institutions in conjunction with the entering into the Brazilian market of foreign banking interests further fueled the tendency toward greater concentration of the banking system as these new foreign banks purchased both state-owned and privately owned banks. The concentration of the industry has strengthened bank employers in relation to the now more vulnerable rank-and-file, often leaving union leaders in disarray and lacking cogent proposals.

Confronted with a large array of issues resulting from the major restructuring of the banking sector, the labor unions have been unable to formulate coherent political strategies to defend the interests of their workers either with regards to job security or the effects of high-tech innovation. As a consequence, union leaders, though continuing to have a major role in national and regional union politics, have been less successful in mobilizing their category while facing setbacks at the hands of government authorities and employers.

Crises in the Social Bases of the CUT: The Case of the Government Workers

Of the occupational groups within the CUT that demonstrated the most militancy, government employees have stood out in the 1980s with the highest strike rates. Growing in organization and militancy over the decade by 1989, civil servants accounted for a little less than half of the strikes that year. In terms of man-hours lost (Almeida, 1994: 94), workers mobilized, and strike frequency, the government employees outpaced the private sector workers in strike activities by almost fifteen times (Sandoval, 1993: 164–169).

In union politics, civil service unions have achieved key positions within the CUT, occupying national and regional director's positions often disproportionate to their numbers in the workforce or even in the rank-and-file affiliated to CUT unions. In 1995, of the twenty-five members of the national board of the CUT, eighteen were representatives of public sector unions and seven from the private sector. In the same year in several state boards, government union representatives held an important proportion of the seats (Nogueira, 1999: 59–66). Within the government employee unionism, some occupational categories stood out in their militancy and influence in union politics: educational workers, health workers, and government employees in the public enterprises (specifically bank workers), steelworkers, and petroleum workers.

Public service workers were not immune to the economic effects of the post-*Real Plan* period. First, one segment of government employee unions, the bank workers, and steelworkers, were severely curtailed in their capacity to exercise collective action pressure due to the impact of privatization of the public banks and the state-owned steel complexes, already analyzed above.

Second, government workers were very hard hit by the fiscal crisis of the state. As stabilization brought a deepening of the consequences of deficit spending, authorities were forced to limit expenditures especially in terms of wage increases for its employees. Since 1994 neither the federal, state, nor municipal governments have given wage increases. Even though this has caused considerable discontent among government employees, frequent demonstrations of the fiscal crisis have made civil servants less predisposed to make proactive demands. In an absolute inversion of previous high strike rates, in the 1990s civil servants have been conspicuously absent from the strike rolls. The few mobilizations registered have been strikes protesting the failure of either state or municipal governments to meet their monthly payrolls or to protest the critical deterioration of working conditions as in the cases of education and health. Only a few sectors, like the subway workers' union of São Paulo, have struck for wage increases.

A third factor that contributes to the demobilization of the public service workers' unions is the effects of decentralization of some key government services like health care, basic education, and social welfare. Among the main points on the political agenda of the Cardoso presidency has been the decentralization from federal and state governments to municipal governments of these three services. As municipalization has progressed, obliging local authorities to assume more of the direct administration of these services, unions face the difficult challenge of restructuring themselves for action on the local city level shifting their organizational base from one primarily focused on state and national governments to one aimed at local municipal administrations. Education, health, and welfare workers' unions were not prepared to handle the mobilization effects of this shift. Both the logic of organization and recruitment and the strategies of mobilization were clearly distinct and the dispersion of power resulting from decentralization meant that unions and their leaders have been hard-pressed to achieve an effective restructuring of their unions conforming to the new geography of public authority. Traditionally, the public service workers' unions have been least successful in organizing and mobilizing municipal workers compared to state and federal employees (Sandoval, 1993: 167–169).

Finally, government employee unions have faced growing disfavor among public opinion, including workers from the private sector, who consider civil servants a privileged category of workers. In 1995, a survey poll in São Paulo indicated that 66.4 percent of those interviewed felt that they were either very much or partially hurt by public employee strikes. At the same time, 84.3 percent felt that employees of the state enterprises were privileged workers. Even though 63.7 percent of those interviewed felt that the real objective of civil servant strikes was politically motivated, 79.3 percent of the interviewees believed that government employees in essential services had the right to strike over economic issues. At the same time 56.3 percent were against political strikes (Rebelião do Funcionalismo, 1995: A14). Thus, confronted with a lack of support among the general public, including workers in the private sector, the various types of protests that government employee unions mobilized in this period have been conducted without any significant support from the rank-and-file workers of the private sector, even though civil service unions occupy a significant number of seats in the upper echelons of the CUT.

Alternative Forms of Working-Class Contention

If until now labor unions have declined in their mobilization capacity to respond to the effects upon urban workers of neoliberalization of the Brazilian economy, segments of the working-class population have not remained altogether passive in seeking collectively to resist this new thrust of capitalism. Alternative forms of working-class contention have emerged, filling the void left by the contraction of union mobilization. Among the more important manifestations of these alternative forms of worker contention that have emerged and that successfully mobilize workers in confrontational actions to challenge government authorities are the following: the Movimento dos Trabalhadores Rurais Sem Terra—MST (the landless workers movement); the Movimento dos *Camelôs* (street vendors confrontations); and the Movimento dos *Perueiros* (the clandestine city transport workers movement).

The *Movimenta dos Sem Terra*—MST

The MST represents the most articulated and extensive agrarian reform movement in Latin America today. Though the MST has its origins in the last years of the military dictatorship in the late 1970s, in fact the movement took

FIGURE 10-5. MST Land Occupations and Families Participating, 1990–1999

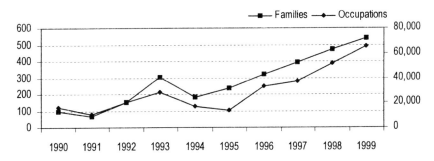

Source: MST, www.mst.org.br, January 2000.

on a new vigor with the progressive neoliberal restructuring of the urban economy and the retraction of urban union mobilization. As the data on collective actions of the MST show, depicted in Figure 10–5, in the period between 1990 and 1993 (Phase I), mobilization in terms of the number of land occupations and the number of families participating in these occupations indicate that the MST gained momentum toward the end of the hyperinflation period in 1992–1993 as the effects of economic instability on workers encouraged rural migrants in the cities to seek a return to the countryside by joining the agrarian reform movement.

Toward the end of Phase I there was an increase in rural workers' contention in 1993, but in the years of 1994 and 1995 when the economy was stabilized under the *Real Plan*, the MST reduced its collective actions while having an important increase in the number of families joining these occupations. The level of mobilization in these two years remains lower than that reached in 1993, 1994, and 1995, indicating a transitional moment between the years of hyperinflation and the beginning of the recession after the *Real Plan*. Certainly, in part, the decline of MST actions is due to the immediate positive effects that the end of hyperinflation has on workers' prospects for a better life in the cities, also reflected in Phase II of urban strike activity (Figure 10–1).

Beginning in 1996, a year prior to the first recessive measures of the federal government, the MST regained the momentum of 1993 with a significant increase in the number of land occupations and a corresponding increase in family participation. As Figure 10–5 shows, 1996 will mark a watershed in agrarian contention. From this year on the MST progressively grew in its mobilization strength as evidenced in the steadily increasing levels of occupations and family participation in these collective actions. As the negative effects of stabilization on the urban and rural working classes made themselves more evident, specific segments of workers turned to the agrarian

movement not only as a reaction against increasing unemployment and falling wages but also against the declining quality of life in the slums and working-class neighborhoods of industrial cities.

FIGURE 10-6. MST Land Occupations and Leaders Arrested, 1990–1999

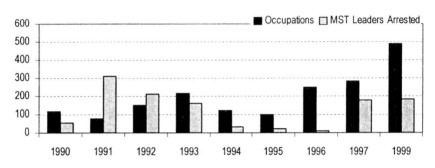

Source: CPT/MST, www.mst.org.br, January 8, 2000.

Over the 1990s the MST occupations met with repression from *latifundiários*, local law enforcement agents, and on occasion federal police.
Under the Collor government the MST suffered its greatest levels of impris-
onments of leaders, as indicated in the data in Figure 10–6, as government
repression exceeded the low number of collective actions conducted in the
three years of the Collor government (1990–1992). After the impeachment of
Fernando Collor, under the Itamar Franco government (1994–1995) arrests
of MST leaders in land occupations declined significantly and remained at
the lowest level until the end of the first government of Fernando Henrique
Cardoso and into his second term when the number of arrests of MST activists reached levels similar to the Collor years. When compared to the greatly
increased number of occupations conducted by the MST in the three years,
from 1997 to 1999, clearly the situation under the Cardoso government has
been more lenient than in the years of Fernando Collor. Overall, though, the
data on land occupation, family participation, and arrests convey a clear indication of the increasing levels of MST militancy in the countryside and widespread support from both the rural and the urban working classes.

As the recession set in after 1997, the MST was also able to raise mobilization in a national campaign for agrarian reform becoming in the eyes of the
general public the predominant expression of working-class discontent and
overshadowing the role of progressive unions in the cities. The deepening
recession affected all segments of the working population, and the MST
became the most visible manifestation of protest among the working class,
especially when the movement initiated another tactic—the mass marches to
government centers like Brasília and other capital cities: at first, as a strategy

of taking rural protests against injustices in the countryside to an urban constituency and, later, as a form of championing the plight of the urban worker against record unemployment and denationalization of the economy.

In April 1997, the MST organized the first of a series of national marches to Brasília, bringing together from across the country in bus caravans more than 40,000 landless rural protesters while catalyzing public display of generalized popular support among urbanites. As the 40,000 *Sem Terras* paraded down the main avenue of the national capital in the direction of the *Praça dos Três Poderes*, thousands of spectators lined the streets with baskets of foodstuffs for the hungry demonstrators and waving Brazilian flags in enthusiastic support of the agrarian movement and against the Cardoso government. While popular support shown to the MST in Brasília was in large measure from the overwhelming civil service–based population that make up the national capital, a national opinion poll conducted at that time indicated that indeed the MST received widespread favor; 80 percent of those interviewed favored the MST goals of agrarian reform (*Eles Chegaram Lá*, 1997: 26–36).

Since this first march on Brasília, the MST has sponsored periodic mass demonstrations in Brasília and other cities calling for agrarian reform and inciting urban workers to react against government recessive policies. While skillfully avoiding any criticism of the labor movement's paralysis, the MST has come to represent the main form of working-class contention in contemporary Brazil.

Following the mobilization repertoire that begins in the countryside with the *Sem Terras* walking to the capital cities recruiting along the way, new demonstrators, and in the cities working-class population, mobilized or not by the unions, joined in a snowball effect and the march along its trajectory. In this manner, the MST has combined mobilization tactics used in the countryside with those familiar to the urban worker into an effective mobilization resource that allies rural and urban workers around the issues of agrarian reform and the challenges facing the urban working class.

By 1999, it was evident that the MST had become a political force to be dealt with. In that year the MST conducted 489 land occupations with the participation of 71,581 families. In addition to these actions, the MST joined forces with the CUT, Catholic Pastorals, and opposition political parties in organizing national demonstrations in Brasília against unemployment and other economic and social exclusion. The *Marcha dos 100 Mil* of August 26, 1999 mobilized 130,000 protesters according to the organizers and 40,000 according to the police, while CUT sources estimated that some 73,000 demonstrators were bused into the national capital from around the country. The state level organizers of São Paulo, Minas Gerais, Rio de Janeiro, Goiás, and the Federal District sent altogether 1,468 buses. In many cities, buses were provided by local authorities as their contribution to the protest, which had also taken its toll on local governments' revenues (*Protestos*, OESP, 8/26/99: A4–A15).

After the success of the August demonstration, the CUT, on its own, attempted to recreate the protest in November of the same year by calling for a national work stoppage against unemployment: *Dia Nacional de Paraliza-ção* and *Protesto em Defesa do Emprego*. Compared to the August action, the CUT event was by all accounts ineffective (if not a failure) in bringing a significant number of workers to strike in protest. Even though the CUT in each state programmed activities for the national stoppage, the very low turnout is symptomatic of CUT's difficulties in activating its mobilization structures among the workers (*Protestos*, OESP, 11/11/99: B5).

An indicator of the underlying competition between the MST and the CUT is the incursion of the CUT in the agrarian reform field. With the success of the MST in the countryside, by 1998 the two major urban labor movement organizations, the CUT and *Força Sindical*, had embarked on sponsoring land occupations by unemployed urban workers as a way to compete with the MST in the countryside as well as to experiment with a weak alternative to the unemployment problem—relocating unemployed workers to agricultural activities. In the state of São Paulo, of the forty-two land occupations in that year twenty-three occupations were lead by the MST, four by the CUT, four by the confederation of rural workers (CONTAG affiliated to the CUT), three by the MAST supported by *Força Sindical*, twelve by independent workers groups supported by local labor unions, and one by the Land Pastoral (ITESP, 1998: 32–33). The idea of settling unemployed urban workers in family farms points out the extent to which urban labor unions have been hard-pressed to come up with coherent and purposeful actions in favor of the beleaguered workers in the cities.

Worker Contention on the Edge: The Neo-*Camelôs* and *Perueiros*

In addition to the growing presence of the MST, the plight of the working class under the recession and the apparent paralysis of the labor movement have also resulted in the emergence of other forms of working-class struggles around the right of workers to gainful activities such as the case of the street vendors. With formal unemployment at about 20 percent in the large urban areas and the interval between jobs now at around one year in São Paulo and Rio de Janeiro, workers have turned to other forms of earning their livelihood such as street vending. In the larger cities, a new type of street vendor has emerged and is becoming commonplace, effectively competing with regular retail businesses for customers on the same street.

This contemporary version of the street vendor, which we have chosen to call the neo-*camelô*, represents a very new and different form of what might still be "penny capitalism."[2] The neo-*camelôs* are by and large industrial workers who lost their jobs as a consequence of the process of restructuring the economy. With the money received from severance pay and *Fundo de Garantia por Tempo de Serviço* benefits they purchase manufactured and imported consumer goods to be sold in street stalls. Unlike the traditional street vendor who sold homemade foods, trinkets, and single cigarettes, the neo-*camelôs* with more resources from severance benefits are able to invest in small electric appliances (telephones, radios, clocks, calculators, etc.), computer accessories (cords, pads, screen shades, etc.), battery-run toys, small leather goods, small tools, clothing, and the like. Because of their numbers, their very low operational costs, and their concentration around the busy commercial streets of the downtown areas, these new street "merchants" have posed serious challenges to the established shopkeepers who find a significant portion of their clientele purchasing goods from these new rivals.

As retail business associations and leaders of commercial workers' unions pressure city authorities to remove the neo-*camelôs* from the sidewalks in front of the stores to less advantageous locations, vendors have reacted in continuous confrontations with authorities, tumultuous mass demonstrations, and an occasional riot against attempts to remove their stands and interdict their access to the main commercial streets. Throughout 1999, the major cities were plagued by civil disorders as the masses of street vendors confronted police over the right to access to the sidewalks. With hundreds of arrests, the use of tear gas and riot police violence, these disturbances became part of the scenario of urban Brazil of the late 1990s.

Reliable aggregate data on the neo-*camelôs* are hard to obtain, as their activity is not legally licensed by government agencies. They therefore evade paying taxes, often because they sell cheaper contraband and/or falsified merchandise. In spite of this, indications of the growing importance of this segment of the working population can be inferred from newspaper accounts of the problems related to the incidences of street vendors confronting authorities and reports of collective protests that neo-*camelôs* stage against official repression and in favor of legalizing their activity.

Figure 10–7 illustrates the growth in the presence of the neo-*camelô* as indicated through two forms of contention. In 1995 the number of articles reporting incidents involving street venders and authorities did not mention any collective mobilizations, but beginning in 1996 street vendors showed a dramatic increase in their confrontations with authorities and, possibly more important, their predisposition to organized collective demonstrations in their

---

2.   *Camelô* is the Brazilian term for street vendor. By "neo-*camelô*" we mean those street vendors that are engaged in retail sales of manufactured products and imported merchandise that is more expensive and aimed at the upper and middle classes as compared to the traditional homemade goods sold by the traditional street vendors.

FIGURE 10-7. Incidents and Protest by "Neo-*camelôs*" and "*Perueiros*," 1995–2000

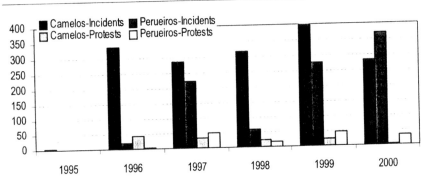

defense. This is vividly depicted in the increase to almost 350 the number of incidents with authorities and almost fifty collective actions reported in the country by the newspaper *O Estado de São Paulo* in 1996.

After 1996 the level of contention remained high, only declining slightly in 1997 and 1998. In 2000, a municipal election year, the number of collection actions declined significantly while the level of incidents with authorities remained relatively high in comparison with the previous years. Thus even though organized neo-*camelôs* refrained from staging mass demonstrations at the time of the hotly contested municipal elections, they were unable to avoid the daily encounters with authorities who attempted to implement the laws that exclude the vendors from the streets. In all of Brazil's major urban centers the neo-*camelôs* have become a vociferous and demanding new segment of the working class with their own organizations.

Street vendor mobilizations further revealed the critical state of the unemployed as they sought gainful employment in activities reserved to businesses. Neo-*camelôs* faced opposition from merchants and from fellow commercial workers, who feared for their jobs as sales dropped in the stores because of the comparative advantages of the low-cost informal retailers. Furthermore, street vendors as they saturated main streets made access to shops difficult, often discouraging customers from shopping in the center city and thereby inducing them to seek the rival shopping centers instead. Because of this, store owners and salesworkers have been adamant in having city authorities remove the thousands of street vendors.

The labor movement was unprepared to respond to this form of contention from among the now near-chronically unemployed. First, the Brazilian labor movement only recently has begun to focus its organizational efforts in recruiting unemployed workers. Traditionally both progressive and conservative unions had regarded as their rank-and-file only those workers employed in the industries under their corresponding jurisdiction. Consequently, street vendor contention revealed an abyss between the organized labor movement and a growing segment of the working class excluded from the reach of institutionalized representation of workers' interests. Furthermore, the CUT has traditionally been less concerned in having a strong presence among the commercial workers' unions, leaving the bulk of these unions to be recruited by the more conservative *Força Sindical*. This has meant that the CUT has largely been absent among workers in growing sectors of the economy, such as the customer service industries, into which the street vendors attempt to enter through their "penny-capitalist" strategies.

The CUT, like the *Força Sindical*, once again found themselves caught in a conflict of interests between two categories of workers, the street vendors (unemployed industrial workers) and store workers; a contradiction that has become common in labor's dilemmas arising from the present phase of capitalist development. The issues raised by the unemployed neo-*camelôs*, the retailers of the informal sector, also point to another lacuna in the Brazilian labor movement: its traditional disregard for urban policies even though most urban policies affect the well-being of the working classes. This has meant that labor is almost impotent in interceding with local authorities as the latter try to deal with the social and political effects of recession when the unemployed workers and their families seek welfare assistance and look toward the municipal government for redress. Consequently, one finds that the labor movement has been unable to systematically bring to bear its weight on local authorities as these seek solutions to addressing the increasing welfare demands of the population.

With labor movement in a declining momentum in Phase II and Phase III (Figure 10–7), "employed" informal sector workers, the neo-*camelôs* show a corresponding inverse increase in their intent to defend their right to work, even if only on the streets.

A similar case is the situation of unemployed workers who used their severance benefits to purchase passenger vans to transport paid riders in competition to the faulty city transit systems. As these "clandestine" transportation services provided by the *perueiros* multiplied in the major cities, the privately owned bus companies and bus drivers' unions joined forces to protest against this informal competition, which neither submitted itself to city vehicle safety regulations, transit management guidelines, nor paid benefits and taxes. Throughout the latter part of the decade of the 1990s, cities were periodically disrupted, on the one hand by bus drivers' strikes against local authorities' lack of suppression of the *perueiros* and in defense of their jobs in lieu of the decline in the number of riders on the city buses and by disturbances from actions of the *perueiros*.

As authorities moved in to curtail the "illegal" activities of the van owners, these workers responded by individual and collective forms of resistance.
In 1999 in the city of São Paulo alone, protests by *perueiros* resulted in the
burning of fourteen buses, the sacking of seven buses, the sequestering of one
bus, the slashing of the tires of another nine buses, and the confiscation of
vans. That year police apprehended 161 vans and in the first two months of
2000 police had already apprehended 1,420 vans and arrested their drivers
(*"Perueiro* é preso," 2000: C4).

Like the neo-*camelôs*, data on *perueiro* contention are likewise scanty.
Newspaper accounts offer the accessible and most detailed information indicating the extent of this form of working-class action. In viewing the distribution of the number of newspaper reports on confrontations between *perueiros*
and police, and van drivers' organized protests, as depicted in Figure 10–7,
the data show that *perueiro* contention rose concomitantly as organized
labor's decline in strike activity between 1996 and 1997 (Phase II) and, after
a brief interlude in 1998, contention in 1999 and 2000 (Phase III) reverber-
ated to higher levels than before.

Once again the labor movement stood on the sideline in dismay at the
spectacle of unemployed workers pitched in battle against police, city inspectors, and bus drivers for the right to gainful employment. As in the case of the
street vendors, the labor movement was neither prepared to represent the
interests of the workers involved in this confrontation nor equipped to interfere in issues of urban planning.

Conclusion

The chapter has attempted to analyze the processes that have led to the weakening of the mobilization capacity of the labor movement and in particular of
the CUT. The effects of stabilization and the restructuring of the economy
produced structural contradictions within the working class. The labor movement has been very slow in dealing with these changes. The contradictions
have been reflected in the overall demobilizing conditions present among
those occupational groups that had been the mainstays of CUT militancy:
metalworkers, bank employees, and civil servants. As the effects of the economic stabilization after the *Real Plan* negatively impacted these occupational categories, unions have been hard-pressed in their ability to respond
collectively to these changes. We have outlined how economic changes in the
decade of the 1990s affected each occupational category and how workers
turned to other forms of collective actions in seeking redress of their grievances and demands for integration into the economy. Among the major forms
of alternative actions have been the MST (Movimento dos Trabalhadores
Sem Terra) in the countryside and the collective actions of the urban unem-

ployed as they engage in street vending and transit activities and as a result confront business interests, other union worker interests, and local authorities. In the ensuing conflicts between these workers, now in the informal sector, and municipal authorities, one finds again the contradictions that have made the labor movement less agile in representing the interests of workers at this point in time.

CHAPTER 11

Brazil and Hemispheric
Integration

João Paulo Machado Peixoto

> *Mercosur is destiny, FTAA is an option.*
> Celso Lafer, Brazilian Foreign Minister
>
> *FTAA is inevitable.*
> Albert Fishlow, Economist

On August 31, 2000, Brazilian President Fernando Henrique Cardoso, exercising leadership in regional governance, convened a meeting of the eleven presidents of South America in Brasília to discuss the integration of the region's economies. As outlined in the *Comunicado de Brasília*, the objective was to connect South American economies through a network of highways, bridges, and river routes, as well as telecommunications, electrical grids, and gas pipelines. A free trade agreement linking and expanding Mercosur (including Chile) and the Andean Community would be the backbone of a South America Free Trade Area led by Brazil. The challenges of developing a South American free area, however, were compounded by serious political instability in most Andean countries and economic uncertainty in Argentina, not to mention the political, diplomatic, and cultural difficulties intrinsic in this kind of integration process.

This chapter explores the choices Brazil faces regarding its role in the international economy and its relationship to the reform process firming up in the second half of the 1990s. It probes Brazilian interests and dilemmas regarding the Free Trade Area of the Americas and Mercosur. Particular attention is paid to relations between Brazil and the United States.

The Free Trade Area of the Americas

The first Pan-American conference, convened by U.S. President Grover Cleveland to consider a customs union of the Americas, was held in Washington, D.C., on October 2, 1889.[1] Mexico, Central America, Haiti, the Dominican Republic, Brazil, and other South American countries were invited. The conference organizing committee considered but did not accept the United States' proposal of creating a hemispheric custom union. Instead, the preference in the conference, presided over by a Brazilian, was the possibility of proceeding with bilateral agreements.

One century later, in 1990, the idea of the FTAA was introduced by President Bush's "Americas initiative," which proposed a triangulation of trade, debt, and aid. It was not until the Miami Summit in 1994, under President Clinton's leadership, that the subject of FTAA was taken up on a practical level, and only until October 1998 that the United States presented a formal proposal for the FTAA.

The preparation phase covered the period between the beginning of the Denver negotiations, in 1995, and the Cartagena Summit in 1996. During this period, the negotiating machinery would be put in place. The Brazilian strategy focused on a few basic points: approaching the FTAA as a process supported by consensus rule, compatible with existing agreements, and negotiated as a "single undertaking." The outcome represented significant victories from Brazil's perspective. The draft of the FTAA agreement was prepared during the Millennium Round (Seattle, 2000). But by 2002 there was no official agreement, only a great number of texts without visible and tangible agreements on the most important issues.

The proposed FTAA took steps forward in the Quebec summit. All thirty-four countries, except Venezuela, endorsed the original schedule, to complete talks by January 2005, and to get the zone started by 2006. In an unprecedented new political deal, the leaders agreed that countries in which democracy had broken down would be excluded from future summits and from the FTAA. President George W. Bush made an important promise at the summit, announcing his intention of getting the Trade Promotion Authority or "fast-track authority" by the end of the year.

Contrasting Perspectives[2]

The U.S. position is that integration itself is advantageous and will benefit all countries in the hemisphere. The introduction of a free trade bilateral agreement between Chile and the United States was an important step toward integration on a larger scale. Cristobal Orozco, Counselor Minister of the U.S. Embassy in Brasília, supports the idea that negotiations between Chile and

1. Simões (forthcoming). Antonio Simões is Counselor at the Brazilian Foreign Affairs Ministry. The Brazilian Chancellery is known as Itamaraty.
2. These perspectives and statements are taken from speeches and presentations given at the International Seminar, "Hemispheric Integration: Political, Economic and Social Dimensions," hosted by the Instituto Teotônio Vilela, in Brasília, December 2000.

the United States do not undermine Mercosur.[3] Canadian diplomats report that the Canadian experience with free trade has been excellent, and that the FTAA will provide valuable economic opportunities for countries like Brazil. Jean-Pierre Juneau, Canadian ambassador to Brazil, argues that Canada has had significant development with NAFTA, just like Mexico, and has accumulated a trade surplus.

Another perspective, held by Brazilian Senator Lúcio Alcântara (PSDB), president of the Senate Economic Committee, highlights the importance of debate about such issues as the FTAA's political agenda, including the participation of the private sector; the institutional aspects regarding hemispheric integration; and the impact of progressive governance. In order to meet such targets, Senator Alcântara suggested discussions combining conceptual and practical aspects of the FTAA. In the following passage, he presents some ideas related to the three great contexts within which hemispheric integration is being constructed: 1) the historical process of economic globalization, 2) the circumstances that generated the current situation of the South American continent, and 3) the experience of inserting South American economies into the global economy:

> I think that the proposal of a continental free trade area will be analyzed from all angles. I hope it happens this way, for it is not by hiding the difficulties or by simply giving the subject a fundamentally ideological appearance that we will debate it appropriately. The recent meeting of the presidents of South America, held in Brasília, provides clear proof of maturity and prudence on Brazil's part: FTAA was not rejected in advance, but there were discussions about some dilemmas that must be solved. . . .
> Finally, I imagine that hemispheric integration will have better possibilities to succeed if it is based on consistent sub-regional blocs; if mechanisms are created to support the participation of private companies, including the small ones (not necessarily attached or subordinated to governmental decisions); if a more direct participation of legislative power in the creation of new policies to be adopted is stimulated . . .; and, finally, if it is based on an idea of partnership which respects differences and the sovereignty of each participating state.[4]

The Brazilian foreign ministry believes that Brazil's participation in international trade could be increased. According to Ambassador Graça Lima, Brazil's chief FTAA negotiator, Brazil does not export at its fullest potential because its production is too focused on the domestic market, and because of its lack of interest in entering international markets. The foreign ministry supports the United States intentions to incorporate the $10 trillion and 800 million person market of all FTAA countries.

---

3. As he puts it, the United States' position looks to disseminate Mercosur's gains throughout the Americas (personal communication with author).

4. Unless otherwise noted, statements in quotations come from notes of interviews by the author.

According to Graça Lima, Brazil is particularly concerned about three issues. First, there are legitimate fears of occasional distortions in regional trade, causing growing imbalances, and related concerns that unemployment may affect the social dimension of integration. Second, Brazil feels that it must have a free trade area with the European Union and its other partners in order to be able to establish competitive relations. Third, the FTAA has the potential to be a new model of a broad integration process, like the World Trade Organization, that provides mutual benefits and equality in the liberalization of products.

Graça Lima puzzles over what the real interest of the United States was in the formulation of a free trade area in the Americas since, according to the patterns of the WTO and the Uruguay Round, 85 percent of international commerce should be free trade. The United States has difficulty defining its own strategy toward FTAA, its long-term objectives, and the advantages for its partners. Brazil is not sure if the United States will be able to make a balanced offer in 2005. Graça Lima emphasizes that Brazil wants an FTAA different from the United States–Chile Free Trade agreement, which was a laboratory for new bilateral trade agreements. He questions the attempt to have bilateral agreements when there is so much pressure to create the multilateral FTAA. Even though he understands Chile's specific reasons, he considers the political impact of the Chilean decision to be negative.

Brazilian policy negotiators also point out the uncertainties about how to form the FTAA, something that must be addressed in order to have a clear proposal that brings advantages to all partners. The agricultural issue, for example, must benefit Brazil and its partners. This critical element apparently was not included in the negotiations of Chile with the United States, but it cannot be separated from a negotiating process that assumes a single undertaking, as decided in the Belo Horizonte meeting in 1997.

Brazil is skeptical of how long it will take to open the largest markets and establish clear rules, and what cost will be incurred during the process. Policymakers feel that the country needs to be prepared by developing Mercosur, increasing the Common External Tariff (CET), and by improving discipline on trade policy matters—that is, by developing a more perfect custom union.

Gianneti da Fonseca, a Brazilian official at Camex (Chamber of Foreign Trade), explains the FTAA as a natural and positive process of regional hemispheric integration. He considers it to be a natural consequence of a new international reality, created in particular by transformations after the Uruguay Round, the deepening of European integration since the Maastricht Treaty, and the launching of Mercosur. These led to intraregional stabilization and trade expansion. He recounts the process leading to FTAA, from its beginnings at the First Summit of the Americas (Miami, 1994), to the Second

Summit of the Americas (Santiago, Chile, 1998), and the third summit in Quebec City, in April 2001.

Gianneti da Fonseca notes the complexity of the negotiations, considering the diversity of the groups and interests involved, and the need for long-run macroeconomic convergence to diminish competitive distortions. The second difficulty is the fact that the FTAA appears to be shaped by the generally conservative and short-term view of entrepreneurs. Together with the negotiating process, it is necessary to have internal adjustments and reforms to correct competitive disadvantages, especially with regard to taxation, finances, and overall logistics. The third are the barriers created by U.S. protectionism against fifteen Brazilian products. The quota on Brazilian sugar is inferior to the quota of a number of Caribbean countries and that of the Philippines. While Brazil exported about 90 percent of the orange juice it produced in 1982, it currently exports no more than 55 percent. These exports are still subjected to taxes of about 44.7 percent. Iron and steel products are still the targets of antidumping actions and other forms of protectionism. Shoes face 8 to 10 percent taxes. Textile and ready-made exports to the United States are today a fraction of what they represented in 1994. The same can be said of ethanol, iron alloys, and silicon-metallic tubes, among other items.

The Brazilian position is quite different from that of the United States, both in agriculture and in other fields such as intellectual property, governmental procurement, services, and bidding policy. Brazil seeks to form a negotiating bloc to achieve more balanced negotiations and avoid the automatic acceptance of agreements. The country must follow the course of structural reforms and increase its competitiveness.

Brazil and the United States

After the Bretton Woods Conference in 1944, the U.S. economy became the principal engine of world economic growth. Following the creation of OPEC in 1973–1974, which increased world energy prices fourfold, the dramatic growth of the economies of Japan, Western Europe, and the newly industrializing countries (NICs) toward export-led growth strategies made the U.S. role even more central to global economic growth. When the U.S. economy expanded or contracted, the same process would take place in economies throughout the rest of the world (Gilpin 1987). The centrality of the U.S. economy continues to shape, for better or worse, the process of trade liberalization and economic integration.

"The big market for the United States is Brazil, and we know that. The big market for us is the United States, and they know that. So, we have more problems and issues to negotiate than smaller countries"—said President Fernando Henrique Cardoso during a press conference early in April 2001, in

Washington, D.C., after a meeting with President Bush. Indeed, 50 percent of Brazilian exports and 70 percent of Brazilian manufactured products go to FTAA countries—not only to the United States, Canada, and Mexico, but also to South American countries, including Mercosur. Brazilian exports to the European Union are substantially composed of primary products, which means that, in economic terms, a free trade zone for the Americas seems to be more important to Brazil than a free trade agreement with the European Union.

At the beginning of the twenty-first century, United States–Brazilian relations continue to be politically and economically defined by their unrealized potential. Brazil and the United States are the most important economies and the most populous countries in the Western Hemisphere. Brazil is the world's eighth- or ninth-largest economy, representing almost half of Latin America's GDP and is second only to China as the most important destination for foreign direct investment among developing countries. Brazil is an economic power and a leader among advanced emerging markets. Brazil is the leader of Mercosur and a regional leader in the "new economy," accounting for more than 40 percent of Latin America's Internet users (Robert and Maxwell, 2001).

The United States is Brazil's main trading partner. U.S. exports to Brazil have more than doubled since 1991 and totaled more than US$13 billion in 1999. Trade with Brazil is particularly important for states such as Florida, where Brazil replaced Japan in 1995 as a top trade partner. About a quarter of all U.S. trade with Brazil passes through Florida. Exports to Brazil from California, New York, Texas, Illinois, Georgia, and Ohio have also expanded considerably. Brazil is a major recipient of direct investment from the United States, attracting an increasing amount over the past three years. U.S. investment in Brazil has been five times greater than that going into China. For many of the top U.S. companies Brazil represents one of their largest overseas engagements. These companies include General Motors, Ford, Texaco, Exxon, General Electric, Citibank, McDonald's, Cargill, Alcoa, Philip Morris, and Goodyear, as well as the largest pharmaceutical firms.

The creation of a free trade zone will force both countries to move into a serious negotiation process aimed at overcoming misinterpretations and stereotypes, political suspicions, ideological barriers, economic uncertainties, and skepticism. In South America, skepticism about the FTAA is caused by a strong historical, social, and political perception that the proposal is a protectionist maneuver by the United States. The economic, financial, political, and cultural asymmetry among several countries of the Americas, disproportionately large when compared to the United States and Canada, reinforces the attitude of distrust.

The trade agenda for both nations will be full of complex topics that must be resolved by 2005, to include the ongoing summits of the Americas, the opening of free trade negotiations between Mercosur and the European Union to be completed by 2004–2005, and the cochairing of an FTAA round beginning in 2002.

The Brazilian government has to overcome a widely held ideological perception, prevalent among key economic and political leaders, as well as in public opinion, that the FTAA will work only to the advantage of the United States. The Brazilian radical left argues that FTAA, as a reflex of globalization, represents one more stage in the process of economic imperialism and political dominance. Even among FTAA's supporters, there are disagreements concerning specific trade topics, such as dumping, tax barriers, agricultural subsidies, and institutional aspects.

In the United States, opinion polls often show a belief that NAFTA has created more disadvantages than benefits for the average citizen, even when considering the long-term prosperity of the U.S. economy. Though this may be extended to the FTAA, the United States is nevertheless the greatest advocate of the FTAA.

Brazil and Canada

According to the Canadian Foundation for the Americas, Brazil should be a priority of Canadian foreign policy. "The South American giant is a major sophisticated and influential player on the multilateral scene, a central actor in the Americas, and shares many points of convergence in its foreign policy with Canada's agenda. Furthermore, Brazil is Canada's first destination of foreign direct investment and largest export market in South America. If nothing else, Brazil's colossal potential as an economic partner should make the case for Canada's attention."[5]

After such a declaration of goodwill, how can the Embraer-Bombardier incident and the subsequent retaliation by the Canadian government through the unprecedented imposition of restrictions on imported Brazilian beef be explained? Business is business? Bureaucratic bungling? Diplomatic miscalculation? Time will make the causes clear. Meanwhile, it is reasonable to expect that Brazil and Canada have much more to gain than to lose from integration, and not only in economic matters.

Canada and Brazil share some mutual experiences that may help Brazil cope with its doubts and anxieties over the FTAA. To sign the Canada–United States Free Trade Agreement (CUFTA), Canada had to promote significant reforms, especially because of the pressure of globalization and the

---

5.   FOCAL, "Canadian Foreign Policy for the Americas. Submission to the Hon. Billy Graham, Minister of Foreign Affairs Foreign Policy Review—2003." (FOCAL Publications, 2003, 12).

requirements of the agreement. Similarly, Brazil has been going through a process of reform, economic liberalization, and fiscal adjustment, since 1990—in no small part to stabilize the economy and enter Mercosur. Compared to Brazil, Canada's economy was more dependent on exports of agricultural products and was oriented not only toward its North American neighbor but also toward Europe.

The reforms introduced in the 1980s in Canada made deep changes in the country's economic policy and challenged the welfare state in force, which had been inspired by social democratic ideas. The reforms constituted a decisive step toward making Canada more competitive within the new rules of the world economy, set by globalization. Brazil began comparable reforms in the 1990s.

After Pierre Trudeau's government (1980–1984), trade liberalization and structural adjustment became major issues in the electoral campaign debates of 1988, known as "the free trade elections." The economic openness inaugurated under the conservative government of Prime Minister Brian Mulroney, after the intense electoral debate, occurred not necessarily as a result of ideological changes, but as a pragmatic adjustment to the economic and political need to adhere to NAFTA. To achieve this, Canada had to correct macroeconomic imbalances and respond to the pressures of globalization. Changes were due to the economic conditions of the country, similar to those found in a number of Third World nations, even the Brazil of the early 1990s, including a negative trade balance, internal debt close to 75 percent of the GDP, a public deficit of around 6 percent, an unemployment rate near 12 percent, and a deep recession. The measures adopted to change this situation and face new political, economic, and cultural challenges centered on the liberalization of the economy, fiscal adjustment, reform of the public sector, and a severe cut in subsidies. The adoption of reforms later contained in the yet unknown "Washington Consensus" (1990) created conditions favoring the process of continental integration.

Entry into NAFTA was positive for Canada's development, because as the American economy expanded, Canadian exporting firms started to approach the American market more aggressively and began to meet an increasing demand for products and services. Certainly, the interdependence between the two economies increased, with trade between the two neighbors reaching more than one trillion dollars.

Like Brazil, Canada has a long tradition of economic intervention somewhat similar to European-style social democracy, while also in tune with American economic liberalism. These political and economic realities forged Canadian institutions and shaped their development. Whereas the role of the state in Canada is more concerned with promoting development and strengthening state-owned and private Canadian companies, the emphasis of the state in the United States is on a free market that allows international capital a major role in promoting development. This is at the core of the important differences between the two countries.

Opinion polls and various studies indicate that Canadians accept and support state intervention more than Americans. "Statism" still prevails in Brazil also, where economic liberalism always lost to development policies sustained by a model attached to state intervention in the economic sphere. In fact, the history of economic development in Brazil is not the history of liberalism but one of state capitalism and economic nationalism, consistent to a degree with Brazil's Iberian colonial heritage.

Deep structural changes took place in Canada and, later, in Brazil. In an unprecedented way, both governments minimized their ideological stands and their pro-state tendencies to change their economic models. Brazil, via constitutional amendments, eliminated monopolies and promoted structural reforms in social security, administrative, and fiscal models. Canada signed the free trade agreement and joined NAFTA as the impetus for change in its economic policy, and promoted a strong fiscal adjustment, implemented reforms in the public sector, and consolidated the openness of the economy. Both countries were pressed by similar domestic and external facts. The national fiscal crisis and the unavoidable economic reality imposed by globalization forced ideological sophistication to be minimized for the sake of pragmatism. The sum of these internal and external pressures made both countries freeze their ideological pasts and enter a new era of pragmatic or neoliberal economic policies, although they kept their engagements with the presence of the state in the social sphere. That is, in both countries the process of reform, and respect for macroeconomic fundamentals create conditions for trade liberalization. Ideological constraints are not as critical. What appears important is the ability of countries to learn how to think positively and be proactive to face new challenges offered by a new world, rather than being strapped by ideological dogma.

The FTAA negotiation will have to address the diversity of perspectives of the private sector, resulting not only from the size of the business involved—the small and medium companies' views differ from those of the major players' views—but also from the fact that transnational and national companies operating in the FTAA countries have different interests. But ideology has lost space to pragmatism as a motivating factor shaping structural reforms and the role of the state in promoting economic integration.

NAFTA, Mercosur, and the European Union

On March 26, 2001, Mercosur, Latin America's main trade bloc, celebrated its tenth anniversary. In its early years, the bloc achieved spectacular success. Trade among its members increased fourfold and investment soared. In January of 1999, however, Brazil allowed the *real* to float, and the currency devalued by almost 40 percent against the U.S. dollar as a consequence of the speculative attack against the *real*, which followed the Russian crisis. The consequences of the devaluation for Argentina and other bloc partners were serious, and criticism of the Brazilian government and its economic policy grew. To many observers, this jeopardized the continuation of Mercosur.

In March, 2001, Domingo Cavallo, then Argentina's new minister of the economy ordered a radical and unilateral change in his country's import tariffs—a measure that was inconsistent with both the letter and the spirit of Mercosur—in an attempt to escape from recession. Those "temporary" measures include abolishing duties on the import of capital goods from non-Mercosur countries and raising those on consumer-goods imports to 35 percent. Brazil's tolerance was largely due to its long-term commitment to subregional integration. Particularly important was the continued interest of the Brazilian private sector in linkages to Mercosur and to the project of a hemispheric free trade area.

Mercosur confirms the Brazilian commitment to autonomy and integration. At the same time, the decision over the trade agreement between Mercosur and the European Union (EU) will become another major political and economic step and will impact the FTAA. Both trade partners are crucial to Brazil—over a half of its imports and exports business (R$100 billion) is done with Europe (29 percent) and the United States (23 percent). This subregional and "triangular negotiation" is at an early stage and has an immense obstacle to overpass, the tariff barriers on agricultural products.

Mexico is already a step further in this process because it avoided agricultural disputes in its recent agreement on nonagricultural free trade with Europe. This will not be the case for Mercosur as a whole, especially in its negotiations with the European bloc. The business community in Brazil is paying attention to the evolution of the Mexican case after entering NAFTA, since its economy has been making great strides and because after almost eight years of integration, it is a good example of what could happen in Brazil. In 1994, Mexico's exports to the world totaled US$61 billion, reaching US$166 billion in 2000—an increase of 172 percent.

The Canadian government lists the follow benefits from NAFTA: a) since the bloc's inauguration its exports to Mexico have grown more than 65 percent; b) in the same period imports from Mexico expanded 105.1 percent; c) in 1993, Mexico supplied 2 percent of Canadian imports, a figure that grew to 3 percent rapidly. Mexico's trade surplus with Canada went from C$2.897 billion in 1993 to C$7.9 billion in 1999—a growth of 172.97 percent. Canadian trade with the United States also improved. Since NAFTA, Canadian exports to the United States grew 104.49 percent; imports grew 89 percent and show a trade surplus of C$92 billion—a growth of 152 percent. The trade surplus between Mexico and the United States and Canada during the period of 1994–1998, amounted to US$50 billion, and US$73 billion respectively.

Prospects

The FTAA negotiations face diverse political and economic challenges. They range from uncertainty over general administrative issues to the insecurity of most participants; from political and economic instability in the region to attempts by some countries to go into direct negotiations with the regional hegemon; from a single undertaking approach to the natural complexity and slowness of negotiating in bloc the political, economic, and commercial interests of thirty-four nations; from a more aggressive posture of Brazil, in the sense of becoming a leader in the region and a major interlocutor for the United States, to the underlying fact that the FTAA could become an incentive to enhance the competitiveness of the Brazilian entrepreneurial sector; from the decisions made by presidents of Brazil and Argentina assuring that Mercosur will negotiate in bloc with the United States, to the desire of the United States to establish trade agreements directly with Chile and other countries; from the lack of competitiveness of key private sectors to nontariff barriers imposed on competitive Brazilian industries; from the high trade deficit of the United States to selective American protectionism.

The United States can be expected to continue to play a central role, even in the face of skepticism and perceptions of neo-imperialism. In fact, partly because of globalization, the hemispheric project is more centered in the United States today than it was ten years ago. Consequently, the actions of the North American giant will be key to the success of integration, particularly since access to its market is a major incentive for all countries involved. The United States' interests include: access to all the markets in the Americas, especially Brazil's; consolidation of democracy and free markets in the region; better laws to protect intellectual rights; and, above all, the prevalence of free trade as a paramount economic policy for the region's economic development.

Just as the United States sees Brazil's market as a grand prize, Brazil wants free entry into the U.S. market without losing Mercosur. Brazil wants access to markets for its products, reduction of nontariff barriers, agreement over rules on antidumping, correction of asymmetries in agricultural products, and the maintenance of the original date to finish negotiations and effectively start the FTAA (obtained at the Trade Ministerial Meeting of April 2001 and ratified in the Summit of the Americas in Canada). In addition, Brazil supports the integration of Cuba in the changing inter-American community.

In the new political economy of international relations accompanying globalization, trade liberalization continues to gain space. In this regard, the FTAA can be seen as a hemispheric reflex of a global phenomenon, and so it appears inevitable. As the 1980s were the "lost decade" for Latin American economies, and the 1990s were the decade of structural reforms, the first decade of the new millennium is likely to be one of freer trade in the Western Hemisphere. With the world partly divided into trading blocs, there is more trade among neighbors than with other countries. In any case, there is growing momentum for the creation of a giant free trade zone from Alaska to Patagonia with a GDP of more than US$11 trillion and a population of almost 800 million people.

One century passed between the preliminary proposals for a customs union for the Americas, and the Free Trade Area of the Americas. This idea will now probably become a reality in a relatively short period of time. The question is how to best insert Brazil into this new and inescapable reality without ignoring national interests. Brazil still faces important strategic and tactical dilemmas. From now until 2005–2006, Brazil will need to make a long-run choice between a genuine free trade area and an unstable customs union. These are the most complex negotiations ever faced by Brazilian diplomacy, with the countries involved in the negotiation being responsible for 50 percent of Brazil's foreign trade and 70 percent of its exports of manufactured products (Nóbrega 2001).

Ideology should not be a complicating factor in the political negotiations surrounding integration. On the contrary, economic rationality should lead to a common understanding of basic principles and values, so long as cultural and political differences among the associated countries are respected.

The reforms adopted to rationalize the state, limit intervention in the economy, liberalize trade and economic activity, and provide for fiscal adjustment are of vital significance in the integration process—even if differences and asymmetries persist in terms of the rhythm and range of structural reform. Evidence from different countries shows that globalization helps firm up two main values: the supremacy of democracy as a political regime, and capitalism as an economic system. A major remaining concern for Brazil and all countries is the issue of social development. Pressures are mounting to deepen the reform process so as to more effectively address social issues, while reinforcing the participation of social actors in the definition of national objectives.

Abbreviations and Acronyms

ABIMAQ	Associação Brasileira da Indústria de Máquinas e Equipamentos (Machine Tools and Equipment Industry Association)
ABIN	Agência Brasileira de Inteligência (Brazilian Intelligence Agency)
ABIPECAS	Associação Brasileira da Indústria de Auto Peças (Auto Parts Industry Association)
ABRINQ	Associação Brasileira da Indústria de Brinquedos (Brazilian Toy Industry Association)
ADIN	Ação Direta de Inconstitucionalidade (Direct Action of Unconstitutionality)
ANC	Assembléia Nacional Constituinte (National Constituent Assembly)
ARENA	Aliança de Renovação Nacional (National Renewal Alliance)
BANERJ	Banco do Estado do Rio de Janeiro (Bank of the State of Rio de Janeiro)
BANESPA	Banco do Estado de São Paulo (Bank of the State of São Paulo)
BNDES	Banco Nacional de Desenvolvimento Econômico e Social (National Bank for Economic and Social Development)
CADE	Conselho de Defesa Econômica (Council for Economic Defense)
CEBRAP	Centro Brasileiro de Análise e Planejamento (Brazilian Center for Analysis and Planning)
CEPAL	UN Economic Commission for Latin America and the Caribbean
CGR	Controladoria Geral da República (Controller General of the Republic)
CGT	Central Geral dos Trabalhadores (General Confederation of Workers)
CGU	Corregedoria Geral da União (Corrector General's Office)
CIESP	Centro das Indústrias do Estado de São Paulo (Center of Industries of the State of São Paulo)
CISE	Interministeral Council for Wages in the State Sector

CLT	Consolidação das Leis do Trabalho (Consolidated Labor Laws)
CMN	Conselho Monetário Nacional (National Monetary Council)
CNA	Confederação Nacional da Agricultura (National Agricultural Confederation)
CNBB	Conferência Nacional dos Bispos Brasileiros (National Conference of Brazilian Bishops)
CNI	Confederação Nacional da Indústria (National Industrial Confederation)
CNPS	National Council for Wage Policy
COFINS	Contribuição para o Financiamento da Seguridade Social (Social Security Financing Contribution)
CONFAZ	Conselho Nacional de Política Fazendária (National Council on Finance Policies)
CONTAG	Confederação Nacional dos Trabalhadores da Agricultura (National Confederation of Agricultural Workers)
CPI	Comissão Parlamentar de Inquérito (Congressional Inquiry Commission)
CPMF	Contribuição Provisória sobre Movimentações Financeiras (Financial Turnover Tax)
CPT	Comissão Pastoral da Terra (Pastoral Land Commission)
CSLL	Contribuição Social sobre o Lucro Líquido (Social Contribution on Liquid Profits)
CUFTA	Canada–United States Free Trade Agreement
CUT	Central Única dos Trabalhadores (Unified Workers' Confederation)
DASP	Departamento Administrativo do Serviço Público (Administrative Department of Public Services)
ECLAC	Economic Commission for Latin America and the Caribbean
EU	European Union
FAT	Fundo de Amparo ao Trabalhador (Worker Protection Fund)
FDI	Foreign Direct Investment
FEF	Fundo de Estabilização Fiscal (Fiscal Stabilization Fund)
FGTS	Fundo de Garantia por Tempo de Serviço (Severance Pay Indemnity Fund)
FGV	Fundação Getúlio Vargas (Getúlio Vargas Foundation)
FHC	Fernando Henrique Cardoso
FIESP	Federação das Indústrias do Estado de São Paulo (Federation of Industries of the State of São Paulo)
FNDE	Fundo Nacional para o Desenvolvimento da Educação (National Fund for the Development of Education)
FPEM	Fundo de Participação dos Estados e Municípios˙ (Fund for States and Municipalities)
FTAA	Free Trade Area of the Americas
FUNDEF	Fundo de Manutenção e Desenvolvimento do Ensino Fundamental e de Valorização do Magistério

	(Fund for the Development and Maintenance of Basic Education and Teacher Development)
GAO	General Accounting Office
GDP	Gross Domestic Product
IADB	Inter-American Development Bank
IBGE	Instituto Brasileiro de Geografia e Estatística (Brazilian Institute of Geography and Statistics)
ICM	Imposto sobre Circulação de Mercadorias (Tax on Circulation of Goods)
ICMS	Imposto sobre Circulação de Mercadorias e Prestação de Serviços (Tax on Circulation of Goods and Services)
IDESP	Instituto de Estudos Econômicos, Sociais e Políticos de São Paulo (Institute of Economic, Social, and Political Research of São Paulo)
IEDI	Instituto de Estudo para o Desenvolvimento Industrial (Institute for Industrial Development)
IMF	International Monetary Fund
INCRA	Instituto Nacional de Colonização e Reforma Agrária (National Institute of Colonization and Agrarian Reform)
INSS	Instituto Nacional da Seguridade Social (National Social Security Institute)
IOF	Tax on Financial Operations
IPI	Imposto sobre Produtos Industrializados (Federal Indirect Tax on Industrial Products)
IPTU	Imposto sobre a Propriedade Local (Tax on Urban Property)
IPVA	Imposto sobre Propriedade de Veículos Automotores (Tax on Property of Automotive Vehicles)
ISI	Import Substitution Industrialization
ISS	Imposto sobre Serviços de Qualquer Natureza (Municipal Tax on Services)
ITBI	Imposto sobre a Transmissão de Bens Imóveis (Transfer of Fixed Assets Tax)
ITCD	Imposto sobre a Transmissão Causa Mortis e Doações (Inheritance Social Security Contributions)
ITR	Imposto sobre a Propriedade Territorial Rural (Tax on Property of Rural Real State)
LRF	Lei de Responsabilidade Fiscal (Law of Fiscal Responsibility)
MARE	Ministry of Administration and Reform of the State
MDB	Movimento Democrático Brasileiro (Brazilian Democratic Movement)
MIRAD	Ministério da Reforma e do Desenvolvimento Agrário (Ministry of Agrarian Reform and Development)
MP	Medida Provisória (Provisional Measure)
MST	Movimento dos Sem Terras (Landless Workers' Movement)
NGO	Nongovernmental Organization
OAS	Organization of American States

OCC	Outras despesas de custeio e capital (Other expenditures)
PASEP	Programa de Formação do Patrimônio do Servidor Público (Government Employee Savings Program)
PBQP	Brazilian Quality and Productivity Program
PDS	Partido Democrático Social (Democratic Social Party)
PDT	Partido Democrático Trabalhista (Democratic Labor Party)
Petrobrás	Petróleos Brasileiros, S.A. (Brazilian Oil Corporation)
PFL	Partido da Frente Liberal (Liberal Front Party)
PIS	Programa de Integração Social (Social Integration Program/Turnover Tax)
PMDB	Partido do Movimento Democrático Brasileiro (Party of the Brazilian Democratic Movement)
PNBE	Pensamento Nacional de Bases Empresariais (National Grassroots Business Association)
PND	Programa Nacional de Desestatização (National Destatization Program/National Divestiture Program)
PND II	Plano Nacional de Desenvolvimento II (National Development Plan II)
PPB	Partido Progressista Brasileiro (Brazilian Progressive Party)
PPR	Partido Popular Reformista (Popular Reformist Party)
PROER	Programa de Estímulo a Reconstrução e ao Sistema Financeiro National (Program to Promote the Restructuring of the Financial System)
PSB	Partido Socialista Brasileiro (Brazilian Socialist Party)
PSD	Partido Social Democrático (Democratic Social Party)
PSDB	Partido da Social Democracia Brasileira (Brazilian Social Democracy Party)
PT	Partido dos Trabalhadores (Workers' Party)
PTB	Partido Trabalhista Brasileiro (Brazilian Labor Party)
SEST	Secretaria de Controle das Empresas Estatais (Secretariat for the Control of Public Enterprises)
SFCI	Internal Control Agency
SINDIMAQ	Sindicato da Indústria de Máquinas e Equipamentos (Machine Tools and Equipment Industry Syndicate)
SINDIPECAS	Sindicato da Indústria de Auto Peças (Auto Parts Industry Syndicate)
SIVAM	Amazon Region Electronic Surveillance System
SRB	Sociedade Rural Brasileira (Brazilian Rural Society)
STF	Supremo Tribunal Federal (Supreme Court)
STJ	Supremo Tribunal de Justiça (Federal Appeals Court)
SUDAM	Superintendência para o Desenvolvimento da Amazônia (Superintendency for the Development of the Amazon Region)
SUDENE	Superintendência para o Desenvolvimento do Nordeste (Superintendency for the Development of the Northeast)
SUS	Sistema Único de Saúde (Unified Health System)
TCU	Tribunal de Contas da União (Federal Accounting Court)
TDA	Título de dívida agrária
TJ	Tribunal de Justiça (State Supreme Court)

TRF	Tribunal Regional Federal (Federal Regional Appeals Court)
TRE	Tribunal Regional Eleitoral (Regional Electoral Court)
TRT-SP	Tribunal Regional do Trabalho, São Paulo (Regional Labor Court, São Paulo)
TSE	Tribunal Superior Eleitoral (Supreme Electoral Court)
UBE	União Brasileira de Empresários (Union of Brazil Businesspeople)
UDR	União Democrática Ruralista (Rural Democratic Union)
URV	Unidade Real de Valor (Real Value Unit)

Bibliography

Abrúcio, Fernando Luiz. 1998. *Os Barões da Federação: Os Governadores e a Redemo-cratização no Brasil*. São Paulo, Brazil: Editora Hucitec/USP.

———. 1994. "Os Barões da Federação." *Lua Nova* 33: 165–183.

Abrúcio, Fernando Luiz, and David Samuels. 1997. "A Nova Política dos Governado-res." *Lua Nova* 40/41: 137–166.

Addis, Caren. 1999. *Taking the Wheel: Auto Parts Firms and the Political Economy of Industrialization in Brazil*. University Park, Pa.: Pennsylvania State University Press.

Addis, Caren, and Eduardo R. Gomes. 2001. "Um Outro Lado da Liberalização: Impac-tos Sociais Transformadores do Apoio do SEBRE às Micro e Pequenas Empresas." In Nadya Guimarães, and Scott Martin, eds., *Competitividade e Desenvolvimento—Atores e Instituições Locais*. São Paulo, Brazil: SENAC.

Affonso, Rui de Britto Alvares. 1997. "Descentralização e Crise Federativa: A Especifi-cidade do Brasil." Paper presented at the Twentieth International Congress of the Latin American Studies Association, Guadalajara, Mexico, April 17–19.

———. 1995. "A Federação no Brasil: Impasses e Perspectivas." In Rui de Britto Álvares Affonso, and Pedro Luiz Barros Silva, eds., *A Federação em Perspectiva: Ensaios Selecionados*. São Paulo, Brazil: FUNDAP.

Affonso, Rui de Britto Alvares, and Pedro Silva, eds. 1994. *Federalismo no Brasil: Desigualidades e Desenvolvimento*. São Paulo, Brazil: FUNDAP/UNESP.

Afonso, José Roberto Rodrigues. 1996. "Descentralizar e Depois Estabilizar: A Com-plexa Experiência Brasileira." *Revista do BNDES* 3 (June): 31–62.

Afonso, José Roberto Rodrigues, and Luiz de Mello. 2000. "Brazil: An Evolving Federation." Paper presented at the IMF/FAD Seminar on Decentralization, Wash-ington, D.C., November 20–21.

Afonso, José Roberto, Erika Amorim Araújo, Fernando Rezende, and Ricardo Varsano. 2000. "A Tributação Brasileira e o Novo Ambiente Econômico: A Reforma Tributária Inevitável e Urgente," *Revista do BNDES* 7(13): 137–170.

Agosin, Manuel R., ed. 1995. *Foreign Direct Investment in Latin America*. Washington, D.C.: Interamerican Development Bank.

Allen, James. 2002. "Corregedoria vai investigar 121 obras irregulares." *O Estado de São Paulo*, January 13, A-7.

Almeida, Ivan Castro. 2001. "A comparação internacional de indicadores de financia-mento e gasto com educação." *Em aberto* 74(18): 121–135.

Almeida, Maria Hermínia Tavares de. 1997. "Unions in Times of Reform." In Maria
    D'Alva Kinzo, ed., *Reforming the State: Business, Unions and Regions in Brazil.*
    Institute of Latin American Studies: University of London.
————. 1996a. *Crise econômica e interesses organizados.* São Paulo, Brazil: Edusp/
    Fapesp.
————. 1996b. "Pragmatismo por Necessidade: Os Rumos da Reforma Econômica no
    Brasil." *Dados—Revista de Ciências Sociais* 39: 213–234.
————. 1994. "O Significado do Sindicalismo na Área Pública: uma Visão Política."
    In *Sindicalismo no Setor Público Paulista.* São Paulo, Brazil: Fundação do Desen-
    volvimento Administrativo de São Paulo-FUNDAP, n.d.
Almeida, Maria Hermínia Tavares de, and Maurício Moya. 1997. "A reforma negoci-
    ada: o Congresso e a política de privatização." *Revista Brasileira de Ciências Soci-
    ais* 12 (34): 119–132.
Almond, Gabriel. 1950. *The American People and Foreign Policy.* New York, N.Y.:
    Harcourt Brace.
Alston, Lee, Gary Libecap, and Bernardo Mueller. 2000. "Land Reform Policies, the
    Sources of Violent Conflict, and Implications for Deforestation in the Brazilian
    Amazon." *Journal of Environmental Economics and Management* 39: 162–188.
Alveal, Carmen. 1993. *Os desbravadores—a Petrobrás e a construção do Brasil indus-
    trial.* Rio de Janeiro, Brazil: ANPOCS/Relume Dumará.
Amaral, Ricardo. 2002. "FHC quer recuperar foro privilegiado." *Valor*, February 4, A-
    7.
Amato, Mario. 1997. Interview with the authors, São Paulo, Brazil.
Ames, Barry. 2001. *The Deadlock of Democracy in Brazil: Interests, Identities, and Insti-
    tutions in Comparative Politics.* Ann Arbor, Mich.: University of Michigan Press.
————. 1987. "The Congressional Connection, the Struggle of Politics, and the Distri-
    bution of Public Expenditures in Brazil's Competitive Period (1946–1964)." *Com-
    parative Politics* 19: 147–171.
Amnesty International. 1998. "Brazil: Corumbiara and Eldorado de Carajás: Rural Vio-
    lence, Political Brutality, and Impunity." AI Index: AMR 19 January. http://
    web.amnesty.org/library/Index/engAMR190011998?OpenDocument&of= COUN-
    TRIES%5CBRAZIL?OpenDocument&of=COUNTRIES%5CBRAZIL.
Amorim, Celso, and Renata Pimentel. 1996. "Iniciativa para as Américas: 'O acordo do
    Jardim das Rosas'." In José Augusto Guilhon Albuquerque, ed., *Sessenta anos de
    política externa brasileira (1930–1990).* Vol. II, Diplomacia para o desenvolvi-
    mento. São Paulo, Brazil: Cultura Editores Associados/NUPRI/USP/FAPESP.
Arantes, Rogério Bastos. 1997. *Judiciário e Política no Brasil.* São Paulo, Brazil:
    Sumaré/EDUSP.
Arantes, Rogério Bastos, and Fábio Kerche. 1999. "Judicário e Democracia no Brasil."
    Novos Estudos CEBRAP 54: 27–42.
Arbix, Glauco. 2000. "Guerra Fiscal e Competição Intermunicipal por Novos Investi-
    mentos no Setor Automotivo Brasileiro." *Dados—Revista de Ciências Sociais* 43(1).
    http://www.scielo.br/scielo.php?script=sci_arttext&pid=S0011-5258200
    0000100001&lng=en&nrm=iso.
Assis, José Carlos de. 1984a. *Os Mandarins da República: Anatomia dos Escândalos da
    Administração Pública.* Rio de Janeiro, Brazil: Paz e Terra.
————. 1984b. *A Dupla Face da Corrupção.* Rio de Janeiro, Brazil: Paz e Terra.
————. 1983. *A Chave do Tesouro: Anatomia dos Escândalos Financeiros no Brasil,
    1974–1983.* Rio de Janeiro, Brazil: Paz e Terra.

Associação Brasileira da Indústria de Máquinas e Equipamentos. 1989. "Política Industrial para a Indústria de Máquinas e Equipamentos no Brasil." São Paulo, Brazil: ABIMAQ, December.

Banco Nacional de Desenvolvimento Econômico e Social. 1989. "Integração Competitiva: Uma Estratégia para o Desenvolvimento Brasileiro." Área de Planejamento, November.

Barbosa, Rubens. 2000. "Barreiras aos produtos e serviços brasileiros no mercado norte-americano." Washington, D.C.: Brazilian Embassy, November.

Barreira, César. 1998. *Crimes por Encomenda: Violência e Pistolagem no Cenário Brasileiro*. Rio de Janeiro, Brazil: Relume Dumará.

Barros, Alexandre C. S. 1978. "The Brazilian Military: Professional Socialization, Political Performance and State Building." Ph.D. diss., University of Chicago, Chicago, Ill.

Barros de Castro, Antonio. 1993. "Renegade Development: Rise and Demise of State-led Development in Brazil." In William Smith, Carlos Acuña, and Eduardo Gamarra, eds., *Democracy, Markets and Structural Reforms in Latin America*. Miami, Fla.: North-South Center, Transaction Publishers.

Bellos, Alex. 2002. *Futebol: The Brazilian Way of Life*. London: Bloomsbury.

Bianchi, Alvaro. 2001. *Hegemonia em Construção—A Trajetória do Pensamento Nacional das Bases Empresariais*. São Paulo, Brazil: Xanã Editora.

Bielchowsky, Ricardo. 1988. *Pensamento econômico brasileiro. O ciclo ideológico do desenvolvimentismo*. Rio de Janeiro, Brazil: IPEA/INPES.

Bilac Pinto, Francisco. 1960. *Enriquecimento Ilícito no Exercício de Cargos Públicos*. Rio de Janeiro, Brazil: Editora Forense.

Biondi, Aloysio. 1999. *O Brasil Privatizado: Um Balanço do Desmonte do Estado*. São Paulo, Brazil: Editora Fundação Perseu Abramo.

Blejer, Mario, Alan Ize, Alfredo Leone, and Sérgio Werlang. 2000. *Inflation Targeting in Practice, Strategic and Operational Issues*. Washington, D.C.: International Monetary Fund.

Bogdanski, Joel, Alexandre Tombini, and Sérgio Werlang. 2000. "Implementing Inflation Targeting in Brazil." Mimeo, Brasília, Brazil: Central Bank of Brazil.

Boito, Armando. 1999. *Política Neoliberal e Sindicalismo no Brasil*. São Paulo, Brazil: Xamá Editora.

Bonelli, Regis. April, 2000. "Fusões e Aquisições no Mercosur." Texto para discussão no. 718. Rio de Janeiro, Brazil: IPEA.

Borin, Jair. 1997. "Reforma Agrária no Governo FHC." In Álvaro Bianchi, ed., *A Crise Brasileira e o Governo FHC*. São Paulo, Brazil: Xamã Editora.

Bresser-Pereira, Luiz Carlos. 2001. "Managerial Administration in Brazil: Reflections of a Reformer." In Ben Ross Schneider and Blanca Heredia, eds., *Reinventing Leviathan*. Miami, Fla.: North-South Center Press.

———. 1996. *Economic Crisis and State Reform in Brazil: Toward a New Interpretation of Latin America*. Boulder, Colo.: Lynne Rienner Publishers.

———. 1993. "Economic Reforms and Economic Growth: Efficiency and Politics in Latin America." In Luiz Carlos Bresser-Pereira, José Maria Maravall, and Adam Przeworski, eds., *Economic Reforms in New Democracies*. New York, N.Y.: Cambridge University Press.

———. 1978. *O Colapso de uma Aliança de Classes*. São Paulo, Brazil: Brasiliense.

Brogan, Chris. 2000. "Brazil." In *Nations of the World: A Political, Economic and Business Handbook*. Place of publication unlisted: Grey House Publishing.

Brooke, James. 1992. "Looting Brazil." *The New York Times Magazine*, November 8, p. 30 passim.

Brunelle, Dorval. 2000. "O Mercosul a cinco anos do lançamento da ALCA: a ALCA é compatível com acordos sub-regionais?" FTAA Continental Forum: political and social actors in integration processes, held by Rebrip, CUT, Cedec, FASE, São Paulo, Brazil, November 29.

Bueno, Ricardo. 1982. *Escândalos Financeiros no Brasil: vinte histórias exemplares.* Petrópolis, Brazil: Vozes.

Bull, Hedley. 1995. *The Anarchical Society: A Study of Order in World Politics.* London: Macmillan.

Burfischer, Mary E., and Elizabeth A. Jones, eds. 1998. "Regional Trade Agreements and U.S. Agriculture." Agriculture Information Bulletin, Washington: U.S. Department of Agriculture, n. 745 (October).

Caldeira, Jorge. 1999. *A Nação Mercantilista: Ensaios sobre o Brasil.* São Paulo, Brazil: Editora 34.

Canosa, Lourdes. 1999. "A Parceria e a Mordaça: A Visão da Firjan sobre as Relações entre Capital e Trabalho." In Ana M. Kirschner, and Eduardo R. Gomes, eds., *Empresa, Empresários e Sociedade.* Rio de Janeiro, Brazil: Sette Letras.

Caputo, Dante. 1990. Lecture presented at CEDEC, São Paulo, Brazil, March.

Cardoso, Adalberto Moreira. 1999. *Sindicatos, Trabalhadores e a Coqueluche Neoliberal.* Rio de Janeiro, Brazil: Editora Fundação Getúlio Vargas.

Cardoso, Eliana. 1998. "Virtual Deficits and the Patinkin Effect." *IMF Staff Papers* 45, no. 4 (December): 619–46.

Cardoso, Eliana, and Ann Helwege. 1995. *Latin America's Economy: Diversity, Trends and Conflicts.* Cambridge, Mass: MIT Press.

Cardoso, Fernando Henrique. 2003. "Além da economia: Interação de política e desenvolvimento econômico." Paper presented at CEPAL, Chile, August 8.

———. 2001. "Democracy as a Starting Point." *Journal of Democracy* 12 (1): 5–14.

———. 1997. "Reforma Agrária: Compromisso de Todos." Brasília, Brazil: Presidência da República, Secretaria de Comunicação Social.

———. 1996. "O Regime Não é dos Excluídos" [transcript of an interview] in *Folha de São Paulo*, October 13, Caderno 5, 6.

———. 1994. *Mãos à Obra Brasil: Proposta de Governo.* Brasília, Brazil: n.p.

———. 1975. *Autoritarismo e democratização.* Rio de Janeiro, Brazil: Paz e Terra.

Cardoso, Fernando Henrique, and José Rubens de Lima Figueiredo Jr. 1992. "Reconciling the Capitalists with Democracy." Paper presented at the Conference on Economic Reform and Democratic Consolidation, Forli, Italy, April 2–4.

Cardoso, Fernando Henrique, and Mauricio A. Font. 2001. *Charting a New Course: The Politics of Globalization and Social Transformation.* Boulder, Colo.: Rowman and Littlefield.

Cardozo, José Eduardo. 2000. *A Máfia das Propinas: Investigando a corrupção em São Paulo.* São Paulo, Brazil: Fundação Perseu Abramo.

Carneiro, Dionísio D., and Eduardo Modiano. 1990. "Ajuste Externo e Desequilíbrio Interno, 1980–1984." In Marcelo P. Abreu, ed., *A Ordem e o Progresso—Cem anos de Política Econômica Republicana, 1889–1989.* Rio de Janeiro, Brazil: Campus.

Carrizosa, Maurício. 2000. "Brazil Structural Reform for Fiscal Sustainability." *World Bank Report* No.19593, Washington, D.C.: The World Bank.

Carvalho, Getúlio. 1987. "Da contravenção à cleptocracia." In Celso Barroso Leite, ed., *Sociologia da Corrupção.* Rio de Janeiro, Brazil: J. Zahar Ed.

Carvalho, Horácio Martins de. 1999. "Banco da Terra: O Banco dos Donos da Terra," *Jornal Sem Terra*, March 10.

Carvalho, Luciana. 2002. "Lei de licitações dificulta corrupção: para Transparência Internacional, a legislação brasileira é a menos vulnerável da AL." *Gazeta Mercantil*, February 4, A-8.

Carvalhosa, Modesto, ed. 1995. *O Livro Negro da Corrupção*. Rio de Janeiro, Brazil: Paz e Terra.

Carr, Edward Hallett. 1979. *Vinte anos de crise: 1919–1939*. Brasília, Brazil: Editora Universidade de Brasília.

Castello, José Carlos Bruzzi. 1989. *Os Crimes do Presidente (117 dias da CPI da corrupção)*. Porto Alegre, Brazil: L&PM Editores.

Castilho, Ela Wiecko V. 1998. *O controle penal nos crimes contra o sistema financeiro nacional*. Belo Horizonte, Brazil: Del Rey.

Castles, Francis G. 1999. "When Politics Matters: Public Expenditure Development in an Era of Economic and Institutional Constraints." Paper for the 11th SASE Conference, Madison, Wi., July 8–11.

Castro, João Augusto de Araújo. 1982a. "O Brasil e o mundo de 1974." Lecture in "Escola de Estudos Internacionais Avançados" at Johns Hopkins University, Washington, January 30, 1974. In Rodrigo Amado. Araújo Castro. Brasília, Brazil: Editora Universidade de Brasília.

————. 1982b. "Relações Brasil-Estados Unidos da América à luz da problemática mundial." Lecture in Escola Superior de Guerra, Rio de Janeiro, June 22, 1974.

Cavalcanti, Carlos Eduardo G., and Sérgio Prado. 1998. *Aspectos da Guerra Fiscal no Brasil*. Brasília, Brazil: IPEA.

Cavalcanti, Márcio Novaes. 2000. "Impactos da Lei de Responsabilidade Fiscal." *Gazeta Mercantil*, January 12, A3.

Centeno, Miguel Angel. 1994. *Democracy within Reason—Technocratic Revolution in Mexico*. Pa: Pennsylvania State University Press.

Chade, Jamil. 1997. "O FMI e as privatizações no Brasil," 'Iniciação Científica' Fellowship Final Report. Universidade de São Paulo, Dept. Political Science, São Paulo, Brazil.

Chade, Jamil, and Fausto Macedo. 2002. "Governo suíço recebe novos dados sobre Maluf." *O Estado de São Paulo*, February 14, A-5.

Cirano, Marcos. 1982. *O Escândalo da Mandioca e a morte do procurador*. Recife, Brazil: Calandra Editorial.

Collier, Ruth Berins, and David Collier. 1993. *Shaping the Political Arena: Critical Junctures, the Labor Movement, and Regime Dynamics in Latin America*. Princeton, N.J.: Princeton University Press.

Collor de Mello, Fernando. 1996. "Impeached Brazilian President Tells his Side of the Story." *Business News*, February 15, 5.

Collor de Mello, Pedro. 1993. *Passando a Limpo: A trajetória de um farsante*. Rio de Janeiro, Brazil: Record.

Comissão Especial de Investigação (CEI). 1994. *A Comissão Especial e a Corrupção na Administração Pública Federal*. Brasília, Brazil: Presidência da República.

Confederação Nacional da Indústria (CNI). 1991, 1992, and 1995. Abertura comercial e estratégia tecnológica: a visão de líderes industriais brasileiros [Commercial opening and technology strategy: the view of Brazilian industrial leaders]. Rio de Janeiro, Brazil: Confederação Nacional da Indústria, December.

Congress 107th. H. R. 3005. 2001. "Bipartisan Trade Promotion Authority Act of 2001." http://thomas.loc.gov/cgi-bin/query/C?c107:./temp/~c`07KIJhWs.

Couto, Cláudio Gonçalves. 1998. "A Longa Constituinte: Reforma do Estado e Fluidez Institucional no Brasil." *Dados—Revista de Ciências Sociais* 41: 51–86.

"Crédito Desafia Reforma, Diz Governo." 2002. *Folha de São Paulo*, January 6, A-8.

Cruz, Antônio. 2000. *A Janela Estilhaçada: A Crise do Discurso do Novo Sindicalismo.* Petrópolis, Brazil: Editora Vozes.

Cruz, Sebastião Velasco. 1996. *Empresariado e Estado na Transformação Brasileira.* Rio de Janeiro, Brazil: Paz e Terra.

Dain, Sulamis. 1995. "Federalismo e Reforma Tributária." In Rui de Britto Álvares Affonso and Pedro Luiz Barros Silva, eds., *A Federação em Perspectiva: Ensaios Selecionados.* São Paulo, Brazil: FUNDAP.

Dantas, Fernando. 2002. "Autoridades do Brasil criticam declarações." *O Estado de São Paulo*, February 2, B-6.

Deland, Robert. 1981. *Exploring Brazilian Bureaucracy: Performance and Pathology.* Washington, D.C.: University Press of America.

Diamond, Larry, Marc. F. Plattner, Yun-han Chu, and Hung-mao Tien. 1997. *Consolidating the Third Wave Democracies: Regional Challenges.* Baltimore, Md.: Johns Hopkins University Press.

Díaz-Alejandro, Carlos. 1984. "Latin America in the 1930s." In Rosemary Thorp, ed., *Latin America in the 1930s: The Role of the Periphery in World Crisis.* London: MacMillan.

DIESSE. 1999. *Boletim.* São Paulo, Brazil.

DIESSE. 1999. *Boletim.* "5 Anos de Plano Real." São Paulo, Brazil.

Dimenstein, Gilberto. 1989. *Conexão Cabo Frio: escândalo no Itamaraty.* São Paulo, Brazil: Ed. Brasiliense.

———. 1988. *A República dos Padrinhos: chantagem e corrupção em Brasília.* São Paulo, Brazil: Ed. Brasiliense.

Diniz, Eli. 1997. *Crise, Reforma do Estado e Governabilidade.* Rio de Janeiro, Brazil: Editora da Fundação Getúlio Vargas.

———. 1988. *Empresariado, sindicatos e política econômica no Brasil da Nova República: 1985–1998.* Santiago, Chile: OIT/PREALC. Mimeo.

Diniz, Eli, and Renato Raul Boschi. 1993a. "Brasil: Um Novo Empresariado? Balanço das Tendências Recentes." In Eli Diniz, ed., *Empresários e Modernização Econômica: Brasil Anos 90.* Florianópolis, Brazil: UFSC/IDACON.

———. 1993b. "Lideranças Empresariais e Problemas da Estratégia Liberal no Brasil." In Eli Diniz and Ary César Minella, eds., *Empresários e Modernização Econômica.* Florianópolis, Brazil: UFSC/IDACON.

———. 1979. *Agregação e Representação de Interesses do Empresariado Industrial: Sindicatos e Associações de Classes.* Rio de Janeiro, Brazil: Edições IUPERJ.

Dinsmoor, James. 1990. *Brazil: Responses to the Debt Crisis. Impact on Savings, Investment and Growth.* Washington D.C.: Interamerican Development Bank.

Domingos, João. 2001. "Governo é derrotado em PEC que muda a reeleição." *Gazeta Mercantil*, May 10, A-12.

Draibe, Sônia. 1999. "A Reforma da Educação no Brasil. A Experiência da Descentralização de Recursos no Ensino Fundamental." In Sergio Martinic, Cristian Aedo, and Javier Corvalán, eds., *Reformas em Educación y Salud em América Latina y el Caribe.* Santiago, Chile: CIDE/ILADES/BID/CIID.

———. 1998. "O Sistema Brasileiro de Proteção Social: O Legado Desenvolvimentista e a Agenda de Reformas." In *1996-Relatório Sobre o Desenvolvimento Humano.* Brasília, Brazil: PNUD/IPEA.

Draibe, Sônia, B. Azeredo, and M. H. Guimarães. 1995. *The System of Social Protection in Brazil: Democracy and Social Policy.* Notre Dame, Ind.: Kellog Institute/University of Notre Dame. Working Paper, n. 3.

Dupas, Gilberto. 2000. "Assimetrias econômicas, lógica das cadeias produtivas e política de bloco no continente americano." Paper presented in "Preparatory Academic Seminar—Meeting of South American presidents." Brasília, Brazil, August.

Durand, Francisco, and Eduardo Silva, eds. 2000. *Organized Business, Economic Change, and Democracy in Latin America.* Miami, Fla.: North-South Center Press.

Dyer, Geoff. 2001. "Fallen Power Behind Brazil's Throne Turns Against Cardoso." *Financial Times,* February 27.

Easterly, William, Norman Loazya, and Peter Montiel. 1997. "Has Latin America's Post-Reform Growth Been Disappointing?" Working Paper 374. Washington, D.C.: Inter-American Development Bank, Office of the Chief Economist.

Economist Intelligence Unit. 1999. *Country Report: Brazil.* November 8: 1. http://db.eiu.com.

"Eles Chegaram Lá: O que fazer agora?" 1997. *Veja* 30 no. 16, April 23: 26–36.

"Em sete anos, SP perdeu 474 empresas metalúrgicas." 1998. *O Estado de São Paulo,* June 27, B4.

Erickson, Kenneth Paul. 1977. *The Brazilian Corporative State and Working-Class Politics.* Berkeley, Calif: University of California Press.

Eugster, Markus. 1995. *Der brasilianische Verfassungsgebungsprozes von 1987/1988.* Bern, Liechtenstein: Verlag Paul Haupt.

Evans, Peter. 1995. *Embedded Autonomy-States and Industrial Transformation.* Princeton, N.J.: Princeton University Press.

Faoro, Raymundo. 1958. *Os Donos do Poder: Formação do Patronato Político Brasileiro.* Rio de Janeiro, Brazil: Editora Globo.

Faucher, Philippe. 1999. "Restoring Governance: Has Brazil Got it Right (at Last)?" In Philip Oxhorn and Pamela K. Strarr, eds., *Markets and Democracy in Latin America: Conflict or Convergence.* Boulder, Colo.: Lynne Rienner Publishers.

Federação da Indústria do Estado de São Paulo. 1997. "Fórum das Reformas: A Nação Tem Pressa." June 23.

Ferraz, Alexandre Sampaio. 2000. "Sindicatos e políticas de privatização no Brasil." M.A. diss. Universidade de São Paulo, Dept. Political Science, São Paulo, Brazil.

Ferreira, José Ignácio.1989. *Denúncia. Crime de responsabilidade do Presidente José Sarney e cinco Ministros de Estado.* Brasília, Brazil: Senado Federal. [CPI Final Report].

Figueiredo, Argelina C., and Fernando Limongi. 2000a. "Presidential Power, Legislative Organization, and Party Behavior in Brazil." *Comparative Politics* 32 (January): 151–170.

———. 2000b. "Constitutional Change, Legislative Performance and Institutional Consolidation." *Brazilian Review of Social Sciences,* special issue, no. 1 (October).

———. 1999. *Executivo e Legislativo na Nova Ordem Constitucional.* Rio de Janeiro, Brazil: Editora Fundação Getúlio Vargas.

———. 1998. "Reforma da Previdência e instituições Políticas." *Novos Estudos* 51(July): 63–91.

————. 1997. "O Congresso e as Medidas Provisórias: Abdicação ou Delegação." *Novos Estudos CEBRAP* 47: 127–154.

————. 1995. "Partidos Políticos na Câmara dos Deputados: 1989–1994." *Dados— Revista de Ciências Sociais* (38): 3.

Figueiredo, Argelina C., Fernando Limongi, and Ana Luiza Valente. 2000. "Governabilidade e Concentração de Poder Institucional: O Governo FHC." *Tempo Social* 11(2): 49–62.

"Fiscal Prudence Goes Local." 2001. *The Economist*, March 10, 35.

Fleischer, David. 2002a. *Corruption in Brazil, Past and Present: Definition, Measurement and Reduction.* Washington, D.C.: Center for Strategic and International Studies.

————. 2002b. Brazil Focus Weekly Report, 5-11 January.

————. 2001. "Como acabar com a praga da corrupção no Brasil?" *Correio Brasiliense*, March 18, 16.

————. 2000. "Reforma Política e Financiamento de Campanhas Eleitorais." In Bruno Wilhelm Speck, Cláudio Weber Abramo, Marcos Fernandes G. da Silva, David Fleischer, and Karl-Heinz Nassmacher, eds., *Os Custos da Corrupção*. São Paulo, Brazil: Fundação Konrad Adenauer.

————. 1999. "Beyond Collorgate: Prospects for Consolidating Democracy in Brazil Through Political Reform." In Keith S. Rosenn, and Richard Downes, eds., *Corruption and Political Reform in Brazil: The Impact of Collor's Impeachment.* Boulder, Colo: Lynne Rienner Publishers.

————. 1998a. "Reelección a la Brasileña: Las elecciones generales de 1998." *Contribuciones* 15(4): 175–195.

————. 1998b. "The Cardoso Government's Reform Agenda: A View from the Congress, 1995–1998." *Journal of Interamerican Studies and World Affairs* 40(4): 119–134.

————. 1997. "Political Corruption in Brazil: The Delicate Connection with Campaign Finance." *Crime, Law and Social Change* 25: 297–321.

————. 1994. "Manipulações Casuísticas do Sistema Eleitoral durante o Período Militar: ou como usualmente o feitiço se voltava contra o feiticeiro." In Gláucio Soares, and Maria Celina D'Araujo, eds., *21 Anos de Regime Militar*. Rio de Janeiro, Brazil: Fundação Getúlio Vargas.

————. 1990. "The Constituent Assembly and the Transformation Strategy: Attempts to Shift Political Power from the Presidency to the Congress." In Lawrence S. Graham, and Robert H. Wilson, eds., *The Political Economy of Brazil*. Austin, Tex: University of Texas Press.

FOCAL. 2003. "Canadian Foreign Policy for the Americas. Submission to the Hon. Bill Graham, Minister of Foreign Affairs." Foreign Policy Review, Canadian Foundations for the Americas.

Folha de São Paulo, 1987–2000.

Font, Mauricio. 2003. *Transforming Brazil: A Reform Era in Perspective*. Boulder, Colo.: Rowman and Littlefield.

Formiga, Marcone. 2000. *O Homem que Queria ser Rei: Ascensão e Queda de Luiz Estevão*. Brasília, Brazil: Dom Quixote.

Franko, Patrice M. 1999. *The Puzzle of Latin American Economic Development*. Boulder, Colo.: Rowman and Littlefield.

Freedman, Eric M. 1992. "The Law as King and the King as Law: Is a President Immune from Criminal Prosecution before Impeachment?" *Hastings Constitutional Law Quarterly* 29: 7–68.

Garman, Christopher, Stephan Haggard, and Eliza Willis. 2001. "Fiscal Decentralization: A Political Theory with Latin American Cases." *World Politics* 53 (January): 205–236.

Gaspar, Malu. 1999. "CPIs dão pouco resultado, diz diretor da entidade responsável por ranking dos países mais corruptos." *Folha de São Paulo*, June 20, 1–7.

Gazeta Mercantil. 1987–2000. Rio de Janeiro, Brazil.

Gazeta Mercantil. 2001, April 21. President Cardoso's speech. São Paulo, Brazil.

Geddes, Barbara. 1994. *Politician's Dilemma: Building State Capacity in Latin America.* Berkeley, Calif.: University of California Press.

Geddes, Barbara, and Artur Ribeiro Neto. 1989. "Institutional Sources of Corruption in Brazil." *Third World Quarterly* 33: 319–347.

Giambiagi, Fábio. 2000. "A Política Fiscal depois de 2002: Algumas Simulações." *Revista do BNDES* 7 (14): 3–28.

Gilpin, Robert. 1987. *The Political Economy of International Relations.* Princeton, N.J.: Princeton University Press.

Gonçalo, José Evaldo. 2001. *Globalização e Reforma Agrária.* January. Available from the PT's Secretaria Agrária Nacional. www.pt.org.br/assessor/agrario.

———. 2000. *Violência no Campo—Ação Orquestrada pelas Elites Rurais com o Apoio de Setores do Estado.* PT Secretaria Agrária Nacional. www.pt.org.br/assessor/agrario.

Gordon, Lincoln. 2001. *Brazil's Second Chance: En Route toward the First World.* Washington, D.C.: The Brookings Institution Press/20th Century Foundation.

Graeff, Eduardo. 2000. "The Flight of the Beetle: Party Politics and the Decision-Making Process in the Cardoso Government." Paper presented at the V Congress of the Brazilian Studies Association. Recife, Brazil.

Grael, Dickson M. 1985. *Aventura, Corrupção e Terrorismo à Sombra da Impunidade.* Petrópolis, Brazil: Vozes.

Graham, Lawrence. 1968. *Civil Service Reform in Brazil: Principles vs. Practice.* Austin, Tex.: University of Texas Press.

Grajew, Oded. 1998. Interview. São Paulo, Brazil.

Gramacho, Waldimir. 2002. "Liquidante do BC é alvo de investigação." *Folha de São Paulo,* February 3, A-6.

Graziano Neto, Francisco. 1998. "A (difícil) interpretação da realidade agrária." In Benício Viero Schmidt, Danilo Nolasco C. Marinho, and Sueli L. Couto Rosa, eds., *Os Assentamentos de Reforma Agrária no Brasil.* Brasília, Brazil: Editora UnB.

Green-Pedersen, CHR. 1999. "Welfare-state Retrenchment in Denmark and the Netherlands 1982–1999. The Role of Party Competition and Party Consensus." Paper for the 11th SASE Conference, Madison, Wis., July 8–11.

Greenfield, Sidney. 1977. "The Patrimonial State and Patron-Client Relations in Iberia and Latin America: Sources of 'The System' in the Fifteenth-Century Writings of the Infante D. Pedro of Portugal." *Ethnohistory* 24 (2, Spring): 163–178.

Greggianin, Eugênio. 2000. "A Lei de Responsabilidade Fiscal e as Despesas Orçamentárias dos Poderes Legislativo e Judiciário e do Ministério Público." Mimeo.

Grieco, Joseph M. 1991. "Anarchy and the Limits of Cooperation: A Realist Critique of the Newest Liberal Institutionalism." In David A. Baldwin, ed., *Neorealism and*

Neoliberalism. The Contemporary Debate. New York, N.Y.: Columbia University Press.

Gros, Denise Barbosa. 1993. "Empresariado e Ação Política na Nova República: Os Institutos Liberais de São Paulo e Rio Grande do Sul." In Eli Diniz, and Ary César Minella, eds., *Empresários e Modernização Econômica.* Florianópolis, Brazil: UFSC/IDACON.

Guadagnin, Ângela. 2001. "A vaca louca e a defesa da Embraer." Linha Direta, São Paulo, Brazil: Diretório Regional do PT de São Paulo, ano XI, n° 486.

Guimarães, Samuel Pinheiro. 1992. O progresso nos processos de integração na América Latina: Mercosul. Brasília, Brazil. Mimeo.

Gurgel, Antônio de Pádua, and David Fleischer. 1990. *Brasil vai às Urnas: Retrato da campanha presidencial.* Brasília, Brazil: Thesaurus.

Gwynne, Robert N., and Cristobal Kay. 1999. *Latin America Transformed: Globalization and Modernity.* New York, N.Y.: Oxford University Press.

Haas, Ernst B. 1956. *The Uniting of Europe.* Stanford, Calif.: Stanford University Press.

Habib, Sérgio. 1994. *Brasil: 500 Anos de Corrupção: Enfoque sócio-histórico-jurídico-penal.* São Paulo, Brazil: Sérgio Antônio Fabri.

Haggard, Stephen, and Robert Kauffman. 1995. *The Political Economy of Democratic Transitions.* Princeton, N.J.: University Press.

Haggard, Stephan, and Steven B. Webb. 1994. *Voting for Reform: Democracy, Political Liberalization and Economic Adjustment.* New York, N.Y.: Oxford University Press.

Hagopian, Frances. 1996. *Traditional Politics and Regime Change in Brazil.* Cambridge, Mass: Cambridge University Press.

————. 1992. "The Compromised Consolidation: The Political Class in the Brazilian Transition." In Scott Mainwaring, Guillermo O'Donnell, and J. Samuel Valenzuela, eds., *Issues in Democratic Consolidation: The New South American Democracies in Comparative Perspective.* Notre Dame: University of Notre Dame Press.

Hammond, John L. 2001. "The MST and the Media: Competing Images of the Landless Farmworkers' Movement." New York, N.Y.: Paper presented to the Seminar on Contentious Politics at Columbia University, April.

Heredia, Blanca. 1993. "Making Economic Reform Politically Viable: The Mexican Experience." In William Smith, Carlos Acuña, and Eduardo Gamarra, eds., *Democracy, Markets and Structural Reforms in Latin America.* Miami, Fla.: North-South Center, Transaction Publishers.

Herrisson, Luiz, and Heliana Frazão. 2000. "Lei Trava Concessão de Incentivos Fiscais nos Estados." *Valor,* June 20.

Hillbrecht, Ronald. 1997. "Federalismo e a União Monetária Brasileira." *Estudos Econômicos* 27 (January/April): 53–67.

Hirschman, Albert O. 1981. *Essays in Trespassing.* Cambridge, Mass: Cambridge University Press.

Hofmeister, Wilhelm, ed. 2000. *Os Custos da Corrupção.* São Paulo, Brazil: Konrad Adenauer Stiftung.

Houtzager, Peter. 2001. "'We Make the Law and the Law Makes Us': Some Ideas on a Law and Development Agenda." *IDS Bulletin* 32 (January 1): 8–18.

Huntington, Samuel P. 1991. *The Third Wave: Democratization in the Late Twentieth Century.* Norman, Okla: University of Oklahoma Press.

IEDI (Instituto dos Estudos para o Desenvolvimento Industrial). 1992a. "Modernização Competitiva, Democracia e Justiça Social." Mudar para Competir, June.

————. 1992b. "A Nova Relação entre Competitividade e Educação: Estratégias Empresariais." Mudar para Competir, January.

————. 1991. "Carga Fiscal, Competitividade Industrial e Potencial de Crescimento Econômico." Mudar para Competir, August.

————. 1990. Mudar para Competir, June.

Ikenberry, John. 1990. "The International Spread of Privatization Policies: Inducements, Learning, and 'Policy Bandwagoning.'" In Ezra Suleiman, and John Waterbury, eds., *The Political Economy of Public Sector Reform and Privatization.* Boulder, Colo.: Westview Press.

Immergut, Ellen. 1995. "As Regras do Jogo: a Lógica da Política de Saúde na França e na Suécia." *Revista Brasileira de Ciências Sociais* 11(30): 139–66.

Instituto Nacional de Colonização e Reforma Agrária. 2000a. *Relatório de Atividades do INCRA 1995 a 1999.* INCRA. http://www.incra.gov.br/estrut/ativ9599.htm.

————. 2000b. Principais Ações do INCRA—1o Semestre de 2000. INCRA. http://www.incra.gov.br/estrut/rel30anos/rel30anos5.htm.

Instituto de Terras do Estado de São Paulo. 1998. Caderno ITESP 6: Mediação no Campo: Estratégias de Ação em Situações de Conflito Fundário. São Paulo, Brazil: Secretaria de Estado de Justiça e da Defesa da Cidadania and ITESP.

Inter-American Development Bank. 2002. *Latin American Economic Policies.* 1st Quarter Vol. 17. Washington, D.C.: IADB.

Jungblut, Cristiane. 2002. "Punidos 20 funcionários por fraudes na Sudam." *O Globo,* January 31, 13.

Kapaz, Emerson. 1998. Interview, São Paulo, Brazil.

Karam, Miram. 2002. "Rombo do Bamerindus é de R$5.7 bi, diz balanço." *Valor,* February 1, C-3.

Kliass, Paulo. 1994. "État et privatisation: aspects du reequilibrage entre le secteur public et le secteur privé au Brésil." Ph.D. diss., Université Paris X, Nanterre, France.

Kingstone, Peter R. Forthcoming. "Why Free Trade 'Losers' Support Free Trade: Industrialists and the Surprising Politics of Trade Reform in Brazil." *Comparative Political Studies.*

————. 2000. "Muddling through Gridlock: Economic Performance, Business Responses, and Democratic Sustainability." In Peter R. Kingstone, and Timothy J. Power, eds., *Democratic Brazil: Actors, Institutions, and Processes.* Pittsburgh, Pa.: University of Pittsburgh Press.

————. 1999. *Crafting Coalitions for Reform: Business Preferences, Political Institutions and Neoliberal Reform in Brazil.* University Park, Pa.: Pennsylvania State University Press.

————. 1998. Corporatism, Neoliberalism, and the Failed Revolt of Big Business: Lessons from the Case of IEDI. *Journal of Interamerican Studies and World Affairs* 40(4): 73–96.

Kinzo, Maria D'Alva. 1993. *Radiografia do quadro partidário brasileiro.* São Paulo, Brazil: Konrad Adenauer Stiftung.

Kirschner, Ana M., and Eduardo R. Gomes, orgs., 1999. *Empresa, Empresários e Sociedade.* Rio de Janeiro, Brazil: Sette Letras.

Kornai, Janos. 1981. "Some Properties of the Eastern European Growth Pattern." *World Development* 9(10): 965–70.

Krieger, Gustavo, Fernando Rodrigues, and Elvis Bonassa. 1993. *Os Donos do Congresso: A farsa na CPI do orçamento.* São Paulo, Brazil: Ática.

Krieger, Gustavo, Luiz Antônio Novais, and Tales Faria. 1992. *Todos os Sócios do Presidente*. São Paulo, Brazil: Página Aberta.

Kruger, Anne O., ed. 2000. *Economic Policy Reform: The Second Stage*. Chicago, Ill.: University of Chicago Press.

———. 1992. *Economic Reform in Developing Countries*. Oxford: Blackwell.

Kuntz, Rolf. 2002. "Mercado teme corrupção no Brasil, diz O'Neill." *O Estado de São Paulo*, February 2, B-6.

———. 1992. "Punição e Corrupção." *Revista da Previdência Social*. Brasília, Brazil, No. 145.

———. 1987. ed. *Sociologia da Corrupção*. Rio de Janeiro, Brazil: Jorge Zahar Editora.

Lafer, Celso. 2001. ALCA não é destino, é opção. *O Estado de São Paulo*, March 3.

Lafer, Celso, and Gelson Fonseca Jr., 1994. "Questões para a diplomacia no contexto internacional das polaridades indefinidas." In Gelson Fonseca Jr., and Sergio Henrique Nabuco de Castro, eds., *Temas de política externa brasileira II*, vol. 1. Brasília, Brazil: IPRI, and Paz e Terra.

Lal, Deepak, and Sylvia Maxfield. 1993. "The Political Economy of Stabilization in Brazil." In Robert Bates, and Anne O. Krueger, eds., *Political and Economic Interactions in Economic Policy Reforms: Evidence from Eight Countries*. Cambridge, Mass.: Blackwell.

Lavagna, Roberto. 2000. Entrevista a Alcides Costa Vaz. Buenos Aires, April 16, 1999. In Alcides Costa Vaz. *A construção do Mercosul: Brasil e Argentina nas negociações do período de transição*. Ph.D. diss., Universidade de São Paulo, São Paulo, Brazil.

Lavoratti, Liliana. 2000. "Atitude Paternalista da União Prejudica Lei Fiscal." *O Estado de São Paulo*, May 4.

Leite, Celso Barroso. 1992. "Punição e Corrupção." *Revista da Previdência Social*, n. 145.

———, ed. 1987. *Sociologia da Corrupção*. Rio de Janeiro, Brazil: Jorge Zahar Editora.

Leite, Janaína. 2000. "Bamerindus: fim da liquidação em estudo." *Jornal do Brasil*, February 12, 6.

Leite, Sérgio. 1999. "Políticas Públicas e Agricultura no Brasil: Comentários sobre o Cenário Recente." In Ivo Lesbaupin, ed., *O Desmonte da Nação: Balanço do Governo FHC*. Petrópolis, Brazil: Editora Vozes.

Leopoldi, Maria Antoinetta. 1984. "Industrial Associations and Politics in Contemporary Brazil." Ph.D. diss., Oxford University, London.

Lewis, Charles, ed. 1996. *The Buying of the President*. New York, N.Y.: Center for Public Integrity/Avon Books. http://www.publicintegrity.org.

Lima, João Policarpo R., and Enildo Meira de Oliveira Júnior. 2000. "Integração regional, Mercosul e os bens intermediários do Nordeste." In Marcos Costa Lima, and Marcelo de Almeida Medeiros, eds., *O Mercosul no limiar do século XXI*. São Paulo, Brazil: Editora Cortez/Clacso.

Lima, Maurício. 2002. "A candidata afundou." *Veja*, March 13, 36–41.

Lima Jr., Olavo Brasil de. 1993. "A Reforma das Instituições Políticas: A Experiência Brasileira e o Aperfeiçoamento Democrático." *Dados* 36(1): 89–117.

Limongi, Fernando, and Argelina Figueiredo. 1995. "Partidos Políticos na Câmara." *Dados* 38(3).

Linz, Juan J., and Alfred Stepan. 1996. *Problems of Democratic Transition and Consolidation: Southern Europe, South America and Post-Communist Europe.* Baltimore, Md.: The Johns Hopkins University.

Lloyd, John. 2001. "Attack on Planet Davos." *Financial Times*, February 24.

Lora, Eduardo. 2000. "What Makes Reform Likely? Timing and Sequencing of Structural Reforms in Latin America." Working paper 424, Office of the Chief Economist, Interamerican Development Bank.

———. 1997. "A Decade of Structural Reforms in Latin America: What Has Been Reformed and How to Measure It." Working paper 348, Office of the Chief Economist, Interamerican Development Bank.

Macedo, Fausto. 2002. "Suíça recebe hoje pedido sobre contas de Maluf." *O Estado de São Paulo*, A-5.

Machado, José Sérgio de Oliveira. 1998. *Reforma Político Partidária: Relatório Final.* Brasília, Brazil: Senado Federal. (Comissão Temporária Interna Encarregada de estudar a Reforma Político Partidária).

Mahar, Dennis. 1971. "The Failures of Revenue Sharing in Brazil and Some Recent Developments," *Bulletin for International Financial Documentation* 25(3): 71–79.

Mainwaring, Scott. 1999. *Rethinking Party Systems in the Third Wave of Democratization: The Case of Brazil.* Stanford, Calif.: Stanford University Press.

Mancuso, Wagner Pralon. 1999. *A indústria da construção e a legislação sobre concessões de serviços públicos.* Ph.D. diss. Universidade de São Paulo, Dept. of Political Science, São Paulo, Brazil.

Maquiavel, Nicolau. 1967. *O príncipe.* Rio de Janeiro, Brazil: Tecnaprint.

Maranhão, Arthur, Luiz Pedone, and David Fleischer. 1998. "Targeting Corruption in Public Bidding." *Economic Reform Today* 2: 14–17. http:// www.cipe.org.

Margolis, Mac. 2002. "A Plot of Their Own." in Newsweek International Online. http:// www.msnbc.com/news (February 6, 2002).

Markwald, Ricardo, and João Bosco Machado. 1999. "Establishing an Industrial Policy for Mercosur." In Riordan Roett, ed., *Mercosur: Regional Integration, World Markets.* Boulder, Colo.: Lynne Rienner Publishers.

Martínez-Lara, Javier. 1996. *Building Democracy in Brazil: The Politics of Constitutional Change, 1985–1995.* New York, N.Y.: St. Martin's Press.

———. 1995. *Building Democracy in Brazil: The Politics of Constitutional Change, 1985–1995.* London: Macmillan.

Martins, Carlos Estevam. 1977. *Capitalismo de Estado e modelo político no Brasil.* Rio de Janeiro, Brazil: Graal.

Martins, José de Souza. 2000. *Reforma Agrária: O Impossível Diálogo.* São Paulo, Brazil: Editora da Universidade de São Paulo.

———. 1999. "Reforma Agrária: O Impossível Diálogo Sobre a História Possível." *Tempo Social* 11 (October 2): 97–128.

Martins, Luciano. 1995. *Crise do Poder: Governabilidade e Governança.* Rio de Janeiro, Brazil: José Olympio.

———. 1985. *Estado capitalista e burocracia no Brasil pós 64.* Rio de Janeiro, Brazil: Paz e Terra.

Mattoso, Jorge. 1996. *O Brasil Desempregado.* São Paulo, Brazil: Editora Fundação Perseu Abramo.

Maxwell, Kenneth. 1999/2000. "The Two Brazils." *Wilson Quarterly* (Winter): 50–60.

———. 1995. *Pombal: The Paradox of Enlightenment.* New York, N.Y.: Cambridge University Press.

McQuerry, Elizabeth. 1996. "Private Sector Responses to Economic Liberalization Pol-
    icies in Brazil: A Look Within São Paulo's Capital Goods Sector." *Revista de Eco-
    nomia Política*, vol. 16, n. 3 (63).
MEC. *Censos Escolares.* 1970–1994.
MEC. *Educação no Brasil.* 1995–2001.
MEC/INEP/SEEC. *Sinopse Estatística da Educação Básica.* 2000. http://www.inep.
    gov.br/basica/censo/Escolar/Sinopse/sinopse.asp.
———. *Números da Educação no Brasil. Grandes Números do Ensino Superior—Gra-
    duação 2000, Brasil.* Available on the Web at http://www.inep.gov.br/estatisticas/
    numeros/brasil09.htm.
Medeiros, Marcos. 1999. "Ajuste Estrutural e Flexibilização das Relações de Traba-
    lho." In Ana M. Kirschner, and Eduardo R. Gomes, eds., *Empresa, Empresários e
    Sociedade.* Rio de Janeiro, Brazil: Sette Letras.
Medici, André C. 1999. "Uma Década de SUS (1988–1998): Progressos e Desafios." In
    Juan Diaz and Loren Galvão eds., *Saúde Sexual e Reprodutiva no Brasil.* São
    Paulo, Brazil: Ed. Hucitec and Population Council.
Mello, Flávia Campos. 2000. "Regionalismo e inserção internacional: continuidade e
    transformação da política externa brasileira nos anos 90." Ph.D. diss., Universi-
    dade de São Paulo, São Paulo, Brazil.
Melo, Marcus André. 1997. "O Jogo das Regras: A Política da Reforma Constitucional
    de 1993/96." *Revista Brasileira de Ciências Sociais* 33 (February): 63–85.
Mignone, Ricardo. 2001. "Marta Diz que Governo Faz 'Carnaval' sobre Mudanças em
    LRF." *Folha de São Paulo*, March 22, 6.
Ministério de Desenvolvimento, Indústria, e Comércio. 2001. Statistical Bulletin.
    Available on the Web at http://www.mdic.gov.br/indicadores.
Monteiro, Tânia. 2001. "Para Anadyr, corrupção caiu a nível 'aceitável'." *O Estado de
    São Paulo*, August 5, A-5.
Montero, Alfred P. 2002a. "After Decentralization: Patterns of Intergovernmental Con-
    flict in Argentina, Brazil, Spain, and Mexico." *The Journal of Federalism* 31: 4
    (Fall).
———. 2002b. *Shifting States in Global Markets: Subnational Industrial Policy in
    Contemporary Brazil and Spain.* University Park, Pa.: Pennsylvania State Univer-
    sity Press.
———. 2000. "Devolving Democracy? Political Decentralization and the New Brazil-
    ian Federalism." In Peter R. Kingstone, and Timothy J. Power, eds., *Democratic
    Brazil: Actors, Institutions, and Processes.* Pittsburgh, Pa.: University of Pittsburgh
    Press.
———. 1998. "State Interests and the New Industrial Policy in Brazil: The Case of the
    Privatization of Steel, 1990–1994." *Journal of Interamerican Studies and World
    Affairs* 40 (Fall): 27–62.
Montero, Alfred P., and David J. Samuels. 2003. "The Political Determinants of Decen-
    tralization in Latin America: Causes and Consequences." In Alfred P. Montero,
    and David J. Samuels, eds., *Decentralization and Democracy in Latin America.*
    Notre Dame, Ind.: University of Notre Dame Press.
Moreira, Maurício Mesquita. 1995. *Industrialization, Trade and Market Failures—The
    Role of Government Intervention in Brazil and South Korea.* New York, N.Y.: St.
    Martin's Press.
Morgenthau, Hans J. 1966. *Politics among Nations—The Struggle for Power and Peace*,
    Fourth Edition. New York, N.Y.: Alfred A. Knopf.

Mota, Carlos Guilherme, ed. 1974. *Brasil em Perspectiva*. São Paulo, Brazil: Difusão Européia do Livro.

Moura, Paulino Rolim de. 1967. *O Livro Negro da Corrupção: O escândalo da "caixinha" dos deputados*. São Paulo, Brazil: n.p.

Moya, Maurício. 1998. As Privatizações e o Poder Legislativo no Brasil. Relátorio final de Iniciação Científica. São Paulo, Brazil: Universidade de São Paulo, Dept. Political Science.

Nardi, Giuseppe di. 1973. *Economia della produzione*. Bari, Italy: Francesco Cacucci Editore.

Nelson, Joan. 1993. "A Política da transformação Econômica: A Experiência do Terceiro Mundo é Relevante Para a Europa Oriental?" In Lourdes Sola, ed. *Estado, Mercado e Democracia*. Rio de Janeiro, Brazil: Paz e Terra.

Nicolau, Jairo. 2000. "Disciplina Partidária e Base Parlamentar na Câmara dos Deputados no Primeiro Governo Fernando Henrique Cardoso (1995–1998)." *Dados— Revista de Ciências Sociais* (32): 4.

Nóbrega, Maílson da. 2001. "Alcafobia." *O Estado de São Paulo*, April 29.

Nogueira, Arnaldo M. 1999. "Novo Sindicalismo no Setor Público." In Iram Jacome Rodrigues, ed., *O Novo Sindicalismo Vinte Anos Depois*. Petrópolis, Brazil: Editora Vozes.

Nogueira, Rubem. 1993. "Considerações acerca de um Código de Ética e Decoro Parlamentar." *Revista de Informação Legislativa*, 118.

Norlin, Kara. 2001. *Rethinking the Principal-Agent Model of Corruption: A Patron-Client Model*. Brasília, Brazil. Mimeo.

Nylen, William. 1993. "Selling Neoliberalism: Brazil's Instituto Liberal." *Journal of Latin American Studies* 25 (2).

———. 1992. "Liberalismo Para Todo Mundo Menos Eu. Brazil and the Neoliberal Solution." In Douglas A. Chalmers, Maria Carmo Campello de Souza, and Atilio A. Borón, eds., *The Right and Democracy in Latin America*. New York, N.Y.: Praeger Publishers.

O'Donnell, Guillermo. 1994. "Delegative Democracy." *Journal of Democracy* 5(1): 5–69.

———. 1973. *Modernization and Bureaucratic Authoritarianism*. Berkeley, Calif.: University of California Press.

O'Donnell, Guillermo, and Philippe C. Schmitter. 1988. *Transições do Regime Autoritário—Primeiras Conclusões*. São Paulo, Brazil: Vértice.

Oliveira, Francisco de. 1995. "A Crise da Federação: Da Oligarquia à Globalização." In Rui de Britto Álvares Affonso, and Pedro Luiz Barros Silva, eds., *A Federação em Perspectiva: Ensaios Selecionados*. São Paulo, Brazil: FUNDAP.

Oliveira, Gesner. 1993. Condicionantes e diretrizes de política para a abertura comercial brasileira [Conditioning factors and directives for the Brazilian commercial opening policy]. IPEA Research Project. São Paulo, Brazil: CEBRAP.

Oliveira, Marco Aurélio Guedes de. 1998. "Mercosul: convergencialismo intergovernamental." Recife, Brazil: UFPe/Núcleo de Estudos sobre Política Internacional.

Oliveira, Vanessa. 1998. O Judiciário e as Privatizações. Relátorio Final de Iniciação Científica. São Paulo, Brazil: Universidade de São Paulo, Dept. Political Science.

Olson, Mancur. 1971. *The Logic of Collective Action: Public Goods and the Theory of Groups*. Cambridge, Mass.: Harvard University Press.

———. 1965. *The Logic of Collective Action*. Cambridge, Mass.: Harvard University Press.

Ondetti, Gabriel. 2001a. *Agrarian Reform in Brazil: Present and Future*. Unpublished manuscript.

———.2001b. *Taking and Making Political Opportunities: The Rise of the Brazilian Landless Movement*. Unpublished manuscript.

Orren, Karen, and Stephen Skowronek. 1995. "Order and Time in Institutional Study: A Brief for the Historical Approach." In James Farr, John Dryzek, and Stephen Leonard, eds., *Political Science in History: Research Programs and Political Traditions*. New York, N.Y.: Cambridge University Press.

Otavio, Chico, and Carolina Brígido. 2002. "Juízes poderão ser afastados." *O Globo*, March 12, 3–5.

Oxhorn, Philip, and Graciela Ducantenzeiler, eds. 1998. *What Kind of Democracy? What Kind of Market?: Latin America in the Age of Neoliberalism*. College Station, Pa.: Pennsylvania State University Press.

Oxhorn, Philip and Pamela K. Starr eds. 1999. *Markets and Democracy in Latin America: Conflict or Convergence*. Boulder, Colo.: Lynne Rienner Publishers.

Padrão, Ana Paula, and Valderez Caetano. 1997. *O Segredo do Cofre: Como os Estados brasileiros chegaram ao rombo de mais de R$100 bilhões*. Rio de Janeiro, Brazil: Editora Globo.

Pastor, Manuel, and Carol Wise. 1994. "The Origins and Sustainability of Mexico's Free Trade Policy." *International Organization*. Cambridge, Mass.: The MIT Press, Summer 48 (3): 459–89.

Paunovic, Igor. 2000. "Growth and Reforms in Latina America and the Caribbean in the 1990s." *Serie Reformas Económicas* CEPAL n. 70, Santiago (36).

Payne, Leigh. 2000. *Uncivil Movements: The Armed Right Wing and Democracy in Latin America*. Baltimore, Md.: Johns Hopkins University Press.

———. 1994. *Brazilian Industrialists and Democratic Change*. Baltimore, Md.: Johns Hopkins University Press.

Pensamento Nacional das Bases Empresariais. 1990. Statute.

Peixoto, João Paulo M. 2000. *Reforma e Modernização do Estado: aspectos da experiência brasileira recente*. Brasília, Brazil: Edições UVA, Sobral.

———. 1998. Notas sobre a liberação econômica no Brasil e Canadá. Anais do Enanpad. Anpad.

Peixoto, João Paulo M., José Flávio S. Saraiva, and Antonio Carlos Lessa. 2001. "Integração Hemisférica: Dimensões Econômicas e Sociais." *Idéias e Debates* 43: 21–22.

Pensamento Empresarial. 1990–2000.

Pereira, Anthony. 1999. "God, the Devil, and Development in Northeast Brazil." *Praxis* XV: 113–136.

———. 1997. *The End of the Peasantry: The Rural Labor Movement in Northeast Brazil, 1961–1988*. Pittsburgh, Pa.: University of Pittsburgh Press.

"Perueiro é preso com carro de placa 'clonada." 2000. *O Estado de São Paulo*, February 4, C4.

Pessanha, Charles. 1997. "Relações entre os poderes executivo e legislativo no Brasil: 1946–1994." Ph.D. diss., Universidade de São Paulo, São Paulo, Brazil.

Pierson, Christopher. 1998. *Beyond the Welfare State?: The New Political Economy of Welfare*. University Park, Pa.: Pennsylvania State University Press.

Pierson, Paul. 2000. "Increasing Returns, Path Dependence, and the Study of Politics." *American Political Science Review* 94 (2): 251–68.

Pinto, Luís Costa. 1996. *As Duas Mortes de PC Farias*. São Paulo, Brazil: Editora Best Seller.

PNBE. 1990. http://www.pnbe.org.br/oq.asp.

Polanyi, Karl. 1944. *The Great Transformation*. Boston, Mass.: Beacon Press.

Policarpo, Júnior. 2002. "O novo show do milhão." *Veja*, March 13, 42–45.

———. 2001a. "A História Secreta de um Golpe Bilionário." *Veja*, May 23, 36–45.

———. 2001b. "As Marcas do Marka." *Veja*, May 30, 38–43.

Pompeu de Toledo, Roberto. 1998. *O Presidente Segundo o Sociólogo: Entrevista de Fernando Henrique Cardoso a Roberto Pompeu de Toledo*. São Paulo, Brazil: Companhia das Letras.

Porto, Mauro. 2001. "Mass Media and Politics in Democratic Brazil." Paper presented at the conference "Fifteen Years of Democracy in Brazil." Institute of Latin American Studies, University of London, February 15–16.

Power, Timothy J. 2000. "Political Institutions in Democratic Brazil: Politics as a Permanent Constitutional Convention." In Peter R. Kingstone, and Timothy J. Power, eds., *Democratic Brazil: Actors, Institutions, and Processes*. Pittsburgh, Pa.: University of Pittsburgh Press.

———. 1998a. "Brazilian Politicians and Neoliberalism: Mapping Support for the Cardoso Reforms, 1995–1997." *Journal of Interamerican Studies and World Affairs* 40 (Winter): 51–72.

———. 1998b. "The Pen is Mightier than the Congress: Presidential Decree Power in Brazil." In John M. Carey, and Matthew Soberg Shugart, eds., *Executive Decree Authority*. New York, N.Y.: Cambridge University Press.

Prebisch, Raúl. 1965. "Proposiciones para la creación del Mercado Común Latinoamericano." *Política Externa Independente*, Rio de Janeiro, Brazil: Editora Civilização Brasileira, ano I, n° 1 (May).

———. 1949. "El desarollo económico de América Latina e sus pricipales problemas." In *ECLA Estudio Económico de la América Latina, 1948*. Santiago: ECLA, UN.

Prillaman, William C. 2000. *The Judiciary and Democratic Decay in Latin America: Declining Confidence in the Rule of Law*. Westport, Conn.: Praeger.

Proceedings of the International Seminar, Hemispheric Integration: Political, Economic and Social Dimensions. 2000. Instituto Teotônio Vilela/PSDB. Brasília, Brazil, December 6–8.

Proner, Caroline. 2000. "O setor de serviços na ALCA." FTAA Continental Forum: political and social actors in integration processes, held by Rebrip, CUT, Cedec, FASE, São Paulo, November 29.

"Protesto" section. 1999. *O Estado de São Paulo*, August 26.

"Protestos contra desemprego tem pouca adesão em todo o país." 1999. *O Estado de São Paulo*, November 11, B5.

Przeworski, Adam. 1995. *Sustainable Democracy*. Cambridge, Mass.: Cambridge University Press.

Purdum, Todd S., and David E. Sanger. 2002. "Two top officials offer stern talk on U.S. policy." *The New York Times*, February 2, 1.

Putnam, Robert D. 1993. "Diplomacy and Domestic Politics: The Logic of Two-Level Games." In Peter B. Evans, Harold K. Jacobson, and Robert D. Putnam, eds,. *Double-edged Diplomacy: International Bargaining and Domestic Politics*. Berkeley, Calif.: University of California Press.

"Rebelião do Fucionalismo: Maioria condena greve no serviços essenciais" 1995. *O Estado do São Paulo*, May 14, A14.

Reich, Gary M. 1998. "The 1988 Constitution a Decade Later: Ugly Compromises Reconsidered." *Journal of Interamerican Studies and World Affairs* 40(4): 5–24.

Ricupero, Rubens. 1987. "O que mudou na política externa." *Jornal do Brasil*, Rio de Janeiro, Brazil, April 1.

Rinelli, Michael. 2001. *Brazil Economic Briefing (BEB)* 01/2001. Washington, D.C.: Brazilian Embassy, 7th edition, April 12.

Robert, Stephen, and Kenneth Maxwell. 2001. *A Letter to the President and a Memorandum on U.S. Policy toward Brazil: Statement of an Independent Task Force Sponsored by the Council on Foreign Relations.* New York, N.Y.: Council on Foreign Relations.

Roberts, Kenneth. 1995. "Neoliberalism and the Transformation of Populism in Latin America: The Peruvian Case." *World Politics* 48 (1): 82–116.

Rodrigues, Iram Jácome, ed. 1999. *O Novo Sindicalismo Vinte Anos Depois.* Petrópolis, Brazil: Editora Vozes.

Rodrigues, Rute Imanishi. 1999. "Empresas Estrangeiras e Fusões e Aquisições: Os Casos dos Ramos de Autopeças e de Alimentação/Bebidas em Meados dos Anos 90." Texto para Discussão, No. 622. Brasília, Brazil: Instituto de Pesquisa Econômica Aplicada.

Rodríguez, Alberto, and Carlos Alberto Herrán. 2000. *Educação secundária no Brasil: Chegou a Hora.* Washington, D.C.: Interamerican Development Bank, World Bank.

Rodriguez, Vicente. 1995. "Federalismo e Interesses Regionais." In Rui de Britto Álvares Affonso, and Pedro Luiz Barros Silva, eds. *A Federação em Perspectiva: Ensaios Selecionados.* São Paulo, Brazil: FUNDAP.

Roett, Riordan. 1999. *Brazil: Politics in a Patrimonial Society.* Fifth edition. Westport, Conn.: Praeger.

Romero, Abelardo. 1967. *Origem da Imoralidade no Brasil.* Rio de Janeiro, Brazil: Conquista.

Rosenn, Keith, and Richard Downes, eds. 1999. *Corruption and Political Reform in Brazil: The Impact of Collor's Impeachment.* Coral Gables, Fla.: University of Miami Press/North-South Center.

Rossi, Clóvis. 2002. "EUA ligam juro alto no Brasil à corrupção." *Folha de São Paulo*, February 2, A-6.

Rossi, Clóvis, and Emanuel Neri. 1995. "Governadores Querem Manter Incentivos." *Folha de São Paulo*, July 24, 1–16.

Rossi, José Luiz Jr., and Pedro Cavalcanti Ferreira. 1999. "Evolução da Produtividade Industrial Brasileira e Abertura Comercial." Texto para Discussão, No. 651. Rio de Janeiro, Brazil: Instituto de Pesquisa Econômica Aplicada.

Sadek, Maria Thereza. 2000. *Ministério Público e administração de justiça no Brasil.* São Paulo, Brazil: IDESP.

Sallum Jr., Brasílio. 1996. "Federação, Autoritarismo e Democratização." *Tempo Social* 8 (October): 27–52.

Sallum Jr., Brasílio, and Kugelmas, Eduardo. 1993. "Leviatã Acorrentado: A crise brasileira dos anos 80." In Sola, L., ed., *Estado, Mercado e Democracia: política e economia comparadas.* Rio de Janeiro, Brazil: Paz e Terra.

Samuels, David J. Forthcoming. *Ambassadors of the States: Federalism, Ambition, and Congressional Politics in Brazil.* New York, N.Y.: Cambridge University Press.

———. 2001. "The Cardoso Administration and 'Predatory' Federalism in Brazil." Mimeo, August.

———. 2000. "Money, Elections, and Democracy in Brazil." *Latin American Politics and Society* 43(2): 27–48.

———. 1998. "Careerism and Its Consequences: Federalism, Elections, and Policy-making in Brazil." Ph.D. diss., University of California, San Diego, California.

Sandoval, Salvador A. M. 1993. *Social Change and Labor Unrest in Brazil Since 1945.* Boulder, Colo.: Westview Press.

Santana, Genilson Fernandes. 1997. "A Indústria de Bens de Capital." Secretariat of Political Economy Paper, December.

Santos, Angela Maria Medeiros M., and Claudia Soares Costa. 1996. "A Reestruturação do Setor de Auto-Peças." BNDES Working Paper. http://www.BNDES.gov. br.

Saraiva, José Flávio Sombra. 2000. Proceedings of the International Seminar, Hemispheric Integration: Political, Economic, and Social Dimensions. Instituto Teotonio Vilela/ PSDB. Brasília, Brazil. December 6–8.

Scheper-Hughes, Nancy. 1992. *Depth Without Weeping: The Violence of Everyday Life in Brazil.* Berkeley, Calif: University of California Press.

Schilling, Flávia. 1999. *Corrupção: Ilegalidade Intolerável? Comissões Parlamentares de Inquérito e a luta contra a corrupção no Brasil (1980–1992).* São Paulo, Brazil: Inst. Brasileiro de Ciências Criminais.

———. 1998. "Governantes and governados, público and privado: alguns significados da luta contra a corrupção, o segredo e a mentira na política." *Revista da USP* No. 37.

Schmidt, Benício Viero, Danilo Nolasco C. Marinho, and Sueli L. Couto Rosa, eds. 1998. *Os Assentamentos de Reforma Agrária no Brasil.* Brasília, Brazil: Editora UnB.

Schmitter, Phillipe C. 1974. "Still the Century of Corporatism." *The Review of Politics* 36: 85–131.

Schneider, Ben R. 1998. "Organized Business Politics in Democratic Brazil." *Journal of Interamerican Studies and World Affairs* 39(4): 95–128.

———. 1997a. "Big Business and the Politics of Economic Reform: Confidence and Concertation in Brazil and Mexico." In Sylvia Maxfield, and Ben R. Schneider, eds., *Business and the State in Developing Countries.* Ithaca, N.Y.: Cornell University Press.

———. 1997b. Organized Business Politics in Democratic Brazil. *Journal of Interamerican Studies and World Affairs* 39 (4): 95–127.

Schwartzman, Simon. 2000. "Brazil: The Social Agenda." *Daedalus* 129 (2, Spring): 29–56.

———. 1982. *Bases do Autoritarismo Brasileiro.* Rio de Janeiro, Brazil: Campus.

Scott, Bruce. 2001. "The Great Divide in the Global Village." *Foreign Affairs* 80(1): January–February.

Selcher, Wayne. 1998. "The Politics of Decentralized Federalism, National Diversification, and Regionalism in Brazil." *Journal of Interamerican Studies and World Affairs* 40 (Winter): 25–50.

———. 1990. "O Futuro do Federalismo na Nova República." *Revista de Administração Pública* 24: 165–190.

Semeguini, Ulisses C. 2001. "Fundef: Corrigindo Distorções Históricas." *Em Aberto* 74(18): 43–57.

Sherwood, Frank P. 1967. *Institutionalizing the Grass Roots in Brazil: A Study of Comparative Local Government.* San Francisco, Calif.: Chandler.

Sicsú, Abraham, and Frederico Katz. 2000. "Nordeste e Mercosul: reflexões iniciais sobre conjuntura e perspectivas." In Marcos Costa Lima, and Marcelo de Almeida Medeiros, eds., *O Mercosul no limiar do século XXI.* São Paulo, Brazil: Editora Cortez/Clacso.

Sigaud, Lygia. 2000. "A Forma Acampamento: Notas a Partir da Versão Pernambucana." *Novos Estudos CEBRAP* 58 (November): 73–92.

Silva, Cleide. 1999. "Pólos industriais empregam 45.9% menos." *O Estado de São Paulo,* November 8, B1.

Silva, Marcos Fernandes Gonçalves da. 2001. *A Economia da Corrupção no Brasil.* São Paulo, Brazil: Senac.

———. 2000. "Corrupção e Desempenho Econômico." In Bruno Wilhelm Speck, Cláudio Weber Abramo, Marcos Fernandes G. da Silva, David Fleischer, and Karl-Heinz Nassmacher, eds., *Os Custos da Corrupção.* São Paulo, Brazil: Fundação Konrad Adenauer.

———. 1999. "The Political Economy of Corruption in Brazil." *Revista de Administração de Empresas* 39(3): 26–41.

———. 1996. "Economia Política da Corrupção." *Revista de Economia da Construção* 2.

Silva, Marcos F. G., Fernando Garcia, and Antônio Carlos Bandeira. 2001. "Evidências acerca dos efeitos da corrupção sobre a produtividade de fatores e a renda agregada." São Paulo, Brazil: EAESP/FGV.

Silva, Pedro Luiz Barros, and Vera Lúcia Cabral Costa. 1995. "Decentralização e Crise da Federação." In Rui de Britto Álvares Affonso, and Pedro Luiz Barros Silva, eds., *A Federação em Perspectiva: Ensaios Selecionados.* São Paulo, Brazil: FUNDAP.

Simoens, Luiz Afonso. 2000. "Os organismos financeiros internacionais e as políticas de integração latino-americanas." Lecture promoted by Fundap, PUC-SP e Cedec, São Paulo, Brazil, June 15.

Simões, Antonio, J. F. Forthcoming. *O Brasil e a Alca no limiar do novo milênio-algumas reflexões.*

Skidmore, Thomas. 1999. *Brazil: Five Centuries of Change.* New York, N.Y.: Oxford University Press.

———. 1988. *The Politics of Military Rule in Brazil, 1964–1985.* New York, N.Y.: Oxford University Press.

———. 1967. *Politics in Brazil: 1930–1964, An Experiment in Democracy.* New York, N.Y.: Oxford University Press.

Smith, William C., and Roberto Patricio Korzeniewicz. 1997. *Politics, Social Change, and Economic Restructuring in Latin America.* Coral Gables, Fla.: North-South Center Press; Boulder, Colo.: Lynne Rienner Publishers.

Soares, Glaúcio A. D. 2001. *A Democracia Interrompida.* Rio de Janeiro, Brazil: Fundação Getúlio Vargas.

Soares, Glaúcio A. D., and Maria Celina D'Araujo, eds. 1994. *21 Anos de Regime Militar: Balanço e Perspectivas.* Rio de Janeiro, Brazil: Fundação Getúlio Vargas.

Sola, Lourdes. 1995. "Estado, Regime Fiscal, e Ordem Monetária: Qual Estado?" *Revista Brasileira de Ciências Sociais* 10: 29–60.

———. 1994. "The State, Structural Reform, and Democratization in Brazil." In William C. Smith, Carlos H. Acuña, and Eduardo A. Gamarra, eds., *Democracy, Mar-*

kets, and Structural Reform in Latin America: Argentina, Bolivia, Brazil, Chile, and Mexico. New Brunswick, N.J.: Transaction Publishers.

Sola, Lourdes, Christopher Garman, and Moisés Marques. 1998. "Central Banking, Democratic Governance and Political Authority: The Case of Brazil in a Comparative Perspective." Revista de Economia Política 18 (April/June): 106–31.

Solnick, Steven L. 1998. "Hanging Separately? Cooperation, Co-optation, and Cheating in Developing Federations." Paper presented at the Annual Meeting of the American Political Science Association, Boston, Mass.: September 3–6.

———. 1995. "Federal Bargaining in Russia." East European Constitutional Review (Fall): 52–58.

Sorj, Bernardo. 1998. "A Reforma Agrária em Tempos de Democracia e Globalização." Novos Estudos CEBRAP 50 (March): 23–40.

Souza, Amaury de. 1997. "Redressing Inequalities: Brazil's Social Agenda at Century's End." In Susan Kaufman Purcell, and Riordan Roett, eds., Brazil Under Cardoso. Boulder, Colo.: Lynne Rienner Publishers.

Souza, Celina. 1998. "Intermediação de Interesses Regionais no Brasil: O Impacto do Federalismo e da Descentralização." Dados—Revista de Ciências Sociais 41(3). Available from http://www.scielo.br/scielo.php?script=sci_arttext&pid=S0011-52581998000300003&lng=en&nrm=iso.

———. 1997. Constitutional Engineering in Brazil: The Politics of Federalism and Decentralization. New York, N.Y.: St. Martin's Press.

———. 1997. Constitutional Engineering in Brazil: The Politics of Federalism and Decentralization. London: Macmillan.

Souza, Maria do Carmo Campelo de. 1976. Estado e Partidos Políticos no Brasil, 1930 a 1964. São Paulo, Brazil: Alfa-Ômega.

———. 1974. "O Processo Político-Partidário na Primeira República." In Carlos Guilherme Mota, ed., Brasil em Perspectiva. Rio de Janeiro, Brazil: Editora Bertand Brasil S.A.

Spanakos, Anthony Peter. 2002. "Realigned Left-Wing: Ready to Share Power?" http://www.InfoBrazil.com (May 4–10).

Spanakos, Anthony Peter, and Howard J. Wiarda. 2003. "Dominican Foreign Policy: From Nationalism to Globalism." In Frank Mora, and Jeanne Hey, ed., Latin American and Caribbean Foreign Policy. Boulder, Colo.: Rowman and Littlefield.

Speck, Bruno Wilhelm, ed. 2002. Caminhos da Transparência. Campinas, Brazil: Editora da Unicamp.

———. 2000a. Inovação e Rotina no Tribunal de Contas da União. São Paulo, Brazil: Konrad Adenauer Stiftung.

———. 2000b. "Mensurando a Corrupção: Uma revisão de dados provenientes de pesquisas empíricas." In Bruno Wilhelm Speck, Cláudio Weber Abramo, Marcos Fernandes G. da Silva, David Fleischer, and Karl-Heinz Nassmacher, eds., Os Custos da Corrupção. São Paulo, Brazil: Fundação Konrad Adenauer.

Stallings, Barbara, and Wison Peres. 2000. Growth, Employment, and Equity. Washington, D.C.: Brookings/ECLAC.

Statistical Abstract of the United States. 2001. In Gilberto Paim, "O patíbulo do embaixador." O Globo, April 20, 7.

Statistics Canada, Ottawa 2000. http://www.statcan.ca/start.html.

Stédile, João Pedro, and Bernardo Mançano Fernandes. 1999. Brava Gente: A Trajetória do MST e a Luta pela Terra no Brasil. São Paulo, Brazil: Editora Fundação Perseu Abramo.

Stepan, Alfred, ed. 1989. *Democratizing Brazil*. New York, N.Y.: Oxford University Press.

Strauss, Jack. 1998. Interview, São Paulo.

Stephen, Robert. 2001. "A Letter to the President and a Memorandum on U.S. Policy Toward Brazil." Statement of an Independent Task Force sponsored by the Council on Foreign Relations, February.

Suassuna, Luciano, and Luiz Antônio Novaes. 1994. *Como Fernando Henrique foi Eleito Presidente: os acordos secretos, o PT de salto alto*. São Paulo, Brazil: Contexto Editorial.

Suetonius. 1957. *The Twelve Caesars*. Baltimore, Md.: Penguin Books.

Sunkel, Osvaldo, ed. 1993. *Development from Within: Toward a Neostructuralist Approach for Latin America*. Boulder, Colo.: Lynne Rienner Publishers.

Tavares, María da Conceição. 1997. "Recentralização Fiscal e Arbítrio Político." *Folha de São Paulo*, July 20, 2–6.

Teixeira, Carla Costa. 1998. *A Honra da Política: Decoro parlamentar e cassação de mandato no Congresso Nacional (1949–1994)*. Rio de Janeiro, Brazil: Relume-Dumará.

———. 1996. "Decoro Parlamentar: A legitimidade da esfera privada no mundo público?" *Revista Brasileira de Ciências Sociais* 30: 110–27.

Teixeira, Letícia Miranda. 2000. "O Combate à Lavagem de Dinheiro no Brasil." Senior Thesis, University of Brasília, Brasília, Brazil.

Thury Filho, Altair. 2001. "O Preço da Ação: Estudo mostra que o Poder Judicário inibe o crescimento industrial brasileiro." *Veja*, February 25, 23–24.

Torre, Juan Carlos. 1997. "Las Dimensiones Políticas e Institucionales de las Reformas Estructurales en América Latina." *Série Reformas de Política Pública* CEPAL, Santiago (46).

———. 1994. "América Latina, el Gobierno de la Democracia en Tiempos Difíciles." *Documento de Trabajo* Instituto Di Tella, CIS, Buenos Aires, Julho (122).

Trebat, T. 1983. *Brazil's State-Owned Enterprises: A Case Study of the State as Entrepreneur*. Cambridge, Mass.: Cambridge University Press.

Tsebelis, George. 1995. "Decision Making in Political Systems: Veto Players in Presidentialism, Parliamentarism, Multicameralism and Multipartyism." *British Journal of Political Science* 25: 289–325.

Uricoechea, Fernando. 1980. *The Patrimonial Foundations of the Brazilian Bureaucratic State*. Berkeley, Calif.: University of California Press.

Valls, Lia. 2000. "O futuro do Mercosul/Brasil diante da ALCA: riscos e oportunidades." FTAA Continental Forum: political and social actors in integration processes, held by Rebrip, CUT, Cedec, FASE, São Paulo, Brazil, November 29.

Varsano, R., E. Pessoa, N. L. Costa da Silva, J. R. Rodriguez, E. Araújo, and J. C. Maciel. 1998. "Uma Análise da Carga Tributária do Brasil." *Texto para Discussão* No. 583, Rio de Janeiro, Brazil: IPEA.

Vasconcellos, Gilberto. 1989. *Collor: A Cocaína dos Pobres. A Nova Cara da Direita*. São Paulo, Brazil: Icone.

Vasconcelos, Adriana. 2001. "Comissão do Senado aprova prazo de desincompatibilização para reeleição." *O Globo*, April 5, 5.

Velasco Jr., Licínio. 1997a. "A economia política das políticas públicas: fatores que favoreceram as privatizações no período 1985/94." Textos para Discussão 54, Rio de Janeiro, Brazil: DEPEC, BNDES.

———. 1997b. "A economia política das políticas públicas: as privatizações e a reforma do Estado." Textos para Discussão 55, Rio de Janeiro, Brazil: DEPEC, BNDES.

Viotti da Costa, Emília. 2000. *The Brazilian Empire: Myths and Histories.* Chapel Hill, N.C.: University of North Carolina Press. Originally published in 1985.

Waterbury, John. 1993. *Exposed to Innumerable Delusions—Public Enterprise and State Power in Egypt, India, Mexico and Turkey.* Cambridge, Mass.: Cambridge University Press.

Weber, Max. 1978. *Economy and Society.* Berkeley, Calif.: University of California Press. Edited by Guenther Roth and Claus Wittich, volumes I and II.

Weffort, Francisco. 1988. "Por que democracia?" In Alfred Stepan, ed., *Democratizando o Brasil.* Rio de Janeiro, Brazil: Paz e Terra.

Werneck, Rogério L. F. 2000. "Processo Orçamentário em Transição." *O Estado de São Paulo*, April 28, B2.

———. 1987. *Empresas estatais e política macroeconômica.* Rio de Janeiro, Brazil: Editora Campus Ltda.

Weyland, Kurt. 2000a. "The Brazilian State in the New Democracy." In Peter R. Kingstone, and Timothy J. Power, eds., *Democratic Brazil: Actors, Institutions, and Processes.* Pittsburgh, Pa.: University of Pittsburgh Press.

———. 2000b. "The Fragmentation of Business in Brazil." In Francisco Durand, and Eduardo Silva, eds., *Organized Business, Economic Change, and Democracy in Latin America.* Miami, Fla.: North-South Center Press.

———. 1998a. "The Fragmentation of Business in Brazil." In Francisco Durand, and Eduardo Silva, eds., *Organized Business, Economic Change and Democracy in Latin America.* Miami, Fla.: North/South Press.

———. 1998b. "Swallowing the Bitter Pill: Sources of Popular Support for Neoliberal Reform in Latin America." *Comparative Political Studies* 31, (5): 529–68.

———. 1998c. "The Brazilian State in the New Democracy." *Journal of Interamerican Studies and World Affairs* 39(4): 63–94.

———. 1996a. "Obstacles to Social Reform in Brazil's New Democracy." *Comparative Politics* 29(1): 1–22.

———. 1996b. *Democracy without Equity: Failures of Reform in Brazil.* Pittsburgh, Pa.: University of Pittsburgh Press.

———. 1993. "The Rise and Fall of President Collor and its impact on Brazilian Democracy." *Journal of Interamerican Studies and World Affairs* 35(1): 1–38.

Whitehead, Laurence. 1993. "On 'Reform of the State' and 'Regulation of the Market.'" *World Development* 21 (8): 1371–93.

Wiarda, Howard J. 1981. *Corporatism and National Development in Latin America.* Boulder, Colo.: Westview Press.

Williamson, John. 1990. "What Washington Means by Policy Reform." In *Latin American Adjustment: How Much Has Happened?* Washington, D.C.: Institute for International Economics.

Willis, Eliza, Christopher da C. B. Garman, and Stephan Haggard. 1999. "The Politics of Decentralization in Latin America." *Latin American Research Review* 34: 7–56.

Wohlcke, Manfred. 1994. *Brasilien: Diagnose einer Krise.* Munich, Germany: Ebenhausen Institute.

World Bank. 2001. *World Development Report 2000/2001.* New York, N.Y.: Oxford University Press.

Zancanaro, Antônio Frederico. 1994. *A corrupção político-administrativa no Brasil*. São Paulo, Brazil: Editora Acadêmica.

Index

About the Contributors

Maria Hermínia Tavares de Almeida is professor of political science at the University of São Paulo.

Cristina Bordin is the outreach coordinator at the Bildner Center for Western Hemisphere Studies, City University of New York.

Eliana Cardoso, an independent consultant and visiting professor of economics at Georgetown University, previously taught at the Fletcher School, Boston University, MIT, and Yale University.

Sônia Draibe is professor of political science at the Economics Institute at the University of Campinas (UNICAMP).

David Fleischer is professor of political science and coordinator of the graduate program in political science at the University of Brasília.

Mauricio A. Font, professor of sociology at Queens College and The Graduate Center, is also director of the Bildner Center for Western Hemisphere Studies, City University of New York.

Eduardo Rodrigues Gomes is coordinator for international affairs and professor of political science at the Universidade Federal Fluminense.

Fabrícia C. Guimarães is a researcher at the Candido Mendes University, Rio de Janeiro.

Peter Kingstone is associate professor of political science at the University of Connecticut.

Alfred Montero is assistant professor of political science at Carleton College.

João Paulo Peixoto is professor of government and public administration at the University of Brasília.

Anthony Pereira, associate professor of political science at Tulane University, previously taught at the Fletcher School of Law and Diplomacy, Tufts University, and the New School for Social Research.

Salvador Sandoval is professor at the Pontifícia Universidade Católica de São Paulo and the Universidade Estadual de Campinas.

Anthony Peter Spanakos is visiting assistant professor of political science at Manhattanville College.